# TURN LEFT AT GREENLAND
## In Search of the Real America

10695717

MARK LITTLE was born in Dublin in 1968 and educated at Trinity College and Dublin City University. He joined RTÉ as a television reporter in 1991 and in September 1995 was appointed RTÉ's first Washington Correspondent. He covered some of the most important events of recent American history, including two presidential elections, and reported on President Clinton's participation in the Irish peace process. He is perhaps best known for his coverage of the Monica Lewinsky scandal. He returned to Ireland in January 2001 to become RTÉ's Foreign Affairs Correspondent, and in October 2001 he joined RTÉ television's current affairs programme *Primetime* as a correspondent and presenter. He has won two National Media Awards for his work, including Television Journalist of the Year.

# TURN LEFT AT GREENLAND

## In Search of the Real America

MARK LITTLE

**NEW
ISLAND**

TURN LEFT AT GREENLAND
First published May 2002
by New Island Books
2 Brookside
Dundrum Road
Dublin 14

ISBN 1 902602 87 0

British Library Cataloguing in Publication Data.
A catalogue record for this book is available
from the British Library.

The author has asserted his moral rights.

**The Arts Council**
An Chomhairle Ealaíon

New Island receives financial assistance from The Arts Council
(An Chomhairle Ealaíon), Dublin, Ireland.

Cover design: Jon Berkeley
Typesetting by New Island Books
Cover photographs courtesy RTÉ
Printed in Ireland by Colour Books Ltd.

3   5   7   9   10   8   6   4

# CONTENTS

## ACKNOWLEDGEMENTS

The inspiration for this book came during a long walk through New York's Central Park with my friend and colleague Paul Reynolds. I am forever grateful for his encouragement that day. There is no way I can repay my partner Tara Peterman for her advice and endurance; she made me believe in the value of a fresh perspective on a country we both love. In the three years it took to write this book, I have been blessed with the support of family and friends, including Tom Little, Bill Owens, Michael O'Kane, Ryan Tubridy, Deaglán de Bréadún and Richard Martin. Without the good humour and experience of my agent Jonathan Williams, this book would never have seen the light of day. Ciara Considine at New Island Books was a patient and objective guide when I needed one most. The students of the publishing programme at NUI Galway gave me honesty and enthusiasm at just the right moment. I would also like to thank my colleagues at RTÉ, in particular the team on the foreign desk, for all their help during my years in Washington, and the two bosses who sent me there in the first place, Ed Mulhall and Joe Mulholland. In the end, this book is a snapshot of places and people that changed my life. To all those people, my eternal thanks.

*for Tara and Sorcha*

# Introduction

## The Day after My Birthday

I celebrated my thirty-third birthday in a hotel room in Jerusalem. I marked the passing of another year with a late night call to room service and a raid on the minibar. It may seem like a sad and solitary way to spend your birthday, but I could not have been happier. I was on the road again, trailing foreign minister Brian Cowen on a tour of the Middle East and savouring every moment of the journey. In the previous five days, I had been in Belfast, Dublin, Amsterdam, Brussels and Cairo. I was a happy addict, getting my buzz from miles travelled and relishing the perverse normality of an abnormal life.

I had not expected to enjoy travelling so much. I had done enough of that in my five years in the United States, and on my return to Dublin in January 2001 I wanted time with family and friends. Yet I had no idea how hard it would be coping with a homeland that had changed beyond recognition. In the first weeks after my return, I was thrilled by Ireland's new spirit, but I also felt increasingly uneasy in company. Whenever I joined a conversation there were constant reminders that I had not lived through Ireland's transformation in the first person. As I waited to pounce on an enlightening phrase in the pub, or listened intently to agonised soul-searching on the radio,

I felt like the latecomer who had heard the punchline but missed the joke. There were things about this new Ireland that I could not fully understand, even though I had read all about them. I had not lived through the changes, and no matter how hard I tried to adapt, I felt that would always set me apart.

Foreign travel was a welcome relief. No matter how inexplicable and chaotic the destination, there was a point in me going there. Sharing coffee with a Palestinian elder among the olive trees of a West Bank farm seemed eminently more logical than struggling to be heard above the thumping rhythms of a Dublin mega-pub. In my first eight months back in Ireland, I never felt more comfortable than when I was heading towards the airport. Whether I was on my way to report on economic woes in Japan, elections in Britain and Israel or Afghanistan's descent into hell, away was generally preferable to home. That's why a beer and a kosher sandwich in the King David Hotel in Jerusalem seemed like the obvious way to celebrate my thirty-third birthday. In fact, it was the perfect end to the perfect day: September 10, 2001.

The next day dawned with absolute clarity. A pure blue sky and a blanket of intense heat had settled over the Israeli capital as the Minister's convoy left the hotel. Brian Cowen was that day's honoured guest at the Yad Vashem memorial on the outskirts of Jerusalem. It records in graphic terms how six million Jews were murdered under Nazi rule and how it was allowed to happen. Almost every visiting VIP is directed here. It is not a memorial, it is an explanation; it is Israel's way of saying: 'This is why we are who we are.'

After we left Yad Vashem, there was obvious tension between the Irish delegation and their Israeli hosts. By the time we reached the Israeli president's office, an Israeli protocol official was arguing with an Irish diplomat. She warned him of the danger involved in Brian Cowen's impending visit to a Palestinian refugee camp near Bethlehem. 'There are gunfire and bombs over there,' she told the diplomat, 'it is war.' The war was not where we expected to see it. As our armoured jeep sped down the narrow alleys of the refugee camp, the first of four hijacked planes was speeding toward the World Trade Centre. As we inspected bullet holes in the walls of a Palestinian classroom, American Airlines Flight 11 exploded high above the streets of Manhattan. As the Irish delegation said goodbye to their Palestinian hosts, United Airlines Flight 175 hit the south tower of the World Trade Centre.

I found out what had happened from my travelling companion, Deaglán de Bréadún of the *Irish Times*. He had called a mutual friend to arrange dinner but instead received news of the attacks. As we drove south towards Gaza in an Irish government jeep, we listened to the BBC World Service with mounting disbelief. I felt nauseous as I listened to the horror unfold in places that I loved. The twin towers had been a presence in my life for years. As I flew up to Manhattan, they would loom large in the window of the plane, not simply announcing New York, but screaming it in my face. From the ground, the World Trade Centre was a gigantic 'you are here' arrow, guiding me around the canyons and gulleys of lower Manhattan. On nights of joyful excess, no matter where the nightclub was, I could always find my way home by reference to the surreal patchwork of lights speckled up and down the twin towers. If I emerged from the club and the towers were on my left, I needed to head right, towards my bed in some Midtown hotel.

In Washington, the Pentagon was more than a landmark. Two of my friends, Sue Shuback and Greg

Burkart, worked in the sprawling office complex. When the passenger plane hit, Sue ran to the crèche to find her son, while her husband Greg was rushing towards the same place from another corner of the building. Neither knew in those first horrifying moments where the explosion had come from and exactly what part of the Pentagon complex had been destroyed. Both would ask the same question: are they safe? I wondered the same thing as we drove down the road to Gaza, each mile throwing up another face or name to worry about. As I listened to false reports of car bombs across Washington and stray airliners heading for the American capital, and heard voices filled with panic from my adopted hometown, I felt physically sick. The last place I wanted to be was on an Israeli highway inspecting a war without end. I wanted to be there, in Washington or New York, sharing the pain of a country that I had learned to love.

I continued on that journey down the highway, welling up inside as the BBC told us that the south tower of the World Trade Centre had collapsed, presumably killing everyone inside. I rang my girlfriend Tara at home in Dublin and she sounded frighteningly remote and calm. She had been watching television since the second plane hit the towers, watching her hometown being attacked and fearing for the lives of friends and relatives, particularly her brother Tommy, a New York firefighter. We eventually found out Tommy was unhurt, but Tara's voice at that moment made me ache with helplessness. She was sitting in an apartment in Dublin, I was on an Israeli highway, the world had gone completely insane, and there was not a single thing we could do about it.

The sense of insanity was never far from me that day, not at Yad Veshem, not in that Palestinian refugee camp, and certainly not as we arrived at the border crossing between Israel and the Gaza strip. A few minutes before we pulled up at the checkpoint, the radio provided a detailed description of the collapse of the north tower. As I listened, I could see an Israeli jet in the distance, scrambling in response to an international outrage that apparently had little or nothing to do with the war between Arab and Jew. I was overcome at that moment with the horrible certainty that nothing would be quite right ever again. At the checkpoint, our convoy passed from under the sullen gaze of a heavily armed Israeli border patrol towards the dubious welcome of gun-toting Palestinian policemen. With the sound of a massacre filling our vehicle, and the sight of Uzis and Kalashnikovs out of the window, it seemed we were being dragged across an invisible threshold into a dark and brutal new world.

In the back of my mind, I wondered why I had not seen this coming. When I worked in the United States, I had played doomsday scenarios through my head and worked out the technical requirements of covering the nightmare terrorist strike on New York or Washington: the massive car bomb near the White House or the nerve gas attack on a Manhattan subway station. In my new role as foreign correspondent, I was employed as an analyst, a person who explains why inexplicable things happen. Yet, when confronted with the unfolding detail of the most significant international event of my lifetime, I could barely keep myself from screaming, 'What the fuck is going on?' On the road to Gaza, I was vaguely aware of another deeply depressing prospect. As the world tried to make sense of the events of this day, it would almost certainly be divided along the same old fault lines of ideology and preconception. Faced with something so incomprehensible, we would fall back on our existing prejudices to make sense of it all, and seek out images that fitted familiar patterns. But the world had changed in a matter of hours; long-established assumptions were outdated and familiar images would prove dangerously misleading.

Less than an hour after crossing into Gaza, I was face-to-face with Yasser Arafat. Minister Brian Cowen had decided to go ahead with a meeting with the Palestinian president at his seaside headquarters, where he urged Arafat to quickly condemn the attacks on America. Arafat was drained of all colour when he and the Minister emerged to talk to Deaglán and me. All around us, Palestinian officials, laden down with documents, were scurrying to waiting cars, preparing to flee a possible Israeli response to the attacks in New York. 'This is a tragedy for the whole world,' Arafat told us, 'not just for the Americans.' I asked him if he would cooperate with the United States in its search for the perpetrators. His eyes opened wide and the words tumbled out of his mouth, 'I will do what the Americans ask of me.'

The interview was brought to an end by Arafat's minders and the Palestinian leader walked Brian Cowen to his car. As he inflicted a bear-hug on the Irish minister, I realised I had a problem. I had to get my video footage back to RTÉ as quickly as possible, but if I left with the departing Irish delegation it would be hours before I reached the satellite link in Jerusalem. If I stayed and used the local link, I would be stranded in Gaza indefinitely. As Brian Cowen's car began to pull away, a local cameraman offered to take my videotape to the Gaza satellite link and feed the interview with Arafat back to Dublin. I gave him the tape, jumped into a jeep at the back of the Minister's convoy and sped away, back towards Israel. Twenty minutes into the journey, I got a phone call telling me the helpful local cameraman had been detained by Palestinian officials and our interview with Arafat destroyed. Luckily, another camera crew had recorded the impromptu interview and the material eventually got back to Dublin.

I was later told that a Palestinian official had wiped the videotape because he thought it belonged to the news agency APTN. The same agency had earlier obtained footage of a crowd of Palestinians celebrating the destruction of the twin towers. By the time Arafat condemned the attacks, those pictures had been broadcast all around the world. Palestinians were incensed by such bad publicity, and in an attempt to punish APTN some anonymous official punished me. It was a crass and vindictive act but I could understand the anger that had inspired it. The celebrations were small and short-lived, involving no more than a handful of people in East Jerusalem and a Palestinian refugee camp in Lebanon, and they took place before the full scale of the assault on America had become apparent. Yet the celebrations fitted a familiar pattern and would define Palestinian reaction in the eyes of the world far more than the words of Yasser Arafat.

As we drove through the dimly lit streets of Gaza City, we saw no sign of celebration. If anything, there was a fearful quiet in those streets. We could see the television images flickering from shops in Gaza's commercial heart and we met silent stares from the people along the side of the street. As we drove on, Deaglán gave an interview to an Irish radio station on his mobile phone. The host asked about the ongoing celebrations on the streets of Gaza. I looked out at sombre faces flying by the window of the car and felt absolute despair.

I spent the next two days probing Israeli and Palestinian reaction to the attacks on America, and early on Friday morning I boarded a British Airways plane at Tel Aviv's Ben Gurion airport and flew towards London, Dublin and home. Tara met me at the airport and on the drive across the city she told me who was safe, who was grieving and who was still unaccounted for. I heard about

Tommy and Pop and Dee and Greg and Sue and Bill and Bud and Laura and a seemingly endless series of names of good people whose lives would never be the same again. When we got home, we sat in our kitchen and talked through the tears. That night I watched Tara, on the *Late Late Show*, tell the Irish people about the members of her family. More than anyone else, they have been the people who have showed me that decency, integrity and sincerity define ordinary Americans far more than the hubris and swagger we often ascribe to them. That's why their suffering was so hard to cope with. As I listened to the pure emotion from other speakers on that show, I felt proud of my nation because it had understood the nature of the wound inflicted on the United States and, by extension, Ireland. I walked through the crowd outside the American Embassy in Ballsbridge the following day and marvelled at the genuine natural empathy of the Irish. Like a big-talking tough guy with a heart of gold, Ireland let its natural cynicism slip in the first few days after September 11 and embraced the concept of solidarity.

I had less than 48 hours to appreciate the wave of Irish compassion. On Sunday morning, I was back in the car driving to the airport and this time I was an uncertain traveller. I was bound for New York with an RTÉ team to film America picking up the pieces. A few hours after our arrival, we took a subway to lower Manhattan and made our way through the streets around Ground Zero towards Police Headquarters where we would get our press credentials. It was 4 a.m. by the time we had been processed and we strolled through the empty streets looking for a taxi. 'Don't Walk' read the blinking traffic light, but there was no one around to heed the warning except us and the occasional cop. It was as if we were the sole survivors of doomsday, emerging from our bunker to look for signs of life, but finding only reminders of death. On the sides of public telephone boxes were photocopies of smiling faces under the word 'Missing'. These were the faces of the victims, placed there by loved ones who dared not give up hope. After a few minutes of drifting, our surroundings became familiar. We had reached the edge of the security perimeter and I could see Chinatown in the distance. I had been there in July on a night out with friends; now I was sharing the street with a squad of National Guardsmen and their Humvee jeeps. We stood on the corner and hailed a taxi. As my colleagues filled up the back of the cab, I climbed into the front seat but was told by an agitated driver to back off. He said that he was taking no chances after what had happened. Fear ruled in the new New York.

There were other raw emotions in the voices we heard over the next three weeks. In New York, Washington and Oklahoma City we heard anger, just as we had expected to, but from those who were most deeply affected by the tragedy there was also caution and restraint. It was expressed by the parents of one young stockbroker who died in the north tower of the World Trade Centre. His mother told us she was worried about the possibility that her son's killers would evade justice, but she also worried about the mothers who would lose sons or daughters when America sought revenge in Afghanistan. A New York firefighter who had helped with the rescue effort at both the Pentagon and the twin towers was the first to express a sentiment I heard again and again: 'We have to respond to this, but it's more important that we do it right than do it quickly.'

Listening to George W. Bush in those first weeks, with his talk of getting Osama bin Laden 'dead or alive', one could easily have assumed that the United States was overcome by bloodlust. That was not the case, even where the wounds were deepest. What was most striking was the helplessness of the ordinary Americans we met. They knew the United States had enemies, but they had assumed they would meet them in foreign battlefields, not on the way to work on a sunny Tuesday morning. Now the enemy was among them, a presence in the small routines of daily life and a threat to what was solid and permanent about their nation. As they coped with the shock, they found themselves asking a number of questions in quick succession: who are the people who want to destroy our way of life; what forces have shaped them and how do we protect ourselves against them? Most European commentators seemed to miss this process of soul-searching, focussing instead on America's instinctive resort to patriotic fervour and its descent into paranoia. Those images fitted the old patterns but they also blinded these outsiders to the American people's quest for knowledge and the growing awareness that the fate of the world's most powerful nation was inextricably linked with the fate of the world's poorest. The sophistication of the American public's response to September 11 was not always reflected in the words and actions of US politicians, but it did exist, even if the sceptics could not see it.

I returned to Ireland at the end of September hoping the pure emotion that I had witnessed in the immediate aftermath of the attacks would prevail. Deep down I knew I was being unrealistic; feelings that strong are, by their very nature, of the moment. There was still genuine sympathy among ordinary people, but that had been overshadowed by what I feared most: a media-led debate about America's role in the world which was being shaped by rival preconceptions and duelling clichés. It was a debate in which there was no grey, just black and white; you were either anti-American or an apologist for American brutality. I began to monitor the commentary obsessively, trawling through the Internet to chart the progression of the debate in the weeks after the attacks on the United States. I found some truly farcical attempts to belittle America's critics in Ireland. A few days after September 11, one former US diplomat wrote on the front page of the *Sunday Independent*: 'The Irish media, in general, bear their share of the responsibility for what happened in the United States.' Other commentators were more reasoned but equally fierce in their defence of the United States. A respected Sunday newspaper columnist wrote there was 'nothing latent about the Anti-Americanism which is the default ideology of most of the Irish media'. My immediate reaction to all this was irritation; scepticism about American foreign policy did not make you anti-American. Five years in Washington had left me deeply sceptical about American politics but had transformed me into an ardent admirer of the United States and its people. Yet, while I was annoyed that the defence of US interests had been framed in such an unsophisticated way, I despaired at the increasingly shrill tone of the verbal assault on America. In particular, I was amazed how much reasoned political argument about US foreign policy was mixed up with reflex generalisations about the nature of American society.

As images of destruction in Afghanistan replaced images from New York on our TV screens, you could hear the Irish conventional wisdom harden against the United States. A few years before, I would have moved right along with the critical mass, but now I was seeing things from a different perspective, an American perspective. I agreed with many of the questions posed about US policy but I found the answers relied too much on images of America that simply did not correspond to the reality as I had lived it. I was unsettled by the extent to which the Irish popular view of the United States was shaped by lazy assumptions about the American psyche and a tendency to think about life in the US in cartoon images. In so much of the comment I read, Americans were reduced to caricatures. In the *Sunday Tribune,* a columnist wrote that America 'would just love if the whole world was American and ate hamburgers, and played baseball, and went to church on Sunday, and watched *Friends* and *The Simpsons.*' In the letters column of the *Irish Times,* citizens of the world's most powerful democracy were compared to the Nazis: 'The current American ethos ... is reminiscent of another powerful military regime I recall from the 1930s.' And in *Magill* magazine one contributor told us that 'the behaviour of America in the decades after 1945 has been that of a bemused, bad-tempered toddler – they want it their way and they want it NOW!'

About a month after the September attacks, I travelled to Egypt and Iran and found a remarkably similar view of the United States. In common with the critics back home, ordinary people in these Islamic countries were deeply suspicious and often openly hostile to the US. They had good reason to be. On the Al Jazeera TV network they watched Apache helicopters and F-16s, supplied to Israel by the American government, pound away at their Palestinian brothers and sisters. But at some point, public expression of hostility to the United States had become parody, prompted as much by self-interest as by genuine grievance. Anti-American sentiment has become a unifying force in societies on the verge of collapse. Many Muslim political leaders actively promote it while repressing other forms of public expression. To the populations of these imperfect societies, America is no longer a real country with real people; it is a useful myth. It struck me forcefully in Teheran, where a man told me, 'I hate America for making me hate America.' Outside the Al-Azhar mosque in Cairo, some of the young men with hateful opinions of the United States were branded from head to foot with symbols of corporate America. Sporting the Nike swoosh, they railed against American interference in their lives.

The Irish critique of the United States is certainly more discriminating and it has an anti-establishment cachet to it that is lacking in Muslim countries. But in the way we talk I sometimes hear an echo of how Iranians talk of America as the 'Global Arrogance'. At the heart of this common critique is a contradiction: the language and images used to define America by outsiders are often just as simplistic as the language and images Americans often use to define the rest of the world. I remember the disdain I felt when I first settled in the United States and read the State Department's official guide to Ireland. My eyes fell on the phrase, 'Slightly larger than West Virginia.' Was that my Ireland? Could it really be summed up with such glib efficiency? However, what strikes me now that I am home is just how glib we can be when looking at the United States.

Europeans do receive a lot more information about Americans than Americans receive about us, but the bulk of that information is filtered through the prism of existing stereotypes. The dirty little secret among foreign correspondents in the United States is that success lies in stories about mad Yanks shooting, executing or sleeping with each other, and not reports that reflect well on Americans. As Washington correspondent, I often despaired at the obsession with tales from the American fringe. I would regularly get calls from Ireland about stories that rated one paragraph at the bottom of page ten of *USA Today*, and half a page in an Irish tabloid. The sensational stories of American excess that fill the Irish airwaves and its newspapers do reflect a reality, but only a partial one. Even when the focus is on more sombre issues, such as presidential politics and foreign policy, I am surprised at the weight given to facts that prove the prevailing Irish thesis rather than reflect the big picture. All this limits our ability to make sense of the intricate code that is America; just because we have the right numbers, it does not necessarily mean they are in the right order.

Today Ireland is more like America than it was when waves of Irish migrants made the journey across the Atlantic in search of a better life. Yet it could be argued that our understanding of the United States has never been so shallow and selective. That makes it more difficult to resolve the great debate that is set to dominate Irish politics in the post-boom era. How can we make the fundamental choice between Boston and Berlin when we have confused the options? In a strictly historical sense, Mary Harney got it right when she said, 'We have sailed closer to the American shore than the European one.' However, having spent years on that American shore looking back at Ireland, I wonder if we really understand the terms of the debate prompted by Harney's insightful comments. If it is simply a question of choosing the most efficient economic model, European or American, then the rules of the game are self-evident, even if the outcome is not. But it's not just about economics. It is about choosing a landmark by which we can judge the changes in our identity, and it is about agreeing a list of priorities by which we can gauge our future success or failure. But how can we use Boston as a guide when we don't have an accurate measure of life in the United States? How can we decide whether or not we would like to become more American when our assumptions about America are both selective and prone to exaggeration?

When I arrived in Washington in 1995, I was convinced that as got to know the people of the United States, my imported assessment of them would prove accurate. After all, I was a member of the most smug generation ever to emerge from Ireland and a self-righteous know-it-all when it came to American politics. But I soon realised how little I understood the dynamics of American society: what drives it forward and what holds it back, what divides it and what keeps it together. All my life, the United States had been a slick one-dimensional surface on which you could project any image you liked, but when I got right up close I discovered that beneath the surface was a labyrinth of endless pathways leading in every direction. For the next five years, I followed the curves and right angles of those pathways, not quite sure what was around the next corner or where the path would eventually lead, but increasingly certain the journey was the most important thing and not the destination.

In the pages of this book are experiences that taught me about Americans and the unique society they continue to build. At times, I have tried to fit these deeply personal stories into a wider context but this is most certainly not some grand sermon about the inner meaning of American life. I have tried to include the sound, taste and smell of these experiences so they have a life beyond the clipped news reports you may associate me with. I have also tried to provide a sense of the fun and excitement that I was blessed with, courtesy of my position. Above all, this is the record of a journey that forced me to abandon my preconceptions about the two countries I now call home.

# One

## The Potato-sucking Moron

If there was a defining moment in my time in the United States it came towards the end and not the beginning. In early 1999, I was searching for a company that would illustrate the enormous changes in Ireland's economic relationship with the United States. American firms had long supported the Irish economy with investment and employment, but a growing number of Irish high-tech companies had reversed the trend, bringing their innovations to the United States and employing American workers. At an investment conference at the Kennedy Library in Boston, I met Eireann Connolly. He was exactly what I needed: a native-born American working as a senior executive for the Irish software firm, Aimware.

I brought a camera crew to the company's offices in Boston's harbour district. It had been restored from a state of industrial decay by high-tech pioneers intent on creating their own limited version of Silicon Valley. The district was so busy on the day of our visit, there were no parking spaces left and we had to park our car illegally. The cameraman left a note on the windscreen explaining that we were filming a story for Irish television. He underlined the word 'Irish', just to be sure. Once inside

Aimware's offices, Eireann Connolly told us that most of
the buildings in the area had once been warehouses
where Irish immigrants packed wool for distribution
across the United States. Eireann's grandfather had
worked in one of these warehouses on his arrival from
Ireland. The Irish grandfather had laboured for the
Americans and now the American grandson was
labouring for the Irish. We had come full circle.

After the interview, as we carried the crew's equipment down the stairs, I tried to write a script in my mind
that would do justice to Eireann Connolly and his grandfather. My concentration was broken by the sound of
laughter. The sound technician had pulled a page of white
paper from under the windscreen wiper of our car. The
paper carried a short message in the neat script of a word
processor: 'Who gives a flying fuck who you are ... your
[sic] illegally parked you potato sucking moron.'

So much for Ireland's spiritual kinship with Boston. In
this most Irish of American cities, my Irishness was
thrown back in my face as an insult. Did the anonymous
author of the note not know about Eireann Connolly and
his grandfather? Had he missed the global explosion of
Irish culture? I don't expect him to remember Yeats,
Beckett or Swift, but surely he must have heard of
Keating, Norton, Corr and Mumba? Potato-sucking
moron, my arse. I'm Irish. I deserve a little respect.

As I worked myself into a fit of righteous indignation,
the camera crew giggled like a pair of cheeky schoolboys.
The cameraman was Italian-American and the sound
recordist didn't seem to care much what came before his
ethnic hyphen, so from their standpoint 'potato-sucking
moron' was not worth getting worked up over. In the
absence of sympathy, my anger faded and I bought the
crew lunch at a seafood restaurant by the edge of Boston
harbour. As I waited for the chowder, I thought about the

sobering reality at the heart of the morning's experience: Seamus Heaney can win a Nobel prize, Westlife and U2 can dominate the charts, and Irish millionaires can multiply like rabbits, but someone will always think the Irish are potato-sucking morons.

Maybe that is not such a bad thing. Instead of brooding over the insults hurled at us over the centuries, perhaps we should embrace them. That piece of paper, with those neatly printed words, stayed on the wall of my office for the rest of my assignment as a correspondent in Washington. It was a strangely reassuring memento. As Ireland was turned upside down by economic boom and as the peace process robbed Irish America of its defining cause, this small expression of prejudice remained pure and absolute. It was a lighthouse in a heaving sea. The Irish might be swept away on an unstoppable wave of smugness and self-confidence, but there will always be at least one person who knows exactly where we and our extended family of potato-sucking morons have come from.

That experience in Boston exposed the big lie every Irish kid brings to the United States: all Americans love the Irish. It is one of the countless false assumptions that underpinned my generation's first-hand experience of the United States. By the time we were old enough to book a transatlantic flight without parental guidance, we had convinced ourselves that there was nothing to fear in America. For the tens of thousands of freshly minted Irish college graduates who left Ireland in the Eighties and Nineties the United States was simply a permanent summer holiday. Emigration was regarded as an indication of a national malaise but on a personal level it was no longer something to be feared or ashamed of. If you left Ireland at that time, you left high unemployment, high taxes and low morale. You left for Boston, New York or Washington with the certainty that things could not be any worse in America and the confidence that they would probably be an awful lot better. I left Ireland with that confidence, and an extra layer of self-belief that came from my upbringing.

I was always fascinated with my family's complicated history. The Littles are not even Irish if you look hard enough. The exact details are lost in the mists of time, but to the best of my knowledge we are descended from the German Palatines. My ancestors ended up in Drogheda, where they made the literal translation of their name from Klein to Little. As many of their fellow Palatines departed Irish shores for the New World, my family moved to Dublin's Liberties. The Littles were working-class Catholics with an unquenchable Protestant work ethic.

I knew the broad brush-stroke of my family history from early childhood, but the details would have to be peeled away in layers. As I grew older, I had a constant niggling feeling there was more to be revealed. Even the things I knew as fact were like pieces in a jigsaw puzzle – it was a struggle to fit everything together. There were a few dramatic revelations down the years, but mostly it was a gradual process and the picture would expand almost imperceptibly each time a story was told at the dinner table or at a family gathering. More and more, I could see the shadow and light in my family. Most of all I could see accomplishment. In this disjointed picture I found inspiration.

My mother and father worked hard to give me the opportunities they never had. The more successful they became, the farther out from the city they moved, finally settling in the comfortable seaside suburb of Malahide on Dublin's Northside (the phrase 'North County' was preferred by the local snobs). My childhood was as close as makes no difference to perfect. Long summers on the beach, steamy weekends at the local disco and a quality education at Malahide's community school turned me into a horribly confident and well-adjusted middle-class teenager. I was good at school but full of opinions which I didn't mind sharing. My religion teacher wrote 'prematurely cynical' on my report card when I was 14. A year later, after I had founded a fairly rebellious school magazine, a local priest described me as 'machiavellian'. It was years before I realised that made me a scheming little git.

In 1985, I arrived at Trinity College in Dublin as a particularly fresh-faced freshman. I had just turned 17 but I was determined to consume every experience the 1980s had to offer. One vital experience was finding out what it was like to be shown disrespect in a foreign country. Along with tens of thousands of other Irish students, I lived the emigrant life for a couple of months every year. I spent the summer of 1986 cleaning toilets in Copenhagen, and the summer of 1987 washing Daimlers and Bentleys at an underground garage near Notting Hill in London. I was called 'White Wog' by a red-faced man in a cheap car when I worked as a car park attendant at Heathrow airport the same year. I had that smug assurance of knowing that, some day, I would be a successful, university-educated White Wog and he would still have a cheap car.

Like hundreds of thousands of privileged students before me, I did a lot of travelling and that helped to create a confidence bordering on arrogance. We had seen the rest of the world and it didn't scare us. We also had the luxury of high expectations because our parents were the last Irish generation to really wonder whether the future would be brighter than the past. I was aware from early childhood that I would have choices my mother and father never had.

The search for success might still mean that I would have to leave Ireland, but despite the national angst about emigration in the 1980s, it was not fear of leaving which worried me, only the fear of not being the best. Half my university classmates left Ireland after graduation, and while it seemed like part of a national tragedy at the time, I do not remember tears in the eyes of the friends and classmates who went. 'Growing up in Dublin,' observed writer Joe O'Connor, 'you expected emigration to happen to you, like puberty.' We all left with the certainty that we would emerge victorious from our promising Irish childhoods. Things were always going to be better for us. If we had to be White Wogs, then we were going to be the best White Wogs we could possibly be.

That confidence translated into our view of the rest of the world, and the United States in particular. My contemporaries looked at America in a very different way from previous waves of Irish emigrants. The privileged among us worked the building sites in Boston or waited tables on Long Island during those endless summers of the J-1 visa. But if we had to go back, it would be to a job on Wall Street or Madison Avenue and a nice apartment in the Village or Brooklyn Heights. However, many of us still regarded America with a confused ambivalence.

It is hard to sort out the fact from the fiction about the United States when you are growing up in Ireland. For me the confusion started way back in early childhood with a jumble of contradictory images, from the ritual violence of Hollywood movies to the simplistic image of contentment on the sit-coms. Any one day on television could be a roller-coaster ride from *Sesame Street* to the *Brady Bunch*; from *Starsky and Hutch* to *Dirty Harry*. If there was some way of making sense of all of this, I must have missed it. Like so many other Irish kids, I just accepted America as a concept and stopped trying to understand it. That made things much easier. It meant I could let that wave of cultural imperialism wash over me and still feel superior to all that American excess and bad taste.

In my early teens, I was into all the fashionable left-wing causes and was fascinated by the history of socialist politics and the ideas of Karl Marx, James Connolly and Antonio Gramsci. From the moment I entered college I was active in student politics. In 1988, I was elected president of the Trinity Students' Union, and spent a glorious year leading the vaguely angst-ridden and idealistic segment of the student body on regular marches, demonstrations and occupations. Yet, at the same time, I could not get enough of American politics and pop culture. By the time I was a student, I could tell you every member of Ronald Reagan's cabinet and reel off that year's list of Oscar nominees for good measure. However, as a student radical I spent countless Saturday afternoons outside the US Embassy in Dublin working myself into a state of outrage at American foreign policy. At 15, I taught my baby sister to say 'Ronald Reagan is a fascist' every time the American president came on television. At 18, my drunken standard was the Christy Moore lyric: 'Hey Ronnie Reagan, I'm black and I'm pagan, I'm gay and I'm left and I'm free. I'm a non-fundamentalist environmentalist, so fuck off and don't bother me.' During the height of my campaign against US interests, I decided I would never apply for the J-1 visa and never spend a working summer in America. I looked with disdain at some of my comrades who worried that all the marching and bellyaching outside the American Embassy would ruin their chances of getting a J-1.

So, instead of waiting tables in the Hamptons, I marched in support of the Sandinistas. I stood beside the liberal nuns and *Socialist Worker* activists hurling verbal abuse at the American Embassy in Dublin. During one summer in London, I worked part-time for *Marxism Today*, the bi-monthly bible of the New Left. Where the Old Left retained a sneaking admiration for Stalin and believed in the primacy of economics, the New Left celebrated glasnost and obsessed over culture. Instead of promoting holidays in Bulgaria, *Marxism Today* advertised futon shops and organic muesli. I spent less time working on thought-provoking journalism and more time selling politically correct fashion accessories. Wherever Lefties gathered, I sold T-shirts emblazoned with a picture of Mikhail Gorbachev. Little did my comrades know that I was also flipping burgers at the McDonalds in Hammersmith to make ends meet.

Just as summer turns to autumn, I knew that part-time politicking would have to be replaced by a real job. In truth, my heart was never in this as a career. Politics was like sport to me. I loved it with a passion, but I didn't have either the staying power or absolute conviction to be really good at it. And by the end of my activist years, I was becoming bored with the sectarianism of left-wing politics. I was sick of judging people by their political outlook and not their character. In retrospect, I see those years of political activity as an essential part of my education, but my heart was already set on a different path.

Some people drift into journalism, but I had always wanted to be a reporter. There was that brief period when I wanted to play centre-forward for Liverpool, but I would soon learn that journalism required far less natural talent. I was a mediocre student, but I knew where I wanted to go and how much work I would have to do to get there. I just about managed to get a second-class honours degree from Trinity College in 1990 and was accepted into the postgraduate journalism programme at Dublin City University.

I was soon making a living from journalism and, like a sponge, I sucked up the experience and advice of more experienced reporters. Like most aspiring journalists, I was prone to wide-ranging, emphatic generalisations. I also tended to express my views with lots of imperious passion and confidence, so my classmates at DCU christened me 'Emperor'. I had no problem tempering my judgements when I was working, but I also came to understand that passion and confidence are two of the most valuable traits in any journalist. A couple of weeks before I joined RTÉ, a veteran reporter leaned over my shoulder as I was writing my first front-page story for the *Sunday Business Post* and said, 'Make it sing.' I have always aspired to make good on that advice, no matter what the story.

On my first day as an RTÉ news reporter in September 1991, I was sent to cover a prison riot. In those days, the only available mobile phone was powered by a battery the size of a brick. I was handed this strange device and told to climb to the top of the Phibsboro Tower in Dublin. The cell phone rang as I stood watching the inmates of Mountjoy Prison sunning themselves on the roof of the cell-block opposite. Three times I ended the call prematurely by pressing the wrong button. Finally, I heard a voice on the line and an exasperated editor back at RTÉ told me it was five minutes to six and they wanted a live report for the *Six-One News* on TV. Ten minutes later, I stood in a stairwell telling presenter Anne Doyle that 'slowly but surely, the prisoners are moving across the roof'. I kept repeating the line, 'Slowly but surely. Surely but slowly.' The same three words, in a different order, over and over again.

I kept my job, despite my underwhelming debut, mainly because I was ambitious and it showed. For the next four years, I was blessed with generous colleagues, good luck and a deep, surviving love affair with television reporting. I was privileged to have a ringside seat in some of the dramas that would lead to remarkable changes in Irish life. I got the first broadcast interview with businessman Ben Dunne on his return from that fateful holiday in Florida, unaware that his self-destruction would shine a light on the dark recesses of Irish politics. As the era of scandal began, I would get a good look behind the brooding, hooded eyes of Charles Haughey as he headed for political oblivion, and I spent a fearful summer in Belfast reporting on the violence and political intrigue that preceded the paramilitary ceasefires. Looking back on those early days, there was a macho ethic in the RTÉ newsroom, which tended to help young male reporters like me. We prided ourselves on being 'hacks', ready to tackle any assignment without complaint but with a great desire to 'make it sing'.

That is how I pitched myself for the job of Washington correspondent late in the summer of 1995. RTÉ had never had a resident correspondent in the United States, so during the selection process I portrayed myself as the candidate who would do anything to make this new position work. I tried to convince my bosses, and myself, that failure was not an option. Pick me, I know America, I'm not afraid. Pick me, I will be the best damn White Wog in Washington. Pick me, I never sleep. They picked me, and within a matter of weeks I was on my way to the United States. One moment I was hugging my parents at Dublin airport and the next I was standing in front of the White House as Washington correspondent.

Despite the frantic pace of those early days, fear bubbled up from my subconscious. The ladder had fallen away from the wall and there was nothing between me and the ground but gravity. I wasn't scared that I would fail at my new job. As long as I worked the late nights and early mornings, the bosses would be happy. What scared me was the realisation that America was no longer a concept; it was my new home. I knew so much about the United States, but in those first few days I realised just how little I understood the country and its people. At one of the first parties I attended in Washington, a veteran Swiss correspondent put it all in context for me. 'You will spend the first six months here getting rid of your old prejudices about America,' she told me, 'and spend years building new ones.'

Good advice could not help me over the deep sense of loss I felt when I arrived in Washington that September. I blamed the sense of dislocation on the sacrifices I had made by coming to America. I had left behind my five-year-old daughter who was living with her mother and just beginning to understand the concept of parents who live separate lives. I had left a beautiful girlfriend behind, and I had left my parents, friends and colleagues. I had left Tayto crisps, Crunchie bars and irony. The three thousand miles between Washington and Dublin felt like a lifetime.

I kept telling myself to snap out of it. 'Suck it up,' as my new American friends would say. This is where my generation's confidence was supposed to come into play. I was a golden boy with a great job. I was St Brendan, Frank McCourt and Bob Woodward all rolled into one, and as I stepped off my flight to Washington, I was truly a master of the universe. I was a cocky ambassador of a new generation of Irish immigrants. I was also a scared little boy with no return ticket and a cheap suit. I was just another potato-sucking moron.

# Two

# My Foggy Bottom

One of my editors used to say, 'The loneliest soul in the world is RTÉ's person in the field.' There's a certain amount of truth in that, but as I tried to make a new life for myself in Washington I discovered that isolation had its benefits. Isolation means you are in control. You are no longer trying to conform to someone else's expectations. You can only rely on your instincts, and not the contradictory advice of multiple chiefs back at base. You work hard because that is the only way you will meet the standards you have set yourself. The problem is that you tend not to know when to stop.

My day could start with a 6 a.m. flight out of Washington and not finish until I had serviced *Morning Ireland* in the early hours of the next morning. My life was an endless series of deadlines and, during a big story, days could stretch into weeks and I wouldn't have time to draw breath. As I travelled outside Washington I started to understand the neurosis that infected every foreign correspondent I had ever met. Your progress is watched by hundreds of thousands of people on a nightly basis, but you never meet any of them. You are separated from your loved ones and forced to rely on strangers with no real interest in your welfare. You eat anything, at any time of day or night, because you don't know when you will eat again. You go to bed too late and get up too early. You spend too much time breathing recycled air on cramped aeroplanes and not enough time in real daylight. You try to cope with the constantly changing time difference but you never know what time it really is. You make a pledge to yourself that you will slow down after the next trip but you know you will speed up. Finally, you try to convince yourself that these are the best days of your life. The truth is they are.

I may have been one of the loneliest men on earth, but I was also one of the luckiest. On my first trip to the West Coast in October 1995, I stayed at the Peninsula Hotel in Beverly Hills, along with then President Mary Robinson and her entourage. At a black tie dinner in the nearby Hilton Hotel, Rupert Murdoch strolled by our table while celebrity lawyers Marcia Clarke and Christopher Darden sat close by (it was their first public appearance since losing the O.J. Simpson trial). The next morning, I was woken by a call from Dublin informing me that I had just won a National Media Award for my radio reporting. An hour later, Gabriel Byrne sat down beside me at a breakfast reception in honour of President Robinson. Immediately afterwards, I got to interview one of my favourite actors, James Woods. The following day, I was ferried to Los Angeles airport (LAX) and a New York-bound flight, in a speeding cavalcade of highway patrolmen and limousines. The strangest part was, I was getting paid for this.

It was hard not to be seduced by the trappings of my new lifestyle. I knew that I would be changed by the world I now inhabited, and I knew the change would separate me further from home. That prospect would have deeply upset me when I first arrived in Washington but as time wore on it mattered less. Where I was now became more important than where I was from. I also began to understand that there is virtue in exile. On that first trip to Los Angeles, I had a drink with an Irish diplomat in the Beverly Hills hotel. The manager in the bar was a particularly elegant young woman who seemed to know the diplomat. 'Wait until you hear this,' he said, as he waved to the woman. She came over to us and let out a cheerful 'Howya' in a broad, flat Dublin accent. She was from Finglas. She had tried to get a decent job in a series of Dublin hotels but she told us her accent and background had always counted against her. She had decided to try her luck in the United States, where a Northside accent can sound vaguely exotic. So instead of cleaning toilets back in Ireland, she was on the management fast track in one of the most famous hotels in the world. There was no bitterness in this woman. She had been forced to leave Ireland because of prejudice, but in exile she had found the life she wanted to live.

I had also found the life I wanted to live, and the place to live it. When I was not travelling, home was an apartment at the top of an office building on M Street in downtown Washington, just a few hundred yards down the street from my office. It was a strange place to live, busy by day and quiet by night, but it was on the margins of two of the most fascinating neighbourhoods in the city. North of M Street was Dupont Circle, with one of the highest concentrations of gay men and women in the United States. To the south of M Street was an area known as Foggy Bottom, which was established by German immigrants in 1771 and later developed by the Irish. The neighbourhood got its peculiar name from the mix of fog from the nearby Potomac River and the foul-smelling smog that belched from the gasworks and breweries that supported the poorest of Washington's poor during the eighteenth and nineteenth centuries. By the time I moved into my chic apartment block, the area had become thoroughly respectable, home as it was to George Washington University, the State Department and the Kennedy Centre. But back in the bad old days it was a vile-smelling slum. A block from my apartment was a long-concealed tributary called Slash Run, which used to carry drainage from the area's slaughterhouses. One local history book gave a frightening account of my neighbourhood back in the early eighteenth century: 'A gang of boys calling themselves the Round Tops terrorised the neighbourhood and, after a heavy rain, swarms of rats infested the muddy streets and Slash Run.'

By the time I arrived, the rats were gone and the Round Tops had been decommissioned, but the weather was still causing problems. Growing up on Europe's western shore does not prepare you for Washington's brand of humidity. This can only be understood if you live through what locals call the '90-90 days', when the temperature rises above 90 degrees Fahrenheit and the humidity index reaches 90 per cent. Other American cities suffer similar conditions but they do not live by an impractical dress code. In Washington, it is suit and tie unless you have some good excuse, like unemployment. So oppressive is this combination that British diplomats used to be awarded hazardous duty pay. Back in the days before air conditioning, one French diplomat killed himself and in his diary wrote that he 'suffered from the heat of midsummer and couldn't stand the iced drinks'.

While May to September is marked by oppressive heat, the rest of the year brings other extremes. The Washington definition of a 'cold snap' takes some getting used to. I flew back to Washington from Atlanta one Saturday night in January 1996 and took a cab directly from the airport to my local cinema where I was due to meet some new friends. As I passed over Memorial

Bridge into the city, the first flakes of snow drifted into the river. The movie that night was Oliver Stone's *Nixon*, and as Anthony Hopkins hammed it up on screen, a snowstorm was blowing through the streets outside the cinema. There was already a carpet of snow on the ground as I set off home. Within minutes I was caught in a blizzard of Arctic proportions. I finally made it to my apartment and took to my bed. By the time I awoke, Washington's biggest winter storm of the twentieth century had dumped three feet of snow on the city, transforming it into a different place; a magical one where the streets were cleared of cars, people skied to the local supermarket, and the Potomac chugged along, laden down by dirty brown icebergs.

The District, as it's known to the locals, is not the most exciting town after dark, but during the day it is breathtaking. When I first arrived in Washington I set out to explore the city on long solitary walks at the weekends. I walked through the narrow streets of Georgetown, past JFK's old home and the beautiful mansions once owned by Washington's liberal elite; down Wisconsin Avenue to the Georgetown waterfront, where the river winds its way slowly past the Watergate Building and the Kennedy Centre. If you sat there long enough, you would eventually see the military helicopters sweep low over the river towards the naval base just beyond the city. One night, I visited the Washington Monument with a group of new friends and stood with my chin pressed up against the cold stone staring up at the top of the 550-foot obelisk as the heavy rain pelted my face. That was a moment of sublime happiness. If you lived in the right part of town, Washington was one of the most beautiful cities in the world.

For an Irish kid obsessed with politics, Washington was Disneyworld. Going to work now meant taking a spot on the South Lawn of the White House or sliding in beside the other reporters under the high ceilings of the Congressional hearing rooms on Capitol Hill. I was surrounded on all sides by the machinery of the most powerful democracy on earth. Everywhere I looked there was another vital piece of the great Washington jigsaw. In a little Mexican restaurant I went to, I could expect to see members of Congress wolfing down a burrito after a hard day at the office. In the Dubliner bar near Union Station, House Speaker Newt Gingrich could sit undisturbed, except for the fawning attention of some Republican groupies. At a reception in the Capitol Building, you might hear the tell-tale Boston inflections of a senator introducing himself – 'Hi, I'm Ted Kennedy' – as if we hadn't realised that the moment he walked through the door. At the annual Radio and Television Correspondents' Association dinner at the Washington Hilton, I sat near the most famous sexual harassment victim in history, Paula Jones, as she was schmoozed by the big names in American journalism. After the dinner, I waited for a taxi at the spot where would-be assassin John Hinkley almost killed President Ronald Reagan in March 1981 with a cheap handgun. Every single square inch of the city seemed to have some enormous significance.

As I tried to negotiate my way into Washington society, I was forced to play a relentless game of first impressions. I was just 26 when I arrived in Washington and I looked even younger. When I got the job, one of my superiors suggested I grow a moustache or begin to wear glasses to make myself look older. To bridge the gravitas gap, a fashion consultant advised me to wear blue because it would make me look more authoritative. She also warned me to avoid white shirts because that would wash the colour out of my face. 'Yellow is the new white,' I was told.

They need not have worried about my appearance; Washington does not suffer bad suits lightly. It is a town where clothes are body armour and the sharper the look, the bigger the psychological advantage. Oscar Wilde once said, 'The true mystery of the world is the visible, not the invisible.' He must have been talking about Washington. As a television reporter in the American capital, your use of language might be subtle and graceful but if your hair is standing on end and there's a coffee stain on your tie then you may as well be reciting the telephone book.

There was a superficial strain to my new life in America that seemed to confirm my imported prejudices. Almost every evening there was another official function or drinks party and another insight into the hierarchy of Washington society. In a first encounter between two Washingtonians, status will govern the conduct of the conversation, and it will also determine the mutual boredom threshold. The more fame and power a person has, the longer they can talk arse before the glazed-eyes of their partner will seek out the location of the buffet. Those farther down Washington's food chain can make up for their lack of status with a quick wit, just like an ugly teenager can make up ground with the opposite sex with a smart chat-up line. In fact, the polite social gatherings that became a central part of my life in Washington resembled high-class singles bars; a glittering few were surrounded by potential suitors while the lesser mortals in the room tried to compensate for their deficiencies with personality and charm.

Being young was a definite advantage on the social circuit. One of the ironies of life in Washington is that while you live cheek by jowl with the mystery of history you are also surrounded by youth. Washington is Hollywood for 'A' students, and just as the siren sounds of Tinseltown beckon a less worldly category of youth, the capital city seduces the intelligent dreamer. In the White House, the young men and women who toiled away in the cubicles of the Lower Press Office seemed barely post-pubescent and yet they were responsible for shaping the image of the most powerful man in the world. In my first encounters with Capitol Hill, I was stunned by the age profile of the congressional staff. Even at my tender age I was over-ripe in comparison with some of the press secretaries and legislative assistants I found myself dealing with. In the corridors of the office buildings around the Capitol, it was hard to concentrate on anything but the confident stride of the stunning young women in sharp suits. 'Poke your eyes out,' one male friend advised me. 'It's the only way you'll be able to keep your mind on the job.'

There are a couple of reasons young people flourish in Washington. The ruling bureaucracy is designed to be in constant transition and that means there are almost always openings for bright young things. The second reason is that the bureaucracy is enormous. During my years in Washington, almost 6000 people worked in what was described as the White House staff community. They ranged from the top advisers crafting major policy initiatives to the mechanics checking the oil on the presidential helicopter. Six thousand staff may sound a bit ridiculous, but the logistics of the modern American presidency are stupefying, turning straightforward tasks like answering the post into epic challenges. (In the first six years of ˌthe Clinton administration, the president received more than 20 million letters and packages, and almost four million e-mail messages.)

The incoming tide of young people surges after each election cycle. Every two years there is some change in the composition of the US Congress and every four years the White House is up for grabs. With every new congressman, senator or president comes another wave of young talent. For some, the bare-knuckle combat of Washington politics is merely a trial run for a more lucrative career in the corporate world, but for others it becomes an addiction. That youthful lust for politics bears more than a passing likeness to alcoholism and I had become just another happy drunk in a town of dipsomaniacs. I was young and I was fascinated with politics. I worked hard and I played hard. In Washington, I was the rule that proved the exception.

Within a few months of my arrival in Washington, I developed friendships that transcended the chatter of the cocktail circuit. I came across people like John Deasy. He had lived in the United States for almost a decade when I met him but he still had an unvarnished Waterford accent. John had worked for two leading US senators before joining a Washington law firm that specialised in lobbying members of Congress. He was an expert guide to Capitol Hill and soon introduced me to the heady pleasures of life among Washington's young politicos. Close to John's Capitol Hill apartment was my favourite bar. The Capitol Lounge on Pennsylvania Avenue was dark, shabby and eclectic. The bartenders served Newcastle Brown Ale and decent Guinness with a sullen rock star cool. Behind them was a giant portrait of dead comedian John Belushi and all over the bar were campaign memorabilia and soccer scarves. Upstairs was the pool table, downstairs the cigar lounge. The jukebox was filled with Ska music and Eighties classics and, as long as you could find a space, it was okay to dance.

On a Friday evening, the Capitol Lounge provided a release from a week of pent-up angst. At around six o'clock, the first wave of young people rolled in from all points on Capitol Hill. By sundown, there was a raw, tense feel to the place, with plenty of aggressive flirting and partisan bitching. As ties and tongues were loosened, party affiliation became subordinate to lust or drunkenness or both. There was an edge to the Capitol Lounge that I had not expected to find in Washington. At first glance, the patrons were characters out of those American high school movies I despised: all bright smiles, perfect hairdos and macho swagger. But nothing and nobody was predictable in that bar. A fierce argument with a Republican about the death penalty would most likely finish off with a couple of shots of tequila and a joint rendition of a Jam song playing on the jukebox. A 22-year-old aide to a right-wing Republican congressman gave me the most astute analysis of Northern Ireland I had ever heard from an American, right there under John Belushi's stare.

The Capitol Lounge was the United States on a barstool. This youthful elite was drawn from all corners of the United States so, during a night at the bar, you could hear accents from Anchorage to Austin and life stories as diverse as America itself. There are large chunks of my time in the Capitol Lounge that I can't remember but I will never forget the energy and optimism that seemed to fill that space. Most of the people who gathered in the Lounge had no real ties to the physical entity that was Washington, but they had embraced the certainty that, in this city, at this time in life, everything is possible.

I had come to understand that the shallowness of the cocktail circuit was only a tiny part of Washington reality. By the end of 1995, I had realised that under the surface glare of the city were sincere friendships, and a world of possibilities. It was as if I had just discovered my sense of taste. The sharpness of each new experience was beyond any expectation I had had before leaving Ireland. When I returned to Dublin for Christmas, I could not help feeling that time away from America was an interruption. I was glad to see my loved ones but I was itching to get back. In less than four months, I had discovered that Harry Truman was right: 'Washington is a very easy city for you to forget where you came from and why you got there in the first place.'

# Three

## Access All Areas

Being Irish was a good thing in Washington in the last years of the twentieth century, thanks to a perceived renaissance in Irish culture, and White House involvement in the peace process. Northern Ireland was what the cynics referred to as a 'boutique' project: while it was inconsequential in the grand scheme of things, it had become a laboratory for Bill Clinton and his foreign policy team. The peace process allowed them to take chances and try out new approaches, without any risk to American lives or their political reputations. As the policy began to pay off, the more interesting it became to the broader Washington establishment. In fact, the political drama in Northern Ireland developed a cult following in the American capital, much like an inspirational foreign film. It was a little bit exotic, there was action and danger, and it seemed destined to have a happy ending. The absence of subtitles was another advantage; all the major characters were white, had names you could pronounce and spoke a form of English you could understand – although there was the odd furrowed brow when a visiting Northerner would talk about 'Norn Iron', 'moving the city-eh-shun forward' or 'On Tea Shock'.

The broad American generalisations about the peace

process were a little bit unsettling to someone who had reported first-hand on the violence in Northern Ireland. Thirty years of low-intensity war was now simply a backdrop, and the complex debate surrounding the peace process had been reduced to scripted inanities. Still, despite the shallowness of it all, the interest in the political intrigue back home in Ireland was a big advantage for me in Washington. One of my priorities was securing press credentials from the White House. The credential comes in the form of a thick plastic card they call the 'Hard Pass'. Not only does it grant you access to the press facilities of the West Wing, it also gives you membership of a relatively exclusive club: the White House Press Corps. I say 'relatively' because, while between 60 and 80 journalists cover the White House as their principal occupation, nearly 2000 Hard Passes had been issued by the time I came knocking on the White House door (many go to the technical staff involved in the network television coverage of the president).

As I went through the application process, I began to worry about the impact of my past exploits on my chances of securing a Hard Pass. The Secret Service performs a background check on every applicant, and the prospect of a couple of suits with ear-pieces and shades trawling through my past filled me with dread. What would they think of my presence at those protests outside the US Embassy in Dublin, or my sustained verbal abuse of Ronald Reagan? How would RTÉ feel, after plunging hundreds of thousands of pounds into their new Washington office, if its correspondent were deemed a security risk? As it turned out, I had nothing to worry about. I got the Hard Pass within six months of my arrival in Washington, while some foreign reporters I knew had waited years. I can't be sure exactly who helped along my application, but I am pretty certain that Ireland's elevated status in the White House firmament was the reason the Hard Pass ended up around my neck in double quick time.

Of all the new routines I treasured in those first months in Washington, the most memorable was the trip to the White House. I loved the self-satisfied thrill of walking through the crowds of tourists milling around Pennsylvania Avenue and presenting myself at the Northwest gate. The Secret Service looked through the Plexiglass at the Hard Pass; the buzzer sounded and I pushed the reinforced door open. Inside the gatehouse, I held my Hard Pass up to a small screen and entered my security code. Once approved for entry, I passed through a metal detector, collected my keys and my phone from a uniformed Secret Serviceman, strolled out the back door of the gatehouse and into the inner sanctum. From the gatehouse, I followed the gentle curve of the driveway, past the forest of TV cameras, lights and monitors to the North Lawn, where the driveway widened slightly and there in front of me was a low-slung extension of the main house, the West Wing. A few yards from the rigid gaze of the marine at the door was the stakeout position, where a row of camera tripods stood sentry in front of a small stand loaded down with microphones. It was where the VIPs came after their brush with power inside the West Wing. It was where senators and congressmen, presidents and prime ministers, dictators and freedom-fighters basked in the reflected glory of the White House, posing for a group of reporters and cameramen who generally could not care less.

Past the stakeout was the door to the White House briefing room. Once inside, I was struck by how small and scruffy the room was. Dominating this tiny space was the podium you see on television, with the instantly recognisable sign behind it. Everything else was just

40

clutter. This was once the site of the White House swimming pool, where President Kennedy reputedly entertained some of the women in his life. In my day it was home to cameramen and technicians who slouched in the solid cinema-style seats reading papers or doing their expenses. The smell of take-away food was almost as unsettling as the snores of sleeping photographers. Occasionally, when the voice on the intercom announced the imminent arrival of the White House press secretary or another top official, the room filled up with some of America's best-known journalists. The reporters made a journey of about 50 feet from their tiny cubicles at the back of the Briefing Room to their pre-assigned chairs in front of the podium. It is about the most exercise some reporters would get all day. Every one of the 48 chairs had a little brass plaque marking the territory of the top news organisations. I used to try and calculate how much those eight or nine big stars in the front row, such as ABC's Sam Donaldson or Helen Thomas of UPI, were earning collectively in a year. I never found out, but I guessed it was more than I would earn in my lifetime.

There were just a few occasions to question the president directly and they had a carefully choreographed routine of their own. When President Clinton met a visiting head of state, it was usually 'stills only', in other words, restricted to photographers. But sometimes, the president would invite the press to what is called an 'Oval Office Spray'. A small group of reporters, who formed 'The Pool', gathered outside the doors of the Oval Office – with the Rose Garden on the left – and waited for an official from the White House press office to escort everyone inside the most exalted workplace in the world. 'The Pool' stood behind the sofa and fired questions at the president, while his bemused guest was often an ornament in the background. I always enjoyed these occasions because they would put me a daydream away from history. These were sublime moments, best captured by Clinton's speechwriter, Michael Waldman, in his memoir *Potus Speaks*: 'At that moment, in that bright room, anything seemed possible.' The first couple of times I stood in the Oval Office I tried to memorise every detail of the room before me, but I soon realised there was no need. 'It's impossible to escape the feeling that you have been there many times,' writes Waldman. 'You could navigate the furniture with your eyes closed.' The ordered floor plan of the room guides you around men and moments that have defined America and the world. As I stood behind the sofa, I imagined John F. Kennedy sitting on his rocking chair during the Cuban Missile Crisis, or Richard Nixon as he contemplated his own political mortality during 'Watergate'. History has never been so real or so vivid as it was when I stood in that room.

Apart from those brief Oval Office encounters, the president occasionally gave a fully fledged news conference. I came to hate these events because they were often a glorified brawl among those of us in the second tier of the White House Press Corps. The big media organisations were guaranteed a question, but the rest of us had to shout and wave our hands like a bunch of hyperactive school children. And we were treated just like kids as we prepared for the news conference.

Half an hour before it began, we gathered at the bottom of a set of steps just outside the briefing room. At the top of the steps an escort from the Lower Press Office waited like a bouncer, ready to check our names. She had a seating plan in front of her and would let by only the reporters with a pre-assigned seat. Everyone else had to wait. The rejects gathered in a pathetic little group at the top of the stairs. They were the lowest form of life in the press corps; like losers who get stopped at the door of the nightclub for wearing white socks and jeans.

I once got stuck with the rejects. I forgot to phone and request a seat assignment. I was stopped by the 'bouncer' and made to stand with the stragglers. It was humiliating. I turned my back so I would not have to endure the pitying stares of my friends in the press corps. The other losers complained loudly in broken English to polite White House staffers about not being allowed in. I just squirmed silently and tried to pretend I had mistakenly been lumped into this multinational group of nobodies. Eventually, even the nobodies were ushered into the East Room, where the press conferences were usually held. It was also where the big White House parties took place. Every day, hundreds of tourists tramped through the room on the regular tours of the house. It was a beautiful setting for the ugly rivalry between those of us in the back rows. With a sense of mounting dread, I would search for my seat and find the little card marked 'Irish TV' sandwiched between the *Jewish Telegraph* and the *Kansas City Star*. The *Hartford Courant* always had a better seat than I did. There are votes in Hartford, Connecticut. There are no votes in Ireland.

Just before the press conference began, a disembodied voice came over the intercom announcing that the 'programme will begin into two minutes'. That was the cue for the network television correspondents to rise from their seats in the front row and fill airtime on live television with predictions about what the president was about to say. Everyone else in the room looked on with amusement. I always hoped the president would silently appear, creep up behind the big TV stars and whisper, 'Watch your house.' But the reality was far more dignified, at least at the outset. The disembodied voice warned everybody to turn off their mobile phones and pagers and a few seconds later the voice said simply, 'The President of the United States.'

Bill Clinton strode purposefully down the corridor beneath the television lights. The reporters, in an uncharacteristic show of respect, rose to their feet as he arrived at the doors to the East Room. When the president reached the podium, he raised his palms, signalling us to take our seats. When he had finished his opening statement, the president called on the Dean of the White House Press Corps, Helen Thomas, to ask the first question, and so battle commenced. What I most remember about those press conferences was the rhythm of the camera shutters; the noise rising and falling with the president's hands, every gesture triggering an immediate Pavlovian reaction from the rows of photographers. Like an overactive Geiger counter, the cameras clicked furiously as they captured the president's every gesture: a finger pointing in anger; a hand raised in frustration; a wry smile creeping across that famous face.

As Clinton and the reporters went through all the major topics of the day, there was a rising panic among those of us in the cheap seats. Each time it seemed the president was about to wind up an answer, I joined the others, put my hand in the air and said firmly, 'Mr President'. Other members of the second tier would rise out of their seats with their arms waving, yelling, 'Sir, Sir, Sir'. It was as if I was back in school, a class swot trying to impress the teacher. I knew the common practice was to provide the president with a seating chart, setting out the location of the various journalists in the room. I would occasionally indulge in the fantasy that on that chart was a big red mark beside the seat marked 'Irish TV', and Clinton would eventually turn his expectant gaze in my direction and call for a beautifully crafted question about Northern Ireland. Of course, that was mere fantasy.

There were only a couple of us who were genuinely interested in the peace process, and Irish-American reporter Susan Garrity had worked hardest to cultivate her contacts at the White House. But once it became known that Ireland was one of the president's interests, an ever-expanding bunch of reporters would come to the press conferences shouting, 'Question on Ireland, Sir.' Generally they had better seats than me. At one press conference, Susan called out the word 'Ireland' and Clinton motioned for the question. Almost before she had finished, a second person, farther back, shouted another question on Ireland and before the president could answer a British reporter was on his feet with a third question on Ireland. Bill Clinton leaned his head on his hand and smiled indulgently. Giggles filled the East Room. It was kind of pathetic and silly and I sat there, the only Irish person in the audience, rooted to the spot, determined not to join in the Irish marathon unfolding before my increasingly cynical eyes.

Those bouts of cynicism would come in frequent waves but would never last for very long. Washington always provided another experience to reawaken a child-like sense of awe. I had been in the United States for just over a year when Bill Clinton won a landslide victory and was inaugurated president for the second time. The inauguration of an American president is a spectacle that brings out the best and the worst of official Washington. No idea is too wacky if it makes the event more memorable. In 1973, the Inaugural Committee wanted to drive the pigeons from the route of the parade that traditionally follows the swearing-in ceremony. I assume they did not want some kamikaze bird crapping on the Commander-in-Chief. They spent $13,000 on a chemical bird repellent that was smeared on tree branches along the parade route. It was supposed to create an itching

45

sensation on the pigeons' feet. Instead, the birds ate the repellent. As Richard Nixon prepared to make his way to the White House, Pennsylvania Avenue was littered with dead and dying pigeons.

It pays to be concise at these glorious events, as poor old William Henry Harrison would find out at his inauguration in 1841. He delivered the longest inaugural address in history, all 8455 words of it. He also insisted on giving the speech without an overcoat or hat. He caught pneumonia and died a month later.

By the time I got to see my first inauguration, the authorities had put a lot of effort into making sure no harm could befall the president. More than 1200 military personnel lined the route of the inaugural parade as well as 3400 police officers. They were so security-conscious that hot food could not be served to the crowds along the parade route. The propane gas cylinders used to heat the food were deemed a security risk. But the powers that be could not do anything to change the weather. It was bitterly cold that January morning. During rehearsal parades, some military band members found their instruments had frozen to their lips.

Despite the arctic chill, 300,000 people had lined the streets between Capitol Hill and the White House as Bill Clinton took the presidential oath for the second time. I sat on top of the Voice of America building watching the VIPs gather for this incredible spectacle. Not everyone who gathered in Washington that day had voted for Bill Clinton. I'm sure there were many there who reviled him as they did the works of the devil. But they had come to participate in what has become a curious amalgam of grand political festival and Hollywood production. Somewhere along the line, it has become one of those traditions that help to regenerate American democracy.

Standing on that building, it was easy to forget that you are in the capital of a country where participation in the political process is the exception and not the rule. Less than half of all Americans turned out to vote in the 1996 presidential election and less than half of those who did, voted for Bill Clinton. Yet here they were, hundreds of thousands of Americans packed together in the brass-monkey cold of a Washington winter, waiting to see the presidency reborn. Without glorious spectacles like this, without reverence for tradition, institutions and common symbols, democracy in America would probably collapse. Maybe the survival of this country comes down to a simple truth: everybody loves a parade.

Not everything about the inauguration is so reverential and inspiring. After a long day of speechifying and parading, the president retires to the White House to prepare for a long night of partying. On the night of his inauguration Clinton made an appearance at 14 inaugural balls. I donned a tuxedo to go to one organised by the Virginia Democrats. It was like a bad wedding at a parochial hall; all that was missing were the mouldy 'hang' sandwiches and sozzled uncles. There was bad food, a bad band and some of the worst dancing I have ever seen in my life. America's political elite may have an enormous sense of their own importance but they have no sense of rhythm. Think of your granny dancing the Hucklebuck at a wedding reception, and you get the idea.

The inaugural ball was proof that Washington is in constant danger of disappearing up its own backside, at least, the Washington that relies on access to power or the powerful. Access would become the most important word in the English language during my time there. I had become like thousands of other reporters, lawyers, lobbyists, consultants and diplomats for whom business begins only when the cocktail party starts and there is a chance to schmooze the member of Congress, sidle up to the senator or have that brief and meaningful word with the president. Without access you are nothing. For many in the American capital, the greatest compliment you can give or receive is 'Washington insider'. An insider has access, and the desire to be an insider becomes an addiction that can consume your life like heroin. After a while I discovered another Washington secret: sometimes it is the people who do not try very hard, or take themselves too seriously, who get the access. And some acquire it by accident.

One night, a group of my friends were having a meal at a trendy Washington restaurant when the former US Trade Representative Mickey Kantor was escorted to a corner table. A few more B-list political celebrities arrived and no one gave them more than a glance. Then a couple of secret service agents walked by, followed by Bill Clinton. After the meal, he shook some hands and ended up at my friends' table. He turned to ITN cameraman Sean Swan, who is originally from the Dublin suburb of Howth. When the president discovered he was Irish, he started to talk about the peace process and soon Bill and Sean were deep in conversation, as if there was no one else in the room.

Joe Carroll of the *Irish Times* enjoyed another great example of access by accident within weeks of arriving in Washington. He was at the media party thrown every summer on the lawn of the White House. That particular year we were entertained by Kid Creole and the Coconuts, a band I had last heard on a dodgy sound system at a teenage disco at the tennis club in Malahide. The party was broken up when a thunderstorm rolled over the city and everybody was forced to seek cover. Joe Carroll ran into a small room just off the White House lawn. As he was drying out, he realised there were just a couple of people in that room and one of them was Hillary Clinton. At first the Secret Service eyed him nervously, but their concentration was broken when the Coconuts arrived, shaking off the rain as they crowded around the first lady. Then Bill Clinton walked into the room and began to shake hands. Joe later explained that he could not pretend to be a Coconut any longer, so he walked straight up to the president, shook hands and began talking about Ireland.

Some Washington reporters would kill for that kind of access but for others it is all very routine and boring. It always amazed me that people I knew, who travelled with the president, could become so blasé about their everyday proximity. As a student, I had devoured all those insider accounts of American politics. *The Boys on the Bus* by Timothy Crouse and Hunter S. Thompson's *Fear and Loathing on the Campaign Trail* were two of my favourite books. Some kids run away to join the circus; I wanted to run away to join the White House Press Corps. But on the few occasions I travelled with the president (or 'POTUS', as he is known on the official schedule) the myth never quite lived up to the reality. Instead of living the glamorous life of hard-working, hard-drinking hard-chaws, armed with rapier wit and a typewriter, the reporters who cover the president resemble a well-heeled group of business executives.

Most people were very welcoming and I did find kindred spirits among the iconoclasts and misfits. They were the kind of people who made the politically incorrect jokes on the press charter or appeared in the lobby of the hotel in the morning with bad hangovers and great stories about the night before. My best friend in Washington was the CBS White House producer, Bill Owens. He was an exceptional journalist and the ultimate party animal but he met his match in Madrid, the last stop on President Clinton's visit to Ireland, Germany and Spain in late 1995. In the early hours of the morning, Bill Owens found himself in a bar, staring at the beautiful woman serving him drinks. Her name was Helena Fernandez and she spoke very little English. While Bill Owens didn't know it then, this woman would eventually become his wife.

Besides the occasional love story, these presidential visits were insufferably comfortable and routine. On the press plane you were pampered within an inch of your life. The trip started off at Andrews Air Force base on the outskirts of Washington, where you dropped off your bags and gave your passport to the staff of the White House travel office. From that point you lived in a bubble. There were no customs forms, no long passport queues and no hassle. The White House Press Corps on tour is a grouchy band of privileged travellers enjoying business class, plush hotel rooms and enough food to feed a couple of developing countries. Too many reporters, producers and technicians travel with POTUS to fit on Air Force One and so a charter plane carrying the press is sent ahead. Over the years, the White House Correspondents' Association has laid down rules about how the travelling press corps is to be treated. In my time, there was a rule that a hot meal must be served on any press flight lasting more than an hour. I just wanted the food to stop. I would waddle off the plane onto a bus and straight to the hotel where a press room had been set up complete with a buffet constantly stocked with the delicacies of whatever country you were in. If it's raw herring, it must be Finland.

Once in that press room you never needed to leave. On the president's first trip to Ireland in 1995, I found out that I could learn more about my own country if I stayed inside the White House press room and simply monitored the constant streams of transcripts, handouts and briefings I was spoon-fed. I expected the Jurys cabaret to come prancing through the door to give us White House reporters a real taste of Irish culture. On the president's final visit to Ireland in December 2000, we were given a pronunciation guide to all those difficult Gaelic expressions like Aras an Uachtaráin (ARR-uss on YOOK-ter-rahn) and Oireachtas (or-YOCK-tuss). The fact that Guinness (GHIN-iss) was included (and described coyly as 'a brewed beverage') led me to believe that this was a rare attempt at official humour. I travelled to Moscow, London, Dublin, Belfast and Helsinki with the White House Press Corps and in each one of those cities I had to make a conscious effort to burst out of the bubble before I lost the capacity for independent thought.

In Moscow, when I ventured out of the hotel, I was given a card with the address of the hotel written in Cyrillic script, just so the taxi driver would know where I was staying. In London, I missed the last press bus to the airport and risked missing the short flight to Belfast. I ran to the US Embassy, just a few streets away on Grosvenor Square, with another panic-stricken White House reporter who had slept late. We were piled into a big black limo and sped to the airport where we were transferred to a waiting police car that deposited us at the foot of the steps of the plane. Now that is what I call service.

Inside the White House bubble, you are a member of an exclusive club, with your numerous plastic passes to prove it and a little card marked 'RTÉ – Irish TV' to tell you where to park your pampered arse. It's the Egon Ronay School of Journalism and now and again I would feel a little guilty about enjoying my time in this rarefied world. You see, I wasn't suffering for my vocation. I had learned my craft chasing Irish cabinet ministers in the freezing cold outside government buildings or scabbing cups of tea from old ladies on Catholic housing estates in Portadown. Now, I couldn't move without someone handing me a press release, a chicken caesar salad and a chilled glass of sauvignon blanc. Where did it all go wrong?

# Four

# My Friend Bill

When I first arrived in Washington I had some serious misconceptions about my place in the grand scheme of things. I really believed it would be just a matter of days before I was summoned to the White House for the first of several intimate on-camera chats with the leader of the free world. That may sound naive but, at the time, there seemed to be grounds for boundless optimism. I began my stint in Washington as Bill Clinton was preparing for his first visit to Ireland. He had invested a huge amount of time and energy in the peace process and I was Irish television's first resident correspondent in Washington, so an interview was a foregone conclusion. I had no idea of the heartbreak and pain that were on the way.

The first disappointment came like the slap of an open hand on a rosy teenage cheek. Just a couple of days before his departure for Ireland, Clinton was supposed to grant an interview to me and the other two members of the Irish press corps in Washington: Conor O'Clery of the *Irish Times* and Susan Garrity. But then the president found himself in the midst of a budget showdown with the Republicans in Congress. As the row over money continued, government offices were closed down and millions of civil servants were sent home. Worse still,

Clinton's advisers were forced to take Susan, Conor and me off the schedule while they set about saving democracy. I got my 'Dear Mark' phone call in a federal building in Boston. I swallowed hard and vowed not to give up. My day would come. The interview would happen sooner or later. It did, but I was not invited. Conor, Susan and Martin Fletcher of *The Times* were given an audience when the president returned from Ireland. The White House decided that only print reporters could share in the president's celebration of his trip to Ireland.

I had witnessed Ireland's breathless affair with President Clinton with my face pressed right up against the glass. Through every magic moment of that first visit in November 1995, I was near the president. I felt a little shudder of childish excitement as the wheels of the press charter crunched down on the runway at Belfast's Aldergrove airport. I sat behind a well-known American television correspondent on the bus ride into Belfast and listened as she got a ten-minute briefing from a producer on my country's 800 years of tortured history.

The bus entered West Belfast and passed through a street jammed with people waiting for the first American president to take them seriously. As I looked into the cheering crowd, I remembered I had been at this spot before – the RUC station on the Springfield Road. I had been here at midnight on the last day of August the previous year when the IRA ceasefire went into effect. I had watched a crowd celebrate the first moments of a new era with elation and uncertainty. They banged bin lids and scrawled slogans on the walls of the station, but someone asked, 'What have we won?'

A year later at the same place, with President Clinton on his way, I thought to myself, At least you have one minor victory. You have made the jaded American hacks on this bus and their audiences back home sit up, take notice and admire you. And you have sent a spine-tingling chill of excitement through a young Irish reporter who cannot believe he is part of all this. By the time I reached Dublin the next day, I had overdosed on the high-grade thrill of history in the making. Like a kid who has gorged himself on Coca-Cola and chocolate, I was wired. On the last night of the visit, I joined my friends from RTÉ in the press centre for a few celebratory pints. I was fairly well oiled when an official from the Department of Foreign Affairs approached me and told me the president had agreed to meet some of the Irish reporters covering his visit. I reached for the breath mints and walked across the courtyard at Dublin Castle to join my colleagues Eamonn Lawlor and Miriam O'Callaghan. We stood and made endless small talk at the foot of the stairs that led to the dining-room. Just when I thought I was in for another disappointment, the President of the United States appeared at the top of the stairs and began to walk in our direction.

I still have the official White House photograph of that first meeting. Clinton has that broad 'Aw shucks' grin on his face and I have my hand outstretched, barely gripping his fist. My face is creased with a determination to say something significant. The Guinness in me wanted to say, 'Mother of Divine Jesus, you will not believe how glad I am to shake your big, fat paw.' Instead, I burbled, 'Hello, it's great to meet you.' Then he was gone; such a brief encounter. I knew there would be other times and was comforted by a friend's advice that once Clinton meets you, he never forgets your face. Of course the same person also told me, 'Beware Bill Clinton when he tells you you're wearing a nice tie. It's his way of saying fuck you.'

As it turned out, there would be other handshakes with Bill Clinton, all part of the ritual grip and grin that happens at White House parties. It's a well-choreographed routine. They announce your name and you step forward to shake hands with the president as the official photographer captures the moment for posterity. Countless others have gone before you but, for that moment, it's just you and his firm handshake and a moment of eye contact. Each time I took my place in the receiving line in the basement of the White House, I would try to think of something intelligent to say to the man. The second time I met him was at a Christmas party at the end of 1995. I was determined to have a brief but substantial conversation about the peace process. When he finally took my hand in his, I croaked, 'How are ya?' Again, I have the photograph and this time there's no grin on his face, just a mildly quizzical stare.

It happened again and again. When I went to shake his hand, my carefully prepared profundity would be replaced by some blubbered silly greeting. It became so frustrating that I soon gave up thinking of things to say. On St Patrick's Day in 1997, I was in the Oval Office where President Clinton was greeting the then Taoiseach, John Bruton. I was the reporter closest to the president, so I got to ask a couple of questions and received some worthy soundbites in return. That night I took my place in the receiving line at the White House party. This time I had absolutely no prepared statement. I had persuaded myself there was no point; grip and grin, that's all this will be. But just as I reached out to grab the president's hand, his eyes lit up in recognition and he said, 'We meet again.' I was dumbstruck. I muttered, 'Thank you for the great conversation today.' He kept shaking my hand waiting for me to say something that made a bit more sense. The leader of the free world was looking for a dialogue, an exchange of ideas or, at the very least, a bit of banter. Once more I said, 'Thank you for the conversation.' I was stunned and maybe he was too. There was a pause and then the president's eye passed to the next guest. The moment had gone. I moved on with a dull pain in my head. 'You tit,' I thought to myself. 'The least you could have said was "nice tie".'

Yet again I comforted myself with the thought that Bill and I had connected. He had remembered me because he was impressed by my questions that morning and, judging by the warmth of the handshake and eye contact, he wanted to hear more. But as usual, I was deluding myself and it would take me just 24 hours to find out. The night after my 'conversation' with Bill, I sat in the dark of a Washington cinema watching a sneak preview of the movie *Primary Colors*, a barely fictional profile of Bill Clinton. The movie opens with presidential candidate Jack Stanton, played by John Travolta, working a crowd of well-wishers. The narrator marvels at how Stanton can tailor a simple handshake to make each and every person feel they have shared a moment of profound empathy. It's a Clinton moment. I know. I'd had one the night before and now, watching the movie screen, I was awed and a little disappointed. These would be the two emotions that would define my relationship with Bill Clinton.

While I was lurching from handshake to handshake, I kept up my soul-destroying search for the big interview. I got so close so many times, but was always the bridesmaid, never the bride. I was once ten minutes away from an interview with Clinton at the Irish-American of the Year award in New York's Waldorf Astoria in March 1997. On a crackly cell phone line to the White House, I was told that I still had a very good chance of 'face time' with the president that night. I was pumped up with premature elation only to be rudely deflated by that old familiar heartbreak. CBS News was escorted behind the wall of Secret Service men to talk to Bill Clinton about

Ireland, while I was left sitting outside with the rest of the audience.

What was the White House playing at? What had I done to deserve this kind of treatment? I let myself slip gently under the warm blanket of self-pity. I imagined that in the White House press office there were a group of demented bureaucrats scheming up ways to screw me royally. Not even this daydream offered me much comfort because I had come to know that the people around the president were anything but malicious. They just do not have the time or the space to play such mind games. The average Irish business executive has a bigger office than all but the most senior White House officials. They work in the cramped and claustrophobic West Wing, 'the crown jewel of the American penal system', as Bill Clinton once described it.

I saw something more in these people than mere endurance. In fact, what attracted me was what I didn't see in their eyes. I didn't see the blind ambition I've seen etched on faces of people whose lives are devoured by politics. There wasn't the stink of cynicism that I remembered from some people in public service in Ireland; those made bitter by a lifetime inside the bureaucracy. Most of the White House staffers I got to know had that sense of place and of history that I have always wanted to believe could exist at the heart of government.

One of those people, Kris Engskov, was among the president's closest aides. Before the White House, Kris had attended an Arkansas college and worked on Bill Clinton's presidential campaign. Initially, his job was to guide members of the press corps into close proximity to President Clinton, control them when they were there and guide them out when time was up. He would go on to serve as the president's personal assistant, known in

Washington parlance as the 'Body Man'. It was a job that gave him more personal access to the leader of the free world than any other living person except the first lady. And I would say at times it was a toss up between Kris and Hillary. I remember thinking that this guy was too good to be true. There was no way his devotion to his job could be real or sincere. Then one Friday night on the way back from the Capitol Lounge, I decided to take a detour by the Jefferson Memorial, one of my favourite places in Washington.

On that cold and crisp winter night, as the lights from the city danced on the tidal basin, I took a big breath of history into my lungs. There was something romantic about the night and the lights of the city but this was still a monument to a dead politician. Who could find romance in that? Then I saw Kris Engskov walking around Jefferson with a pretty young woman. They stopped to look at the inscription above the statue's head. Kris turned and saw me and we traded hellos and spoke briefly. As he walked on to the next inscription, I wondered about this man. Every day he goes to work in the White House, the most potent symbol of American democracy. Yet, at night, when he's trying to impress a woman, he goes to a place that honours American democracy.

It might have been wrong to look at Kris and see something more than a boring civil servant, but I was convinced that the people who worked in the White House deserved more respect than my homemade begrudgery would at first allow. What really convinced me were my dealings with a handful of officials who ended up giving more time and effort to the search for peace in Ireland than anyone back home had the right to expect. There was Nancy Soderberg and Tony Lake, the top brass at the National Security Council. Then there were the anonymous people like Colonel James L. Fetig of the United States Army. For the first two years I was in Washington, he was the assistant press secretary for foreign affairs at the White House, the mouthpiece for the National Security Council, the well-placed source I quoted in my reports, and the man who interpreted every nuance of American policy on Ireland. What he said and how he said it had an influence on the search for peace in Ireland merely because of whom he represented. Yet he was a most unlikely player in the Irish peace process.

Jim Fetig had no Irish ancestors that I knew of. But he had almost 30 years of life in the military. He was the son of an army officer, joined the infantry at the height of the Vietnam War and rose through the ranks to become the spokesperson for the army's Chief of Staff. He had worked at the Pentagon, served in Panama and Korea and was the army spokesperson during the Gulf War. Then he was called to the White House.

I came to value the time I spent with Jim Fetig not because of any high-grade information he shared with me. What I liked about the man was that he was a walking American cliché. He strode around with a straight back, a ready smile and an aura of unshakeable confidence. He talked in clipped and efficient sentences like a character from an old TV detective series: 'Just the facts, ma'am, just the facts.' Jim could be brutally honest about American attitudes to Ireland. It was from him that I learned the first immutable rule about White House policy on Ireland: 'There is always less than meets the eye.' At some point, the work he did on Ireland became personal. I stood beside Jim in the Guildhall Square in Derry during that first presidential visit to Ireland. Thousands had jammed into the square waving little American flags and shouting in unison, 'We want Bull.' 'Who's Bull?' asked the Americans. 'Bull Clinton,' answered the locals. I remember Jim gazing out into that sea of Stars and Stripes. As an army officer, in some of the most troubled parts of the world, he had seen his national flag burned and abused. Now, here he was in a country he would normally never have cared about, watching thousands of people saluting his nation and its most potent symbol.

One of the most interesting individuals I got to know during that presidential visit to Ireland was White House press secretary Mike McCurry. I pestered him and his office during the trip for a brief interview with the president, so he could tell the people of Ireland once more how brilliant they were. Mike could not deliver the president but he did agree to stand in for Bill Clinton on the *Six-One News*. He was due to meet me and the RTÉ satellite truck at the front gate of the US Ambassador's residence in the Phoenix Park for the interview. Just minutes before he was supposed to go on air, a speeding car screeched to a halt and McCurry clambered out. He stood without complaint, ankle deep in mud in the freezing cold, waiting for his live interview. He didn't even get fazed when his ear-piece fell out and a technician jumped over the barricade to jam it back into place. Mike McCurry was almost too good to be true.

He was among the most popular press secretaries of modern times, partly because of his sense of humour. On one trip during the 1996 presidential election campaign, McCurry jumped fully clothed into a swimming pool to win a bet. His lopsided grin and constant wisecracks were also a shield against the onslaught he faced during the Monica Lewinsky scandal. Once, during Bill Clinton's year of living dangerously, McCurry came to the podium in the White House briefing room with a brown paper bag over his head and announced that he was the anonymous source everyone was quoting. But jokes were a fragile defence when faced with the Lewinsky scandal. The day the scandal broke, McCurry spent 36 minutes in the briefing room and answered 148 questions in front of a live television audience of countless millions. During this period, there were briefings where he would crack and angrily denounce the press corps for recycling rumour and innuendo. After he had left the White House, he would talk of the misery of those months and the terrible realisation that his boss had lied about his relationship with a young White House intern. Every day, from January to October, McCurry stood on the podium as the first line of defence for his boss. Sometimes he would brag about his limited knowledge of the details of the scandal and by the time he left the White House his credibility had been undermined and his halo dented. But when President Clinton said McCurry had set the standard by which future White House press secretaries would be judged, few in the briefing room disagreed.

Nevertheless, when it came to getting the big interview for RTÉ, McCurry was a disaster. A few months before he left the White House, I did get close. In May 1998, I was certain I had the interview. The people of Ireland were about to vote in a referendum on the Good Friday Agreement. On the morning of the vote, I had been led to believe there was a good chance that Bill Clinton would sit down with me. Then the White House rang to tell me that he could not do an interview, but what about a conference call with the president and a couple of other reporters? I had been through so much that I would have accepted a nice postcard from the man. But even the consolation prize of a conference call was taken off the table because of the president's busy schedule. That night, I watched pictures of him on the golf course with a big cigar in his mouth. I consoled myself with the words of a White House official: 'When he's ready to talk about Ireland, he will talk to *you*.' After years of waiting, that seemed like a good deal. When would I ever learn?

It was June 1999 and I was trying to escape the suffocating humidity of a Washington summer morning. I sat in the air-conditioned refuge of my office, my feet on the desk, reading about efforts to save the Good Friday Agreement. The phone rang. It was the RTÉ foreign desk with the message that the BBC had got an exclusive interview on Northern Ireland with the president. I felt the familiar dry taste in my mouth and tightening in my gut, but instead of agonising disappointment there was seething anger. Downing Street had asked the White House to give the exclusive interview to the BBC in an attempt to soften up the Unionists. It was the ultimate kick in the teeth. That night I stalked around a party at the Irish Embassy trying to collar a senior White House official for an explanation. When I finally cornered him, all I got was an apologetic smile and a shrug.

For the first time, I had to contemplate the appalling prospect that I would never get an interview with President Clinton. In some ways it was a liberating thought. It's like the moment you realise that your girlfriend really means it when she says she doesn't want to see you anymore. Now I could hear Bill Clinton's voice and not feel a little sad. I could walk down the streets of Washington and see his motorcade and not have a little tear well up in my eye. I could even see him with other interviewers and not feel jealous. I was making progress. Maybe some day I would have that most elusive part of the American dream: closure. But just when I thought I was over him, the bastards went and gave me that interview. No warning. It just happened.

It was the end of November 1999, and Northern Ireland was about to get a new power-sharing executive. I rang the White House to request an interview with one of the president's foreign policy advisers. The National Security Council spokesman said that he thought the president himself might talk to me later in the week from Seattle, where he was attending the ill-fated World Trade Organisation conference. There were conditions to the offer of an interview. I would share it with a BBC reporter and it would take place on the phone. But for once it sounded as if it could happen. I had to make a quick trip to Dublin on some personal business and all through a sleepless plane journey across the Atlantic, I kept thinking, Something will go wrong. I was afraid to mention the possibility of an interview to anyone in case I put a jinx on the whole thing. When I returned to Washington, there were three messages on my answering machine, all confirming that the interview was on.

The next day history was made in Northern Ireland with the formation of a new power-sharing executive. Bill Clinton was about to leave Seattle and the plan was that once he got to King's County International Airport, he would take a phone call from me and Steven Grimason of the BBC in Belfast. The BBC offered to let me use their studios in Washington to record the interview. I sat there with a cameraman, ready to capture the image of me, my headphones on, talking to the leader of the free world. I sat there for almost an hour in silence, waiting for the call, thinking about the three or four questions I would get to ask. Mostly I thought of how long I had waited for this moment and how much effort I had put into my search for an interview with the president. It wasn't the same as sitting down with him face to face, but it was something.

I was roused out of my reflections by the sound of a BBC producer telling me that the White House telephone operator was on the line. The operator had a perky little voice, so perky it sounded like she was computer-generated.

'Mr Little, this is the Camp David operator. I apologise

for keeping you waiting. Please hold the line for the secure voice operator.'

I wrote down the words 'secure voice operator' on my notepad. It sounded delicious. I wondered what a secure voice sounded like. Was it like a football coach or a kindly teacher?

'Hello, is that Mike Little?' the secure voice operator enquired. For a moment, I wondered, Who's Mike?

Steven Grimason joined the conference call from Belfast, then a National Security Council official was on the line and finally White House press secretary Joe Lockhart talked to us from Seattle. We chatted briefly and in the background I could hear the faint sound of a voice on another telephone line. It was Bill Clinton. Joe Lockhart came back once more to check that Steven and I were still there and then there was a worrying silence that was finally broken by a voice.

'Hello,' the voice said.

It sounded like a question, like the voice of someone that has walked into a dark room and is unsure of who is there. The word hung in the air for a moment before I realised it was him.

'Hello, Mr President. This is Mark Little with RTÉ in Washington.'

Steven introduced himself from Belfast and we both thanked him profusely for his time.

'I'm just glad to hear your voices on this day,' he said. Jesus, that's right, I remembered. They've just formed the new executive in Belfast. That's what we are here for.

The interview lasted for 13 minutes. Clinton was quick-witted but careful. He spoke as if he was facing us in a small, quiet room. His voice and his language combined to create a carefully controlled flood of intimate understanding. When I looked back over my notes of the interview, I saw a pattern in the phrases he had used.

They were so exact it seemed impossible that they were the product of a spontaneous conversation. It was like reading a script that had been revised and revised. It appeared that the president had either memorised phrases passed to him by a top adviser, or this perfect syntax was the product of a mind so engaged with the Irish peace process that he had the power of total recall. He was instinctively aware of nuances even the most seasoned observers could miss. I asked him about the decision to drop Articles Two and Three of the Irish constitution. He used the word 'noble'. It was an unusual word and I had never heard it from the mouth of an Irish politician, but it was a beautiful word to use in that context.

'So I think the Irish Republic did a noble thing here,' he said. 'And they ennobled the people who agree with them and who still support the concept of a united Ireland, because they gave them the only chance they could ever have to achieve their dreams. They gave them the only chance they could have to have a full life along the way.'

I knew the president's advisers and these were not their words. This was Bill Clinton on a riff and you could hear the commas dropping into place along the way. When the interview came to an end, I thanked Clinton for his time. Steven and I told him that we would see him in Belfast soon and he joked that he would visit every two weeks if it were up to him. We laughed and said goodbye and there was a loud, almost stage-managed, click as the line went dead. It was 11.09 a.m. Pacific Time.

# Five

# Melting Pot, My Arse

For all its obvious majesty, my new hometown had a squalid side to it. By the early 1990s, Washington had the second highest murder rate of any city in America. There was almost one killing a day. In the five years I lived in the US capital, more than 1400 people were murdered inside the city limits. Family life was a luxury many Washingtonians would never enjoy. In 1998, 63 per cent of children born in the District of Colombia were born to single mothers and three out of five kids were growing up in homes where the father was absent. Homelessness was like an open sore the city would not treat. There seemed to be nobody who would confront the problems of mental illness among those who were living on the streets of Washington. Most were black and many were Vietnam veterans, still trying to cope with the psychological scars of a distant war. The streets themselves were pockmarked with evidence of neglect. The traffic-light at one pedestrian crossing near my street was out of order for three months. They couldn't be bothered to fix a pot-hole near my office, so they put a heavy sheet of steel over it. Every few seconds, for weeks, there was an enormous bang as each successive car bounced over the rusting steel plate. When Washington was hit by the blizzard of 1996, cars remained buried for weeks because the city's snowploughs never made it to some neighbourhoods. And this was the capital of the most powerful nation on earth.

By the time Washington celebrated the new millennium, things had got a lot better, but in those first years it was clear that DC was paralysed. Paralysed because the city's population had chosen to live with a strange form of racial segregation. When I arrived in the city, 70 per cent of the people in Washington were African-American. The vast majority lived in three of the four quadrants of the District: south-east, south-west and north-east. These areas are home to some of the most stable communities of true Washingtonians; the human soul of the city. But in these areas lie some of the scariest neighbourhoods in America. These are where the grim statistics of the urban massacre are calculated and where the vast majority of Washington's murders are committed. Gang-bangs, drive-by shootings, teenage homicides filled the Metro section of the *Washington Post* and most of the crime was Black on Black. Tucked away on the inner pages of the newspaper were stories that would bring tears to your eyes: mothers cut down by a stray bullet, infants killed while sleeping in their cribs, and teenagers killing teenagers for the designer labels on their clothes.

However, to a privileged white boy like me, the senseless violence was never a pressing concern, even though it was happening only a few miles away. That's because I lived in the one affluent quadrant of the city: north-west. Two or three nights a week, I walked the few blocks home from my office in the early hours of the morning and in the five years I lived in the city I never felt any serious threat to my personal safety. In contrast, on my trips home to Dublin, I would get very nervous walking down O'Connell Street after closing time, always aware of the possibility of random attack.

If you are wealthy and white and live in Washington, you can generally assume that the city's most serious problems will affect other people. But no matter how privileged you are, there is no way of ignoring the dire state of public services. Generally, white Washingtonians held their noses and wrote off the problems with two words: 'Marion Barry'. He was the Washington mayor who had been arrested in January 1990 in a city hotel room in possession of a large amount of cocaine and in the company of a couple of call girls. He served a term in jail but always insisted he had been set up. Soon after his release, he appealed for understanding from Washington's African-American majority and was duly re-elected. To the white population of Washington, the infamous mayor was a crack-smoking charlatan who had built up a corrupt and overstaffed bureaucracy. But to the black majority, electing Marion Barry was an act of self-governance and the more he was attacked, the more he became a symbol of resistance. There was one city, but two radically different views.

On issue after issue, I would find out that Washington was a microcosm of the broader reality of race in America. The first big story I covered in the United States was the verdict in the O.J. Simpson trial, handed down in October 1995. I chose to watch the verdict in the mock-courtroom of Howard University's Law School. Howard is the one of the most prestigious African-American colleges in America and is located in the inner city of Washington. There must have been a couple of hundred people in the room that day, watching two television screens set up by the witness stand. There were four white people among them: a sound-recordist, a local journalist, a lecturer and myself. I hadn't noticed that fact until the room had filled up and a black cameraman casually mentioned it to me.

In the front row, three young women were sitting together holding hands. Every now and again, one of them would break free to join her palms together in prayer. Behind her, a row of young men sat in silence, grim expressions etched on their faces. I ignored the two television screens because I wanted to watch these faces when the verdict was announced. I also wanted to stay out of the way if the verdict went against OJ. I heard the court official call the spokesperson for the jury and I watched a woman in the front row grimace and pull her hands to her face. I heard the verdict in slow motion. '… Orenthal James Simpson, not guilty.' The scream of delight was immediate. It erupted almost before the words had emerged from the television. The women in the front row grabbed each other and tears streamed down their faces while the young men behind jumped up and down, swinging their fists in a circle in salute of the verdict. There were some silent members of the audience. I guessed they were a little embarrassed at the ferocity of the reaction, but there was no doubt that the vast majority in that room welcomed the verdict.

It was a scene repeated in black neighbourhoods across America. The man they called 'The Juice' had become a powerful symbol to African-Americans, one of their heroes caught in the grip of a modern judicial lynch mob. Some people I talked to in that mock-courtroom hailed the verdict as progress, showing that there were indeed checks and balances on racial bias in the American legal system. Most of my white friends thought a murderer had walked free. But then most of my friends, people who lived in a small, racially polarised city, also felt some relief. Washington and other American cities would be spared the kind of deadly rioting that had broken out after the Rodney King verdict in 1992.

I was stunned to see America's racial fault line open up before my eyes. But I was more surprised by how subtle racial tension in America could be. What amazed me was how desensitised Blacks and Whites have become to the mutual suspicion that is still an important part of their daily interaction, especially in the big cities. The best cameraman I worked with was an African-American. Darryl Johnson was lanky, laid back and a joy to work with. On one trip outside Washington, I was lagging behind Darryl as we left an airport terminal building. He was about 20 yards in front of me when he tried to hail the shuttle bus that was supposed to take us to our rental car. It passed him but when I put out my hand, the bus stopped almost immediately. As I looked back to Darryl, he tipped his head to the side and raised his hands in a gesture of impotence and frustration. We would never know if the bus driver had acted out of racial bias. It is quite possible he did not, but Darryl never had any doubt. Later over a beer, he wouldn't talk about the incident except to say, 'It's the Man.' 'The Man' is a generic description for the white establishment. When you hear the phrase spoken it's usually an expression of hope-lessness and weariness. It's a declaration that unseen but powerful forces are keeping the black man down, just as they have done for centuries. Those two words sum up both the real and imagined racism of American society.

It soon occurred to me that maybe that fabled melting pot just doesn't exist in the United States, at least not in the way we commonly understand it. In the past, the different ethnic and racial groups built a common identity and culture as they started to work, live, eat, dance and sing together. Those things that are unique to each group enter into the mainstream and become at some stage 'American', such as pizza and pretzels or jazz and gospel. These days, popular music is dominated by African-

American and Latino artists or by the forms they pioneered. White kids have adopted the styles of their black heroes and, in turn, this has started to filter back into the music. Take the case of an angst-ridden white boy called Marshall Mathers. He emerges from the deeply unfashionable Midwest, takes the name Eminem, adopts rap lyrics and sensibilities and becomes a dominant figure in American pop-culture; all with the support and patronage of the veteran black rappers who spawned this musical genre in the first place.

There are limits to this type of cultural crossover. Outside the mainstream, 'America' is an ever-increasing number of racial and ethnic groups struggling to maintain their distinct identities by separate development. You walk into a record shop in America and you see one section that is 'Urban' and another side that is 'Alternative'. They may as well have signs saying 'Black Kids' and 'White Kids'. White Americans who drink and drive fear arrest on a charge of DWI: Driving While Intoxicated. Black Americans joke that every time they go out on the highway, they risk being stopped for DWB: Driving While Black. You can watch a stream of prime-time sit-coms on the major networks dealing with everything from lesbianism to jailhouse love, but you will never find more than one black character per show. Meanwhile, when you look at the Warner Brothers' television network on any given evening, there's nothing but comedies dealing with the black experience.

In no other country in history have so many lived so far apart in such close proximity. It is not just a black and white thing. Shortly before I left the United States, I took a flight from Miami to New York. The plane was filled with a rich mixture of 'hyphenated' Americans. A large group of Hasidic Jews occupied the seats immediately in front of me, while across the aisle a stunning black woman was sitting on her own; she was tall, with the sharp features of a model. Behind me, a Muslim man and his wife were trying to pacify their infant child. A Latino couple on the other side of me cuddled and whispered sweet nothings in Spanish. Shortly before departure, we were joined by a very distinguished gentleman with his hand on the shoulder of a handsome younger man with dyed blond hair, a South Beach tan and tight jeans; a gay couple, I assumed, returning from holidays.

A turbulent flight was topped off by a ninety-minute delay over Long Island. As we circled in the holding pattern, we all knew we still had to face the baggage claim at Kennedy Airport, which on any normal evening is a scene from a disaster movie. I spent more than three hours with that multicultural mix of people and never once did any of us exchange words of greeting, sympathy or even frustration. At one point, as we waited for our bags, I realised that all the white people in suits were standing together like Custer and his men at the Little Big Horn. I travel enough to know there is very little communication between passengers on aeroplanes these days, but this was a remarkable spectacle. In Manhattan the next day, I kept thinking back to that bizarre flight and it made me look around more closely. New York City is supposed to be the ultimate celebration of diversity. On every sidewalk there are people who look and sound different. The smell from the street corner is of food from every part of the world. The average taxi driver can whip up blood-curdling curses in 15 different languages and people can be rude in a dizzying array of accents. But as I travelled from midtown Manhattan to La Guardia airport that afternoon, through the affluence of the Upper East Side, through Spanish Harlem and across the bridge into Queens, it occurred to me that living in urban America you no longer find strength through a common humanity.

Strength comes from the things that make you different in a world that constantly threatens to overwhelm you. It is about always sticking with what you know and what makes you feel comfortable.

That's the way it is along Calle Ocho in Miami. The main drag of Little Havana is known simply as Eighth Street to English speakers and is far less impressive than you hoped for. There are crusty old men playing draughts in the shadow of an authentic Cuban coffee house, but the long street is littered with the generic urban clutter of any American suburb. In many ways it reminded me of the Shankill Road, or any other main street in a Protestant area of Northern Ireland. Beneath the modernity there is a simmering tension. The memory of past sacrifice and the fear of future betrayal are never very far from the surface. In the spring of 2000, the tension spilled out into the open on Calle Ocho because of a little boy called Elián Gonzales.

By the time he was found floating in the Atlantic, his mother and most of her companions were already dead. Elián was pulled aboard a fishing boat, brought to shore and reunited with his exiled relatives. While the US Justice Department decided what to do with him, his Uncle Lazaro took the boy and retreated behind a wall of Cuban-American activists. By the time it became clear that the American government was determined to send Elián back to his father in Cuba, Lazaro's modest bungalow home, off the Calle Ocho, was already besieged by the media and the massed ranks of Cuban America.

I spent too much time outside that house, waiting for words of wisdom and a glimpse of little Elián. Just two days before the official deadline for Elián's deportation, I stood shoulder to shoulder with the rest of the hack pack, craning my neck to see the boy play in the back garden of his uncle's house. He finally emerged into the late afternoon heat through the back door of the bungalow, with two little playmates trailing behind him. For the next ten minutes, he delighted the camera crews by crawling around the climbing frame and practising kick-boxing techniques he had picked up from countless hours in front of the TV. He was like any six-year-old boy from any working-class neighbourhood in any big city in America, except he was a little better turned out. There were no mysterious stains and scabby knee-caps on this child, just spotless runners, a snazzy Tommy Hilfiger T-shirt and a squeaky-clean face with 'spoiled rotten' written all over it.

It was hard not to feel enormous sadness watching that child. It was not just the terrible journey he had endured or the loss of his mother on that ill-fated raft trip from Cuba. It was the raging exploitation of this little boy by the media and the Cuban exiles. Elián had become a symbol, a saint, a martyr, a problem, a controversy and a cause. He was no longer a little boy.

A few days before his scheduled deportation, tens of thousands of Cuban exiles massed along Calle Ocho. From the air, the crowd looked vaguely like a crucifix, with the main intersection of Eighth Street the centre of the cross. Each member of the crowd had been asked to bring a flashlight or torch and, on command from the main stage, they pointed their lights up towards the aeroplanes taking off from nearby Miami airport and chanted, 'Cuba Sí, Castro No.' They listened respectfully as the American national anthem was played. But it was only when the old Cuban national anthem filled the air that you heard real passion. This was less a political rally and more a religious gathering. Everywhere there were posters of Elián standing with a statue of the Blessed Virgin. One man stood with a poster that read, 'Elián is an Angel, Castro is Satan.' When I could find people in the crowd who felt comfortable speaking in English, they told me Elián was special. God had meant him to come to Miami. He must stay.

That's what framed the debate for many Cuban-Americans. Their conversations about Elián were peppered with religious terms. Stories circulated on the grapevine about supernatural involvement in the rescue of this little boy. 'When they found him in the water off Fort Lauderdale,' one local told me, 'he was surrounded by dolphins and they protected him from the sharks.' One Cuban-American magazine published a full-page photo of Elián with the headline 'The Cuban Moses.' And that's at the heart of the passion that filled the streets of Little Havana during that Miami spring.

There were young people in the crowd on Calle Ocho but many more were first generation exiles who desperately needed to believe that Castro would not outlive them. After four decades of struggle, stretching from the Bay of Pigs to Brothers to the Rescue, Cuban exiles used all means necessary to try and topple Fidel. And they were still left with a question, 'What have we achieved?' Someone needed to deliver them from doubt. And then along came Elián: a God-given symbol of resistance. There was a silent majority of Cuban-Americans who believed Elián was not the saviour but a little boy who needed to go home to his father. One Cuban-American academic told me he believed about 25 to 30 per cent of his community would support Elián's return to Cuba. But the silent minority stayed largely silent. The microphone stayed where it always has been: in the hands of those who saw salvation in the eyes of Elián Gonzales. Deliver us from evil, little boy.

The Elián Gonzales saga threw the limits of the melting-pot theory into stark relief. The Cuban exile community is one of the most powerful ethnic groups in America, but no matter how much they achieve, there is still a crippling sense of dislocation in their ranks. Those who have chosen to integrate themselves into the mainstream of American society have, like other waves of immigrants, made great progress. But the community still has a messianic streak running through it. Too many wait with a growing sense of desperation for deliverance from Castro, and ultimately America. The most telling symbol of protest during the Elián saga was the flag carried by many Cuban protestors. It was the Stars and Stripes turned upside down: a symbol of uncertain loyalties and sullen resentment.

There are ethnic minorities in the United States who have grievances deeper and wider than the Cubans. There are so many reasons the melting pot should be at a constant boil. So why, if there is such tension inside the various different groups, is the United States not permanently in the throes of race riots? When I looked at those black neighbourhoods in Washington and the Calle Ocho in Miami, my first instinct was to say, 'I don't know.' But when I look at those ethnic groups that have been rejuvenated by waves of new immigrants, I find some plausible answers.

Whenever I visited San Francisco, the first thing I would do was make my way to Chinatown. I loved the sounds and smells of the streets, especially at the weekend. One Saturday, while a festival played out on the crowded streets, I dawdled by the Karaoke stalls where young and old belted out Chinese standards. The food stalls did a brisk business, as did every form of commerce, from faux oriental antiques to household staples. And for as long as you stayed in those few city blocks of San Francisco, you never had to listen to a word of English.

On the other side of the city, I sought out the string of Irish bars on Geary Avenue: the Abbey Tavern, Ireland's

32 Counties and the Blarney Stone, where the sign outside the door reads, 'We cheat drunks and tourists.' What is remarkable about these uninspiring bars is the company they now keep. To get to them, you must first pass by Japan Town and a restaurant called We-Be-Sushi. Geary Avenue is also home to Russian émigrés who shop at the Moscow Bakery and worship at the Russian Orthodox Church, right next door to Jimmy's Mexican Restaurant.

The Chinese, the Irish, the Russians and the Mexicans are staking their claim to real estate in a cultural turf war. The difference between this battle and the racially motivated violence of the past is that each of these groups is confident that it will hang on to what it has. The different ethnic groups no longer have to conform to succeed. They can accentuate their differences and still be American. The reason this works is because the disparate groups have no problem sharing the symbols and institutions of the country they have chosen as their new home. Those symbols and institutions are of no threat to the survival of their language and heritage; if anything, they will be their ultimate protection.

On St Patrick's Day 1996, I attended a ceremony at the Department of the Interior in Washington where more than a hundred Irish people were due to become American citizens. Some had been living in the United States for years, others were doing it for the children they were rearing in America, and one woman told me she was taking American citizenship to honour President Clinton, 'after all he has done for Ireland'. A man with a heavy Drogheda accent recited the pledge of allegiance. A young mother raised her hand to take the pledge as her infant daughter sat in the chair beside her, chewing on the top of a little Stars and Stripes. And yet as these Irish people made the ultimate commitment to their new country, they would not give up their link to 'home'.

Everyone I talked to that day planned to keep dual Irish and American citizenship. Even as they swore 'to reject all foreign potentates', they insisted that they would not break their formal links with Ireland.

That day at the Department of the Interior helped me to understand why the melting-pot theory no longer fully explains America. And so did an experience on the Mall in Washington a few months later. On 4 July, hundreds of thousands of people turn the Mall into a vast picnic area. They fight for space from the Capitol Building to the south, past the vast obelisk of the Washington Monument, all the way up to the Lincoln Memorial to the north. Under the shadow of the dome of the Capitol Building, I sat drinking beer with a few Irish and American friends. Beside us was a big Latino family, spread out with deckchairs, tables and umbrellas. The children played and the older generations kept up a constant animated conversation. During the four hours we shared that space, I did not hear a word of English from them. Yet when the fireworks lit up the night sky and the crowd began to sing 'The Star-Spangled Banner', every member of that family stood and belted out their adopted national anthem in perfect English, while my friends and I stood mute. Most of us didn't know the words. It was a humbling experience.

It also made me understand the difference between nationalism and patriotism. America is built up of many different nations with different outlooks on life, different languages and different grievances. But as soon as they take that simple pledge and learn the national anthem, they are part of the United States. They are citizens of a country where you can be an Irish nationalist and an American patriot all on the same day.

# Six

## The United States of Everything

They used to say that if you want to know America, go to a baseball game. That may have been true in the past, but today if you want to understand America then you must go to CostCo. CostCo is not just a wholesale discount supermarket. It's a temple to the God of Choice, a sacred place where you will uncover the secrets of America's success and its persistent problems.

I paid my first visit to CostCo in 1996 when I was still new to Washington. I was on a date of sorts with my American girlfriend Tara. As I wheeled my trolley through the aisles, I lost the power to connect my desire for material goods with my ability to decide what I actually needed. I tried to control myself but when I got to the checkout counter, I looked into my trolley and found a slab of Brie cheese the size of a lorry wheel, two cacti, six bottles of fine Italian wine and a vacuum cleaner. I couldn't remember ever deciding that I needed this stuff. I felt like I had just woken up on a beach in Ibiza with a tattoo on my bum and a bad hangover. However, I was not alone in my consumer excess. Right beside me, a woman had piled a computer and what looked like a year's supply of toilet paper into her trolley. The contented smile on her face told me she would soon be surfing the net from the comfort of her own bog.

As I loaded my purchases into the back of the car, I paused for a moment of quiet reflection. I had just crossed the border into a whole new world. I think every foreigner who settles in America passes that boundary at some point. It is the moment when you ask yourself how you ever survived without the things Americans take for granted: valet parking, garbage disposal units in the sink, bagels and cream cheese, Thanksgiving dinner, and more than two cubes of ice in your drink. As a kid, I learned that you don't know what you have until it's gone. In America, you don't know what's been missing until it is sitting in your trolley at CostCo.

The concept of unlimited choice is the key to understanding America. In other countries choice is conditional: you can have it if it's in stock, if you want blue or if your name begins with a vowel. In the United States of America, you can have it in varieties you never believed possible: 'Cheeseburger without the cheese, no problem.' Of course, this concept of choice takes some getting used to. I was happy that I could get 65 channels on my TV at four in the morning, but I wished there was something to watch other than reruns of *I Love Lucy* and 'infomercials' selling vegetable juicers and sadistic exercise devices. I really appreciated the fact that I could choose among competing telephone companies to find the service that suited me, but within a couple of months of arriving in America I had 16 different phone bills covering the expanding list of phone, modem, fax, ISDN, pager and calling card facilities I was using. You would need a degree in advanced mathematics to understand the ten-page monthly bills I received for each one of these services.

Then there were the numbers I had to remember each

day. Before leaving home, I had to check the voice mail on my mobile phone and use an access number to retrieve my messages. I would stop to get cash with my ATM card and use my pin number. When I got to the office, there was more voice mail, which I could access only by using my security code and an additional numeric pass code. To check my e-mail, I first had to remember the password to get logged on to the Internet. To book a flight for an upcoming trip out of Washington, I quoted the membership number from one of six frequent flyer cards I had been issued with. I would take a walk to the White House and have to remember my security code to get past the Secret Service checkpoint. When I got back to the office, I might have to apply for credentials for some upcoming event and quote my date of birth, my passport number and my social security number. At the end of the day, I'd pay bills over the phone by following the instructions from an automated voice and punching in my credit card number. There were simply too many numbers, too many choices and too many people trying to get their hands on my wallet or a stake in my life.

Even at times of crisis, someone was always hawking another choice. In September 1999, I had just finished reporting on Hurricane Floyd, the biggest Atlantic storm in a generation. I was on a highway in North Carolina racing to catch a plane to my next story in California when I saw a set of flashing lights in my rear-view mirror. A very pleasant highway patrol man pulled me over and told me I had been doing 85 miles an hour in a 70-mile-an-hour zone. I smiled sheepishly while he wrote me a ticket. He told me I could contest the fine at a court hearing two weeks later. I wanted to say there was no way I was coming back to face a bunch of inbred hillbillies in a courtroom but I just bit my lip and drove away, slowly.

When I got back to my apartment in Washington the

following week, there were letters from six lawyers in North Carolina offering to help me fight my speeding fine. One letter began: 'While performing some of my duties at the courthouse, I came across your name ...' I imagined my face on one of those old wild-West posters: 'Wanted. Mark Little – for claim-jumping, sheep-rustling and speeding.' The letter was signed Reed N. Noble. I was tempted to write back and tell him I could never hire a lawyer who sounded like the star of a daytime soap opera. Another lawyer told me that with a plea bargain and what he called 'a prayer for judgement considered', he could ensure that no final conviction would be entered. None of the solicitors who wrote to me charged less than 150 dollars. The fine was 95 dollars.

This ridiculous concept of false choice intruded into my life every time I opened the post. A daily torrent of junk mail flowed into my house. I used to wonder from what bizarre database they had got my name. I once received two sheets of stickers, each printed with my name and address and a couple of Italian flags. That came from the League of Italian-Americans with a plea for money to support their work. Every month, I received a mailing from a singles club that began, 'Looking for love?' Yes, but not from you.

My real enemies were the telemarketers who called up at all hours of the day and night. At the beginning I had some pleasant conversations with these strangers. I especially liked one young woman from a telephone company with a dainty southern accent who kept referring to me as 'Mr Nettle'. However, it didn't take long before my patience wore thin. There must have been a hidden camera in my apartment. Some telemarketer was watching me and waiting for that moment when I got into the shower or sat down to dinner before dialling my number and making that unwanted sales pitch. I lost my rag with increasing frequency. I would angrily demand that each caller give me his home phone number so I could wake him up at 8 a.m. on a Saturday morning. I was amazed that so many Americans seemed to feel comfortable with this kind of intrusion. There must be a lot of people seriously interested in hearing what these telemarketers have to say; otherwise, it wouldn't be worthwhile employing them.

After a while, I felt my resistance to the all-knowing and all-powerful beast that is the American marketing industry begin to wane. At first, I couldn't stand the idea that my TV programmes were constantly interrupted by ads for pizza and adult nappies. But I was soon looking forward to some of the quirky ads. You start to develop favourites. You even talk about them in work. I am not a great fan of American football, but I watched the Superbowl every year just to see the multi-million dollar ads. I once caught myself in a crowded lift humming the music to an advert for tampons.

One of the distressing things about American advertising is that it is subject to the prudishness of the major television networks. You can find plenty of soft porn on television by paying for extra cable stations, but when the networks adapt a movie to the small screen they will dub in the word 'damn' when you know the character said 'fuck'. Where they cannot easily cut out a sex scene, they will electronically cover up the nipples, buttocks and pubic hair. One night, I found myself channel-hopping between two great films: Stanley Kubrick's *Full Metal Jacket* and *The Unbearable Lightness of Being*, based on the novel by Milan Kundera. Kubrick's movie is about the moral dilemmas posed by the Vietnam War, and the TV network faithfully broadcast every graphic image of violence. But on the other channel, some of the most artfully erotic scenes of modern moviemaking were hacked out of *The Unbearable Lightness of Being,* leaving it almost unrecognisable. One moment, Daniel Day Lewis is engaged in energetic foreplay with Juliette Binoche and the next moment he has a post-coital smile on his face and is putting his shoes back on. With a quick click of the remote control, I'm back with *Full Metal Jacket* at the point where Matthew Modine puts a bullet into the head of a young female Vietcong fighter. In a nation that worries about the messages that TV is sending children, citizens should ponder this paradox: a man can kill a woman on prime-time television but he cannot make love to her.

The double-think seems to extend into the world of advertising. You will not see any graceful images of naked flesh but you will hear bodily functions discussed in stomach-churning detail. There was a great commercial for a product called Beano that stops you farting. The ad featured a man judging a competition for the best baked-beans at a county fair; one capsule of Beano and you can kiss your gas goodbye, or at least that seemed to be the fine print of the commercial. Adverts for adult nappies always involved an incredibly attractive middle-aged woman who was supposed to represent an incontinent granny. It was Doris Day with a bladder the size of a pea. Then there was the remedy for piles that showed a beautiful businesswoman who looked like she had stepp-ed straight off the cover of *Vogue*; a supermodel with an itchy bum. One of the most important commercials that appeared during my time in America was part of the marketing campaign for Viagra. On prime-time TV we could all discuss E.D.: erectile dysfunction, or impotence. Former presidential candidate Bob Dole kicked off the campaign for Viagra with brutally honest adverts about his problems with E.D., even as his wife Elizabeth was working hard to promote her own campaign for the

Republican presidential nomination. Dole soon faded from the adverts, to be replaced by a succession of good-looking men, none over fifty, hugging their wives or swinging them around in preparation for a vigorous bout of rumpy-pumpy.

The best part of these commercials was the small print. While advertisers can claim pretty much anything about a medical product, American law does compel them to reveal any potential side-effects. So while the advert might show a couple hand in hand against a glorious sunset, the small print at the bottom of the screen is warning you that this product might cause nausea, dry mouth, constipation, temporary blindness and breast tenderness. Of course, the advertiser might try to dress up the hazards a bit, so they don't sound quite so bad. A friend of mine swears he saw a commercial warning that the product might cause 'anal leakage'.

The bodily orifice that gets most attention is the mouth. It is remarkable that even as one group of advertisers offers remedies for everything from acne to angina, another group is doing its best to make Americans bigger, fatter and less healthy. An ad break might start off with a commercial for Burger King – 'Have it your way', move to IHOP (International House of Pancakes), wind its way past Chili's – 'Home of the baby back ribs', and end up with some indigestion medicine. Yet Americans continue to be amazed by statistics telling them that they are expanding quicker than a balloon at a kids' party. Official statistics show that slightly more than half of all Americans are overweight and one in four is clinically obese. Despite the obsession with low-fat food, Americans are eating more fat. Fat consumption by the average adult man rose by 13 per cent between 1990 and 1995.

America's waistline is expanding at such a rate

because there is no good reason to feel guilty anymore. Plump is a valid option. It's like choosing an off-beat hair-style or bright colour for your car; not everyone's going to like it but they will respect your right to make a dodgy lifestyle choice. Here again, choice is the key word. The prospect of limitless consumption provides you with ways to stuff your face with fat, cholesterol and calories and still feel like you're looking after your figure. The double cheeseburger with bacon is OK as long as you wash it down with a Diet Coke. Don't worry about wolfing down half a pound of jellybeans; they're fat free.

I would love to say that I was completely resistant to this form of self-delusion. When I arrived in Washington, I laughed at an Irish friend who told me that I would gain at least ten pounds in my first year. 'Everyone does, Mark. There's no way of avoiding it.' Maybe it was the size of the portions, the frequency of those business lunches or the lack of exercise. Or perhaps I was simply eating like a pig. Whatever the reason, I did gain those extra pounds on schedule. It took me a while to realise that I was getting fatter. My American friends were too polite to say anything, or else saw nothing wrong with my gradual expansion. But when I'd go back to Ireland, there were too many people telling me that I was 'filling out' or that I wasn't 'that skinny young fella anymore'. One Irish friend in Washington was even more blunt: 'My mother watches you on the TV and she asked me to tell you that you're getting a fat face.' All my life, I convinced myself that dieting is the preserve of losers, but I had to admit that it was time for me to try something.

In America, while there's someone on every street corner trying to convince you to eat yourself into oblivion, there is also another kind soul ready to sell you the most effective diet in the history of the world. One of the reasons I love America is because it will give anyone a hearing, even if they have no idea what they are talking about. And that applies to all the diet gurus who are busy trying to reinvent the wheel. Each generation learns the same painful lessons about weight loss and each generation is seduced by a different false hope, whether it's colonic irrigation, stomach staples or miracle pills.

The never-ending stream of weight-loss schemes was a constant source of entertainment to me. My favourites were the brace of high-protein, low-carbohydrate diets that sprouted up as a result of the theories of one Dr Atkins. *Dr Atkins' New Diet Revolution* was followed by bestsellers with titles like *Sugarbuster* and *Protein Power*. The books promoted the theory that protein is good and carbohydrates are bad because they disrupt the balance of sugars in the body and promote fat storage and weight gain. In practice, the diet is just too good to be true. Bacon and eggs for breakfast is fine; just forget the toast. There is no limit to the sacrifices you don't have to make. Take the suggested recipe for a 'Swiss snack', taken from Dr Atkins' book. You wrap bacon strips around cubes of Swiss cheese and deep-fry them in hot oil. The recipe serves one and calls for four strips of bacon and a quarter pound of cheese. I felt I had gained a couple of pounds just by reading the recipe.

Despite my cynicism, friends who tried the high-protein diets told me that they did work. Most of them lost weight rapidly. Apparently they were not bothered when they didn't have a bowel movement for days, or that their arteries were screaming out from the pressure of all that extra cholesterol. In some ways those drawbacks were merely the proof that the diet was working. No pain, no gain. But after a few months, the people I knew who flirted with Dr Atkins and his Swiss snacks were back to the fat-free jellybeans and Diet Cokes. Just like every other adult living in America, they could not escape the grip of a feverish consumer culture that promotes consumption as a virtue in itself, a consumer culture in which your lack of restraint is not your fault; it's the carbohydrates or genetics or heavy bones or your over-loaded schedule. For once, I wanted someone to come on TV, between all those fast-food commercials, and say, 'It's your own fault. You're fat because you are weak. Put down that Diet Coke and get on the Stairmaster, you tubby bastard.'

Of course I am the ultimate hypocrite. Like anyone drawn from the Celtic gene pool, there was a special place in my heart for alcohol, cigarettes and red meat. Yet I would stand in my local bar at closing time, a whiskey in my hand and a cigarette in my mouth, ridiculing my American friends for their country's obesity. I was hurtling down the bottomless well of smugness which all foreigners in America fall into at some stage. I always had some pretensions to healthy living. I drank lots of water, took extra vitamins and ate plenty of fruit and vegetables, but by my second year in Washington I was smoking a packet of Marlboro Lights every day and there was an increasingly evil tinge to my occasional hangovers. I was also developing bizarre routines based on my addiction to nicotine.

Smoking is banned in most public spaces in Washington, and so, outside every office block, there is a hardy band of smokers braving the elements to feed their addiction. The people you tend to be most friendly with in your building are the people you meet on your cigarette breaks. Your friendships are based on a bond you cannot share with the non-smokers in your building. You gather together, sometimes to ward off the elements, but mostly to provide emotional support in the face of increasing intolerance from the rest of society. You look forward to those cigarette breaks and, as you take the lift down to the ground floor, you wonder which one of your smoking buddies will be there. It sounds pathetic to those who have never taken up the habit, but every smoker in America knows the power of the friendships forged around that collective ashtray.

I valued my membership of the 'American Smokers Club'. I would get a happy feeling when a person I had just met pulled out their cigarettes and said, 'Mind if I smoke?' In bars, I would gravitate towards the smokers and stay around them longer. I really believed I had more intimate conversations with my fellow smokers. But man cannot live by cigarette smoke alone. I could not block myself off from the reality that smoking in America is up there with public urination and loud belching. I would feel embarrassed when friends of mine waved their hands in the air to clear the wisps of smoke coming from my cigarette. I would be with a big group of people in a restaurant and realise that I was the only one smoking. My girlfriend tolerated the smoking, but I started to see the ashtray through her eyes and it looked pretty disgusting.

The end of my days as a regular smoker came without any great fanfare. This key decision in my life was the by-product of an especially severe hangover. I woke up one Saturday morning with the carbon-monoxide headache you get from a combination of cigarettes and drink. I rolled out of bed and saw that crumpled packet of cigarettes on the floor where I had dumped my clothes. I felt absolutely no desire to pick it up; cigarettes were no fun anymore. I made a modest pledge to myself: I would get through one day without a fag. One day turned into two and with the help of Nicorette gum, the days rolled by.

At first I thought I had done a very un-American thing: I had taken personal responsibility for one of my failings and so had set out to rectify it. But that's not the way it was. Once more, I was exercising my very American right to choose; to choose to be nicotine-free, to choose to be a functioning member of society and to choose to be among normal members of society, and not those dysfunctional addicts around the ashtray outside the office block.

The concept of choice explains success but also helps undermine the concept of failure. If I cannot lose weight with that diet, then I simply choose a better diet. If I cannot give up cigarettes with the Nicorette gum, then I simply get the nicotine patch. Since there is unlimited choice, there are unlimited reasons to avoid responsibility and avoid failure; because I can always avoid failure, I never need to fear it. That is the American dialectic, a force so powerful that it provides forward momentum to a society that always seems to be on the verge of crisis. Those who hate America always portray it as self-indulgent, corpulent and one step from collapse. However, they consistently underestimate the principles that sustain it: as long as you have a choice, you will be free, and there will always be another choice. The overpowering optimism is based on a considerable amount of self-delusion, but it is still optimism and it is still a powerful force.

Just look at how the United States has coped with problems in the frontier-land of cyber-space. The siren call of dot-com happiness through consumption once provoked rapture, but now it prompts scepticism. Just a few years ago, investors were throwing millions of dollars at any young Internet pioneer with a service to sell and a website to sell it with. Today, the money has dried up and only the fittest in e-commerce have survived. Wall Street has learned a valuable lesson and so have those Internet pioneers, although it's not the lesson you might imagine.

For instance, take Kosmo.com. The company's big idea

was to take orders over the Internet for movies, magazines and food, and deliver these to your door in less than an hour. It started off with ten employees and operated solely in New York. Infected by dot-com madness, venture capitalists put $28 million into Kosmo.com, even though they had been given no clear idea of when and how the company would make a profit. The money kept flowing and the company kept expanding. Two years after it was founded, the business had received $280 million in capital, employed 3000 people in ten cities and planned to go public. Kosmo.com was a balloon ready to burst.

Once the extent of dot-com madness dawned on Wall Street, Kosmo.com's days were numbered. The company was forced to withdraw plans for an initial public offering and begin laying people off. The company folded in April 2001. What is remarkable about the Kosmo.com story is the almost complete absence of the word failure. Indeed, conventional notions of success or failure never seemed to be important standards for the young capitalists behind Kosmo.com, and other Internet pioneers. One of the company's founders said, 'If I just absolutely fail, what's going to happen? I'm going to apply to business school and have an incredible application.'

To a new generation, failure had become a business plan. I got to know some of the people at the cutting edge of e-commerce and it was a refrain I heard time and again: 'You have nothing to fear from failure.' I met one young Irish pioneer in Silicon Valley who told me of the pride some of his contemporaries take in the collapse of previous businesses. 'It's proof they've tried.' Even among hard-nosed financial journalists in the United States, there was a certain admiration for the Philosophy of Heroic Failure. One Wall Street hack summed it up like this: 'Don't think, do. Make a decision every day, check the decision the next day and if it doesn't work out, then make another decision.'

There is the germ of a good idea in this philosophy. If pursued to its logical conclusion it's the basis for a subversive manifesto. If enough Americans adopted this credo they might embrace the social disorder that results from radical change instead of fearing it. Such disorder would no longer be an indication of failure. Instead, it would be proof that they were trying to make their society better. In line with America's omnipotent culture of choice, citizens would choose change over status quo. The problem is that like every other great subversive idea in America, the establishment has realised the power of this radical interpretation of choice and used it for its own ends.

The ruling elite in the United States is no longer a blue-blooded caste of White Anglo-Saxon Protestants. At the end of the last century, it was the Baby Boomers who ruled with their irresistible mixture of diversity and self-indulgence. The generation of Americans born immediately after the Second World War had been able to shape the world because of its unprecedented affluence and demographic power. The relative wealth of the Baby Boomers had been an unstoppable market force: their outlook on the world dominated modern American politics, and their desire for self-gratification fuelled cultural trends for close to half a century. Bill Clinton was their president, the Mini van their celebration of suburban bliss, and the continued existence of the Rolling Stones testament to their nostalgia.

Now that they exercised absolute power over the commanding heights of civil society, the Baby Boomers abandoned the notion of subversion they had celebrated during the Sixties. Instead, they took counter-cultural ideas and a bohemian lifestyle and used them to strengthen the power of the establishment. They became what American author David Brooks has called 'Bobos': Bourgeois Bohemians. Their primary goal was to sustain America's economic power but they did so by bringing the appearance and language of their former radicalism to the marketplace. In his book, *Bobos in Paradise*, Brooks writes: 'The bohemians have decided that commercial culture is wonderful, so long as they can wear jeans and black T-shirts to work ... they have brought those aspects of the counterculture that enhance profits and discarded those that don't.' Brooks cites examples of the language of modern American business: 'Sometimes you gotta break the rules' was one of Burger King's advertising lines, 'Born to be wild' was Lucent Technology's motto, and hardware supermarket chain, Home Depot thundered: 'Think Revolution, not evolution.' Of course the timing of that revolution would be coordinated by a small group of palm pilot-wielding Boomers over non-fat lattes at Starbucks.

The notion of unlimited choice and the Philosophy of Heroic Failure were absolutely essential to the Baby Boomers as they approached their twilight years. By inculcating the next generation with their brand of excess, they have guaranteed their survival. One self-confessed American Boomer, David Owen, put it like this in *The New Yorker*: 'Members of Generation X and Y have not displaced us; they have merely become our worker bees, toiling away in their windowless cubicles in Silicon Valley, mindlessly generating the capital gains on which we will retire.' In short, what's good for the Baby Boomers is good for America, and by extension the world.

America's love affair with choice is not a new thing, but the level of passion reached intoxicating levels under the influence of the Bobos. Generations to come will struggle to free themselves of that legacy and the backlash has already begun. The mass demonstrations that rocked Seattle in the winter of 1999 spawned a movement which, at least in part, is dedicated to resisting the spread of corporate brands and fighting back against the false choices promoted by advertising. In this movement there is great hope but also some risk. A previous generation made an honourable attempt to combat vices like racism and sexism with notions of 'political correctness', but their backlash begat a backlash.

Today, we should take a realistic look at the notion of choice that is buried at the heart of American consumer culture. Of course, there is much to despise in a philosophy that encourages citizens to consume but not to question and which covers up dysfunction with empty slogans of empowerment. But there is also something to admire in the energy that flows directly from the concept of choice as defined by most Americans. That energy is used for profit, but it also powers innovation. The culture of unlimited choice creates slobs, but it also creates pioneers. And, of course, valet parking and great bagels.

# Seven

# The Girl with the Floppy Hat

It was 15 June 1996, the first day of Mary Robinson's first visit to Washington as president. The official arrival ceremony had all the pageantry of a royal wedding. A colonial pipe band pranced across Summerall Field under the blazing sun of a Washington summer as the cannons roared in salute. Hundreds of Irish-Americans waved their little Stars and Stripes and tricolours behind a wall of VIPs and then stood silently when 'Amhran na BhFiann' was played by the Marine Band.

I was there with cameraman Darryl Johnson. He scanned the crowd with his lens and settled on a young woman with long black hair, a baggy cotton summer dress, a pearl necklace and a floppy hat with pink roses around the brim. I am sure I cast an eye in her direction. I might even have taken mental note of her presence, but my gaze had not lingered. Thankfully, Darryl's had. Maybe it was because she was the only adult amid a crowd of cheering kids. Maybe it was her unconcealed glee at getting a close look at Mary Robinson and Bill Clinton, or maybe it was the bright red lipstick and the blinding white dress. It certainly wasn't because her name was Monica Lewinsky; it would be another eighteen months before she was to become perhaps the most famous woman in the world.

The footage of that day sat on the shelves in my office for another two years before I realised what Darryl had filmed. I was watching CNN one evening in September 1998, a broadcast of all the events where Bill Clinton and Monica Lewinsky had been seen in close proximity. Suddenly there were a few seconds of footage with just three people in it: Bill Clinton, Mary Robinson and a young woman with a long white dress and a floppy hat. I lurched out of my seat and started ripping tapes off the shelves until I found the footage Darryl had shot that day. I shoved the videotape into the editing machine and spooled along until she was revealed in glorious technicolour. The video shows her with a big smile, waving a tiny tricolour and a tiny Stars and Stripes behind the rope line with all those little kids. Kids who would soon be asking some awkward questions: 'Mommy, what's oral sex?'

I spooled further along the tape to the point where Mary Robinson and Bill Clinton set out on their walk along the rope line. They pass the VIPs and there's Hillary Clinton, looking elegant in her own summer hat and a pair of designer sunglasses. Three seconds later they pass Ireland's then foreign minister Dick Spring, and just six seconds later Bill Clinton pulls his hand up from his side, raises his palm and salutes someone in the crowd. A few steps later Monica appears on the screen. She gives Clinton a little baby-girl wave. As the president walks past, he points to his head as if to say 'nice hat' and Monica replies with a big lipstick grin. Mary Robinson doesn't know it, but she has just played a walk-on part in a drama of epic proportions.

I have sometimes wondered what I would have done if I had known Monica Lewinsky was in the crowd that day, just as I often wish I had been better prepared for her arrival in my life. I had been predicting for the previous two years that the sexual harassment suit pursued by Paula Jones against Bill Clinton would have destructive and potentially fatal consequences for the presidency. But I don't know if I ever really believed it. It's like a child waiting for snow on Christmas Day. You know it's technically possible and you listen intently to the weather reports in the run up to the big day, but you have a feeling that there's more chance of finding Santa passed out cold on the kitchen floor on Christmas morning in a congealed pool of whiskey and pudding. To most Washington insiders, Paula Jones was just a carnival act that had temporarily pitched its tent in their backyard; she was the 'bearded lady' and 'monkey boy' rolled into one. There was a serious charge of sexual harassment at the heart of the case, and most hacks like me were convinced Bill Clinton was guilty. But wherever reporters gathered and talked about Paula Jones, the conversation would descend into giggles and tasteless jokes about trailer parks and big noses.

On the morning of 17 January 1998, I joined hundreds of other reporters in a scrum around a taxi carrying Paula Jones to a Washington law office to testify in her lawsuit against the president. By this stage she had undergone a complete makeover and no longer looked as if she would burst into flames if you lit a match too close to her hair. But she had the air of a hunted animal as our happy band of carnival-goers crushed her against the side of the taxi. A few minutes later, the president travelled the five hundred yards from the White House to the law office in a stately convoy of limousines, his route lined with police officers and secret servicemen. Bill Clinton was asked to talk about alleged affairs with people he had worked with and one of those people was a young woman called Monica Lewinsky. The president's denial of a sexual relationship would plunge the United States into its most serious political crisis since Watergate. Five days later, Bill and Monica's relationship became public knowledge.

I woke up that morning, went to the front door and picked up the *Washington Post*. I carried it back into the apartment and looked at the headline. Although I didn't realise it at the time, that may well have been the last truly normal moment in my life for over a year. Ironically, I had to be dragged into this story. When the call came from the RTÉ newsroom in Dublin asking for a report on the latest Clinton scandal, I wondered aloud whether this really mattered. 'Bill Clinton was shagging some young staffer. And why would that be news?' But as the day wore on, the scale of the story began to dawn on me. I remember composing the opening line of my first report, writing those three words, 'White House intern', and realising the phrase would dominate my life for months. Even as I typed, I was having trouble remembering the woman's name: Melinsky, Leniskwy, Walinsky. Why couldn't Clinton have picked a Murphy?

The next three or four days were a blur for everybody reporting the story. The anchors for the three main networks' news programmes were whisked out of Cuba, where they were covering the Pope's first historic visit, to present breathless bulletins from the White House lawn. New York's tabloids splashed banner headlines across their front pages: 'The big creep told me to lie', 'Bombshell stuns Clinton'. News executives at one network instructed their staff to use the word 'crisis' and not 'scandal' when covering the story, while some talk show host was first out with the eminently predictable 'Zippergate'. A reporter who had covered Watergate and Richard Nixon's resignation said, 'The same sense of smelling blood in the White House in 1973 is what I smell today.' An anonymous White House official said, 'I'm sleeping like a baby. I wake up every couple of hours and cry.'

The media blitzkrieg that followed the revelations was shaped by a powerful combination of celebrity and politics. It was as if O.J. Simpson and not Bill Clinton was in danger of being dragged from the Oval Office. But what really distinguished this story was the speed at which it reached critical mass. It was the first great story of the new media age. Twenty-four-hour rolling television coverage, wall-to-wall commentary and the vast possibilities of the Internet intensified the battle for every scrap of information and tawdry detail. Get it right, but for God's sake get it first. I knew one CBS News producer who lived in the Watergate complex near the banks of the Potomac, in the apartment block next to Monica, who by this stage had locked herself away from the world. His instructions were to take a home video camera supplied by CBS and use his status as a resident of the Watergate to sneak exclusive pictures of his famous neighbour. He tried everything, including loitering in her building in the hope that she would bring her laundry out, and waiting by the bakery just outside her building in case she popped out for a doughnut.

Another producer friend was sent by an American TV network to stake out the Watergate building. She stood with all the camera crews and photographers in the cold January rain waiting for Monica to emerge. One photographer decided to take a group shot of the assembled media pack and send it up to Monica's apartment to remind her they were all still there. A short while later, a plate of freshly baked cookies was sent out. Monica had baked the cookies and the note attached read, 'When this is all over we'll all go and get a pizza.' Somehow, the note ended up at the offices of Monica's nemesis, the independent counsel, Ken Starr, for handwriting analysis by the FBI. I don't think they ever found any hidden message and I know for a fact that the media pack never got that pizza.

The frantic days and sleepless nights finally gave way to an oddly comforting routine. The story just wouldn't go away but it had settled down somewhat. The scandal revolved around three or four locations and none was more than a ten-minute walk or taxi ride from my office. On any given day, I would stroll out and do a quick report from the White House lawn, or I would walk around the corner onto Connecticut Avenue and join my media friends outside the offices of Monica Lewinsky's lawyers. I might slip down to the Watergate to record a piece-to-camera, and on the way back I could stop off at the George Washington University in Foggy Bottom to interview one of the legion of experts in the law department there. But my favourite place to visit was 'Monica Beach', the media encampment outside the Washington District Courthouse.

When Bill Clinton first ran for the presidency, Republicans made up a bumper sticker: 'Annoy the media – re-elect George Bush.' In those glory days of scandal, the quickest way to annoy the media was to get between a camera and Monica Lewinsky. One foolhardy soul discovered this outside the courthouse when Monica turned up to testify before the grand jury. He held up a handwritten sign, which read 'Good Luck, Monica', right in front of the wall of cameras filming the crucial arrival scene. The camera crews jumped up in unison and unleashed a tidal wave of profanity. But it was too late. By the time the man with the sign had been removed, the intern was in the building.

The army of cameramen, correspondents, technicians and producers camped outside the courthouse was usually a fairly even-tempered lot. They lived on a patchwork of concrete and grass that used to be called 'Barry Beach'. It was so named in honour of Marion Barry, who had stood trial in that courthouse. When Ken Starr and his Grand Jury reported for duty, it became 'Monica Beach'. The tourists had a habit of spoiling the ambience with their constant questions and smart-ass comments. The camera crews got so cheesed off with the passers-by that they posted signs on the satellite trucks which read, 'Yes, we're here covering the Ken Starr Grand Jury, and no, Monica Lewinsky is not inside.' It was the visitors with their own signs and opinions who most annoyed the regulars on Monica Beach. Every day there seemed to be some new slogan scrawled on crumpled cardboard. 'Mothers for Monica' read one; 'Who cares?' read another.

Aside from these occasional irritants, life on the beach had a fairly predictable routine. Reporters from all over the world kept up a stream of multilingual commentary about semen stains and subpoenas while the camera crews jostled for those few seconds of arrivals and departures. Life in front of the courthouse was like life on any beach. There were soft drinks, packed lunches, paperbacks and fairly regular sunshine. Now and again, the beach-dwellers would engage in a brief period of frantic activity before reclining back into their chairs to eat, drink, sleep and dream of all the things they would do with their overtime pay.

The real pillars of the beach community were the hardy band of regulars who had been racking up the overtime since the scandal broke. With a slight hint of disdain, the veterans endured the part-time beach-goers; the ones who came just to see the big witnesses appear before the grand jury. The veterans soldiered through rain, sleet, snow and regular abuse from passing motorists sick of this everlasting scandal. And as summer approached, they pondered the sacrifices which they were making for the story. The big topic became the family holidays that had to be cancelled. One reporter said, 'The only trip I'm making this year is a guilt trip.'

But then who really needs two weeks by the sea when you have Monica Beach?

The beach would continue to be a focal point for the story until September 1998 when the action shifted to Capitol Hill, which is where I started to run into the whackos. I suspect the people I met there were already crazy before Monica Lewinsky came into their lives, but given the madness gripping Washington I wasn't 100 per cent sure. During the months of the impeachment hearings, I used a camera position in 'The Swamp', a little clearing in the shadow of the Capitol Building. It seemed that every time I arrived, at least one person in the vicinity was gripped by mental illness. One very well-groomed young man walked around in circles reading loudly from a bible just feet away from my camera. On the first day I worked out a little code with him. Just as I was about to go live on air, I gave him a wave and he stopped reading and walking. When I had finished my report, I would turn and shout 'Thank you', and he would resume his public performance of the good word.

Some of the crazies were not so accommodating. One day I arrived at The Swamp to find a young African-American man in black paramilitary-style clothes, armed with a loudhailer. He was screaming about how the Jews who controlled the American media had whipped up the Monica Lewinsky scandal as part of a plot to take over the United States. At least I think that's what he was saying. Just a few minutes before I was due to go live on air, I asked him to give me a couple of minutes to finish my report. Before I got within 20 feet, he started to scream, 'Don't come near me!' into his loudhailer. Finally, two policemen took pity on me and moved the man on. But a few minutes later, just as I started my live report on the nine o'clock news, he came back and started to scream even louder about the 'damn Jews'. My blood was boiling. I finished up, ripped off my microphone and ear-piece and turned to walk straight towards this nutcase. He started to scream again. 'Get away from me! Where's the cops? This guy's going to assault me.' The idea had passed through my mind, but instead I spat out the inane statement, 'Some of us are trying to work over here.' I stood there for a few moments venting my anger until finally he screamed into the loudhailer, 'This guy just called me a nigger.' The words had the force of a punch. I froze and then turned to see a crowd of about 30 people staring at our strange confrontation: an angry white man in a suit and tie facing off against a black man in urban guerilla uniform. He might have been nuts, but he was smart. He knew I had not made any racial remark, but he also knew that the accusation would stop me dead in my tracks.

The nastiness of that encounter was a wake up call of sorts. It confirmed what I had known for some time but was afraid to admit: the Lewinsky story was no longer any fun. It was still interesting because it was about momentous political events, but there was a bad smell about the story. I was tired of fighting my way through the other reporters and camera crews outside the courthouse or the lawyers' offices. I'd had enough of the sweaty lunchtime dash to the White House lawn or The Swamp and I was troubled by the questions I found myself facing, such as how to explain a blowjob on the nine o'clock news. Most of all, I was sick of the exhausted cynicism that I was feeling about this story and everyone connected to it.

For other reporters in Washington, however, the Lewinsky scandal was an answer to their prayers. When he was first elected, Bill Clinton had worked his southern charm on many American journalists, but that had long worn off. By the time Monica Lewinsky came along, the media had seen Clinton slip and slide through more scandals than any other American president of modern times. There were plenty of people who wanted to nail him. Now suddenly, after years of near misses, Clinton was in a ten-car pile up. And the media were a crowd of onlookers gawking at the blood and guts with sick fascination and a little mordant satisfaction. There was an unstoppable momentum behind the scandal. Washington is a city that needs intrigue and rumour just as other cities need a good sewage system or decent housing. And if there's even a whiff of scandal, it wakens the slumbering beast that is the Washington press corps.

On the Sunday after the scandal broke, one prominent American newsman declared emphatically that Bill Clinton would have to resign within days. I heard the same man on the phone a couple of weeks later, in the cramped offices of the White House Press Corps, telling a colleague that, by definition, the president had been unfaithful. 'Eatin' is cheatin',' he said. It took me a few moments before I realised he did mean what I thought he meant. I travelled to Ireland with President Clinton and the same newsman in September 1998. The night we stayed at the Shelbourne Hotel in Dublin, news came through that Senator Joseph Lieberman of Connecticut had delivered a blistering attack on Bill Clinton for his conduct with Monica Lewinsky. Lieberman was one of Clinton's political allies and his speech raised the prospect that the president's friends were about to desert him in droves. The very same prominent American reporter read Lieberman's speech to a group of fellow hacks gathered in the lounge of the Shelbourne, punching the air for emphasis and taking great delight in the senator's attack.

Even reporters with a more reasoned approach to Bill Clinton found themselves searching hopelessly for the fine line between outrageous rumour and absolute fact.

And those of us who would have been fairly sympathetic to Clinton were convinced that he was lying about his relationship with Monica Lewinsky. As time went on, we knew that even some of the unbelievable gossip about the president's conduct was true: the jism on the blue dress, the early-morning phone sex and the blowjobs in the Oval Office. Each time a rumour was proved true, it would make the next rumour more credible. After a while, it became impossible to separate rumour from fact.

In Washington, I shared a building with 14 other foreign news organisations, including the BBC, and NHK, Japan's national broadcaster. Next door was the CBS Washington bureau. Each Friday night during the scandal, a crowd of news people would gather at our local bar, the Red Tomato. We traded rumours and the latest Monica jokes, and as the drink flowed there would be plenty of heated arguments about the rights and wrongs of our collective scandal coverage. One night, in the early days of the story, there was a good crowd at the bar when some of the American journalists heard their pagers go off. It was a sure sign that there was a new development, so they rushed back to their offices. The story they returned with was unbelievable.

The networks were setting up a satellite link from Stanford University in California where the Clintons' daughter, Chelsea, was due to give a press conference the next day. The word was that she would allege that her father had sexually abused her. It was sick and it was incredible, but then so was everything else about this saga. For a moment, I believed that the story was true and wondered how I would break the news to a bleary-eyed Irish public the next day. The story was like an electric shock to the patrons of the Red Tomato, but no sooner had we all started to drain our glasses than someone came back with news that it was a hoax. Not for the first time, and not for the last time, I felt queasy. I had been prepared to believe the very worst about a man, without the slightest sliver of proof, and had enjoyed the voyeuristic thrill that goes along with such a presumption of guilt.

But the shame would never last that long. It would wear off in the face of the smugness and hypocrisy I saw in Clinton's supporters. They seemed to have a blind indifference to the danger of this scandal. On the one hand, here was a president who could get up in front of the world and tell us, 'I never had sexual relations with that woman, Miss Lewinsky.' On the other, the same man would testify to a grand jury, picking his way through words like a spoiled child picking at food. He was indignant at the questions asked of him, telling his interrogators at one point, 'It depends what the meaning of the word "is", is.'

I watched the president's cabinet members, friends and supporters announcing to the world that Clinton was telling the truth. And even if he was lying, they would say *sotto voce*, he was lying about sex. It was a lie told by millions of mere mortals every day of the week. But it was also a lie told by the most powerful man in the world. A lie that led to other lies and prompted the leading lights in the government of the world's last remaining superpower to spin a web of half-truth and denial. I never put it that way in my reports because it wasn't for me to tell the Irish people what to think about Bill Clinton and his deception. But I must have let something slip through in my reporting because I found myself under attack for allegedly revelling in the president's misfortune.

I was back in Dublin shortly after the House of Representatives had voted to impeach Bill Clinton in December 1998. I was in a bar with a group of friends when an acquaintance took me aside and started to tell me what he thought of my work. He began, 'Mark, I want to tell you that your reports are absolutely ...', and then he paused. I thought he was about to say 'excellent' or 'compelling' or at least something nice. But the next word out of his mouth was 'abysmal'. He said I seemed to take pleasure in the president's difficulties, before delivering a well-argued and reasonable attack on Ken Starr and the president's enemies.

I found myself agreeing with him in part, but I also wanted him to look into Bill Clinton's eyes and see the cold, hard look of defiance. I wanted him to talk to the advisers and friends who had defended the president but who were eventually forced to slink into a corner, laden down by humiliation, anger and betrayal. I just wanted people to recognise that this mattered. An over-zealous prosecutor should never have pursued Bill Clinton in the first place. It was just and it was right that he remained in office and that his Republican enemies were defeated. It is right that the history books should remember him as a man who helped to save lives in Northern Ireland. But it is wrong to forget the pain that the president was willing to inflict on those around him and on the nation just so that he could escape responsibility for the deep flaws in his character.

One piece of testimony from the Monica Lewinsky scandal stands out for me. It came from Dick Morris, the president's former political adviser. Morris had resigned in disgrace in the summer of 1996 after his relationship with a prostitute had been revealed. But just a few days after the Lewinsky scandal broke he took an opinion poll for the president. The question asked if the American people would forgive Bill Clinton if he admitted the affair with the former White House intern. The poll showed that they would not. Dick Morris gave the president the results of the survey and Clinton replied, 'Then we're going to have to win, aren't we?' It sums up the whole scandal for me. The president was prepared to win at all costs, no matter who got hurt. Ken Starr and the Republicans were prepared to win at all costs, no matter how much damage they inflicted on the American political system. And we in the media were prepared to get the story on air first, no matter what.

When I think about the winners and losers of the Monica wars, I remember that girl with the floppy hat. She was so perfectly cast in the starring role of this pathetic and puerile scandal. You just had to listen to her on the famous tapes, talking to that Baby Boomer-misfit Linda Tripp telling her so-called friend that she had called the president 'butthead' to his face and might address him as 'boo-boo' in her next angst-ridden letter. Then, seconds later, she is wracked by heaving sobs as she realises the trouble she is in.

I saw Monica Lewinsky about a year after the scandal ended. I had just left my apartment building and walked about fifty yards when I saw a couple snogging on the roadway by a hastily parked car. I knew Monica's new boyfriend lived in my neighbourhood and so was intrigued by the sight of a man kissing a woman with distinctive, thick black hair. Her face was partially obscured and she was thinner than on television, but when she pulled back from the man, I got a look at that profile, the corner of her smile, and it was Monica Lewinsky. I wanted to go over and say hello, but it would have been bad manners to get in the way of her romantic clinch. Anyway, I don't know what I would have said. I just walked on and remembered the first time I had seen her, the day that she was just a face in the crowd, a girl with a floppy hat and a lipstick grin. If only she could have stayed that way. Life would have been so much simpler for everybody.

# Eight

## The Boy from Hot Springs

At the end of the day in Hot Springs, Arkansas, the evening sun lights up the town's towering centrepiece, the Arlington Hotel. Yellow turns to orange as the sun slowly disappears behind the Ouachita Mountains. Walk out of the hotel and you find yourself on Central Avenue. Even in the twilight you can see the steam rising off the waterfalls to your left. A little farther on, you come to a row of bathhouses that feed off the natural springs on the mountainside: Hale, Superior, Ozark, Buckstaff and Quapaw are just a few of the names of these monuments to southern gentility. Yet, as you continue your stroll around Hot Springs, there are reminders that this town did not become famous for being genteel.

Al Capone was a regular visitor. Legend has it that he took a corner suite on the fourth floor of the Arlington so he could keep an eye on the comings and goings of the gamblers at the Southern Club across the street. Hot Springs was famous for casinos, booze and big-name entertainers well into the 1950s. Liberace and Tony Bennett played at the famous Vapors Club just up the road from the Arlington. Side by side with the casinos and clubs were the churches. A few yards from the Vapors was the Park Place Baptist Church, and a short walk from the church is 1011 Park Avenue. Today, there is a well-tended flowerbed outside the modest house and a sign that reads 'Childhood home of Bill Clinton'.

The campaign ads said that Bill Clinton was the boy from Hope, Arkansas, but it was Hot Springs that made him. To understand the contradictions at the heart of this American president, you must see the light and dark in the soul of this mountain holiday resort. 'It was poetic to be born in Hope, but it meant more to grow up in Hot Springs,' observed David Maraniss in his definitive Clinton biography, *First in His Class*: 'Hot Springs was a vaporous city of ancient corruption mingling with purely American idealism.' Locals remember young Billy Clinton, a bible under his arm, walking alone to the Park Place Church. They also remember his mother, Virginia, as a regular at the Oaklawn Racetrack and a flamboyant presence at the Vapors. Virginia had brought Bill to Hot Springs to live with her second husband, a car dealer called Roger Clinton. He was a heavy drinker with a capacity for violence, which he would occasionally direct at his wife. Throughout that long and difficult marriage, Virginia would rely heavily on her son.

Virginia was full of contradictions. She was a nurse and would occasionally come home with a traumatic tale from the hospital, complaining about the unfairness of the American health system. 'Mother was everything,' one of young Billy's close friends told me. 'When she talked, it was very much black and white.' Yet this was a woman who was deeply suspicious of people with a narrow interpretation of what was good and proper. She lived in a richly permissive town, and that seemed to have shaped her view of life. 'I'm not one for rules and the only rule in Hot Springs was to enjoy yourself,' Virginia wrote in her memoir, *Leading with My Heart*. 'Too many people seem to think life is the tablecloth, instead of the messy feast that's spread out on it. That's not life. Done right, life leaves stains.'

During the 1992 campaign, a good friend of mine interviewed Virginia. While the camera was on, she gave the approved text of the Clinton biography but when the cameras were turned off, she kept talking. One day, she told my friend, she was baking cookies while young Billy worked on his homework at the kitchen table. She put the cookies out to cool on a baking tray and then left the house on an errand. When she came back, Billy had finished his homework and the cookies were gone. She turned angrily to her young son and asked what had happened. 'What cookies? You never baked any cookies,' he replied. Billy kept talking until he had persuaded his mother that she had not baked that night. 'That's when I knew he would be a politician,' Virginia said.

As he grew into a chubby teenager, Clinton's passion was music. He played tenor saxophone with his high school band by day and jazz at the Majestic Hotel by night. His high school band director was Virgil Spurlin. I met him at his house just outside Hot Springs when I was preparing my first profile of Bill Clinton in November 1995. Mr Spurlin was an ex-Marine and Baptist deacon and had been a father figure to Billy when he was a teenager. He was a precious role model for the child of a dysfunctional family. He remembered the collective pride that surrounded Billy's trip to Washington in the summer of 1963. He had been chosen to attend Boys Nation, a prestigious conference of America's most promising youth leaders. The trip ended in the Rose Garden of the White House, where Bill Clinton shook hands with President John F. Kennedy. That moment changed Clinton's life and he returned to Hot Springs and his mentor with his heart set on a life in politics. 'If he had met Elvis that summer, he would have been a musician,' said Virgil Spurlin. The old band teacher was there the day young Billy announced his first bid for a seat in the US Congress in 1974. He was also at the reception marking Arkansas Attorney General Bill Clinton's elevation to Governor. And when Spurlin had a stroke, Bill Clinton phoned him from his campaign bus; it was 1992 and he had just been nominated as the Democratic candidate for president.

'I went to see him at the White House after he was elected and he asked me how I was doing. He asked *me*!' Mr Spurlin recounted the events of that day with unrestrained glee. 'I said I don't agree with everything you're doing, but I think you're doing fine and I wish they would just leave you alone and let you be president.'

Mr Spurlin had his collection of Clinton memorabilia close to hand the day I met him. He took out a copy of the Hot Springs High School Yearbook of 1964, opened it up and handed it to me with a smile. On the opening page was an inscription from eighteen-year-old Bill Clinton to his band director. When we came to do the interview, Mr Spurlin had the yearbook on his lap, so I asked him to read the inscription for the benefit of our camera. A cloud of doubt passed briefly across his face. 'The first time I was asked to do that, I said no. This is a private deal between me and Bill.' Then he seemed to relent. 'But I suppose there's nothing that the public should not hear.' He dipped his head and began to read. His voice grew louder and stronger and there seemed to be a bitter-sweet flicker of lost joy in his eyes as he read the words Clinton had written to him more than 30 years before: 'I honestly tried to do a good job for you. I think I almost made it. Now it's time for me to leave and make the best I can of myself, and I know no matter how I do, I'll be better because of my association with one the greatest Christian men that the Lord ever gave life.' As Virgil

Spurlin finished reading these words, he lifted his head to reveal tears under the reddening rims of his eyes.

That episode helped me understand the fundamental dynamic of Bill Clinton's career: there would always be people who would see nothing but the best in him, even when confronted with the worst. Without their bottomless well of support, Clinton would be nothing. He would break their hearts again and again, but he would keep coming back for their forgiveness and they would give it to him every time because they shared in the warm sunshine of his success and the joy of promise fulfilled. To many of the people I met on that first trip to Arkansas, Bill Clinton was still the gilded youth in that high school yearbook, the teenage leader who would go out and conquer the world in the name of the God-fearing folk of Hot Springs. But in their hopeful hearts there was a silent, sad certainty: the hometown hero had left Hot Springs, but Hot Springs would never quite leave him.

Not everyone who knows Bill Clinton is willing to accept the ambiguity at the heart of his character. There are those who deny that there is a dark side to him. David Leopoulos spent almost every day with Bill Clinton when they were kids running around Hot Springs. In that 1964 high school yearbook is a picture of Clinton cradling Leopoulos in his arms as they both clown around in a variety show. 'They were very simple times,' Leopoulos told me. 'Hot Springs was simply a wonderful place to grow up.' I could not help feeling he had a selective memory of this contradictory town and his complicated friend.

Clinton's childhood was overshadowed by the violence and alcoholism of his stepfather, Roger. 'What was curious,' David Leopoulos told me, 'was that we never knew one thing that was happening in that family.' I found that hard to believe. Leopoulos visited the Clinton home almost every day for years, and yet he still claims he never saw the darkness in the lives of Bill and his mother. It would make no sense even if this was the story of a normal human being, but this was the story of Bill Clinton. His old friend put it like this, 'He internalises anything that is a problem and solves it himself.' Leopolous was reflexive in defence of his childhood friend, but between the lines was another important clue.

On my first visit to Arkansas, I got more clues from a man who had resisted the legendary Clinton charm. Paul Greenberg had spent two decades writing newspaper columns about life in Arkansas, and many of those columns were about Bill Clinton. He never stopped liking Clinton, but he slowly began to lose all respect for him. 'When I look back on all those columns over 20 years, I see how often I wanted to give him the benefit of the doubt. But again and again when you look for him to use the political credit he had built up, and all the popularity he had gained by compromise, he would compromise again.'

Greenberg was the man who coined the Clinton nickname, 'Slick Willie'. He had come up with the name when Clinton served as Governor of Arkansas. 'I'm not sure there is a real Bill Clinton. I've never been able to identify a single political principle he would not compromise in some way, or sacrifice in some way, for the next election. I've never been able to find something solid to stick with at the core of this hollow man.'

That view of Bill Clinton, the permanent campaigner with no moral compass, is consistent with the story of the young Billy Clinton of Hot Springs. He was the over-achieving young star who tirelessly campaigned for the love and admiration of those around him. Each successive stage of his life was a competition and, while victory came easily, it would come at a price – a warped view of the surrounding world. If the reality doesn't suit, then it must be ignored. If it cannot be ignored, it must be changed.

The Monica Lewinsky scandal was the ultimate test of a man who was used to twisting reality in the face of overwhelming adversity. Crucially, it was a self-inflicted adversity. In the seeds of every great moment for Clinton, there are the seeds of the next crisis. So it was when he turned his presidency around by defeating the Republican Party in a battle over the budget in October 1995. As he led the fight that would guarantee him victory in the following year's presidential election, he was beginning an affair that would almost destroy his presidency.

Hubris was at the heart of the cycle of boom and bust in Clinton's career. The over-confidence of his golden youth comes back to haunt him repeatedly. On 4 May 1998, the president was in Senegal during a whistle-stop tour through West Africa when he received news that the Paula Jones sexual harassment lawsuit had been thrown out by Arkansas Judge Susan Webber Wright. Clinton is the master of understatement when he wants to be. Deep feelings are acted out in slow motion, with a mid-sentence pause, a ripple of the muscles in his jaw, a curl of his lip and a serious, sombre presidential look at the ground. But in Senegal, a rogue television camera captured Bill Clinton in the glory of unguarded and adolescent joy. The president sat in his hotel room, with a wide grin and an unlit stogie clenched between his teeth (this was in the days before we thought of a presidential cigar as a sex toy). He was beating away on a bongo drum like a ten-year-old with a new toy on Christmas morning.

That image remains locked in my subconscious. Bill Clinton had every reason to celebrate. If logic prevailed, the end of the Paula Jones lawsuit meant that there could be no basis for the Republicans to pursue the Monica

Lewinsky affair, which was the product of a lie in the Jones case. But there was too much arrogance in that image, and in Clinton's life there is an immutable law: the greater the celebration, the greater the subsequent humiliation.

So it came to pass. Months of denial came to an end with the report of an FBI examiner: 'Based on the results of those seven genetic loci, specimen K39 (CLINTON) is the source of the DNA obtained from specimen Q3243-I, to a reasonable degree of scientific certainty.' In other words, it was Clinton's semen on Monica's dress.

The proof of the illicit relationship with Lewinsky forced the president to make a partial confession of his sins in the Map Room of the White House on a rainy day in August 1998. He spent four hours in front of a video camera, answering questions from the independent counsel Ken Starr and his deputies. Later, he made a televised address to the nation: 'Indeed I did have a relationship with Monica Lewinsky that was not appropriate. In fact it was wrong.' But this was not the *mea culpa* some advisers had urged on the president. This was as much denunciation as it was admission. It was 543 words boiled down to four: 'Fuck you, Ken Starr.'

'It is time to stop the pursuit of personal destruction and the prying into private lives and get on with our national life.' While there was talk of seeking forgiveness, there was no talk of apology. If there was any trace of sorrow, it was the sorrow of getting caught. 'This has gone on too long, cost too much and hurt too many innocent people. Now this matter is between me and the two people I love most, my wife and our daughter, and our God. I must put it right.'

That last phrase was straight out of the mouth of young Billy Clinton. 'I must put it right' by shaping reality to my own ends. More important than what was said was what was not said. Bill Clinton did not say the words 'lie', 'guilt' or 'sorry'. By expressing his wrong-doing in religious terms, and not in terms of law or fact, he was preparing his escape route. He was appealing to an admirable American attribute: an absolute belief in the power of redemption.

With this in mind, Bill Clinton presented himself as a sinner who deserved forgiveness. Only his family and his God had the right to punish him; everyone else should back off until the process of redemption was complete. He was back in Hot Springs again, where devout observance and self-indulgence coexist without contradiction, and where there is no sin that cannot be forgiven. And so, in those last few months of 1998, Bill Clinton launched the fight for his political life with those words, 'I must put it right.' He would seek forgiveness from those who were willing to forgive and destroy those who were not. There was no room for compromise in this situation. You were either with him on the road to redemption or you were an enemy he would simply run over.

Bill Clinton was well prepared for this defining battle. Ever since he had been a student at Oxford, the desire to be elected to public office provided order and logic in his life and that remained the case even after he had won his second presidential election in 1996. He loved the smell of political combat and at every stage of his career he could count on the loyalty of experts who specialised in 'slash and burn' political tactics. These partisans eventually became policy-makers, but they conducted the affairs of the nation like a presidential election, with one eye on the opinion polls and the other on their enemies. It was an atmosphere summed up by White House press secretary Joe Lockhart: 'There was this view that every news cycle was important, that every story was important, and that it was important never to give an inch.'

In the autumn of 1998, many of Clinton's foot soldiers had been alienated by the lies of their Commander-in-Chief. Even those still loyal to the president could not help him out. They could not talk to him about the scandal for fear of being summoned to testify before Ken Starr's grand jury – there lay madness and crippling legal fees. Bill Clinton was left to fend for himself with the help of a rapidly depleted inner circle composed of his lawyers and his wife, the only people in the world legally exempt from testifying against him.

In the end, salvation for this lonely man came from Hillary Clinton and it came in two stages. The first was her silence in the wake of her husband's public and private admissions of limited guilt. There was obvious anger in her body language after that television address in the summer of 1998, and Washington was obsessed with every full stop and comma. If there was one image that sums up that smouldering, silent rage, it was the sight of Bill Clinton leading his dog, Buddy, across the White House lawn to a waiting helicopter the day after his address to the nation. Holding his left hand is daughter Chelsea, who in turn grips her mother's right hand. Hillary doesn't wave, smile or tilt her head to the waiting media. She stares straight ahead and hides her eyes behind a pair of sunglasses. The dark cloud of anger and detachment followed the first couple for the next couple of weeks, on their holiday in Martha's Vineyard and through the early stages of their official visit to Ireland in September 1998.

It ended in Limerick, at the junction of Thomas Street and O'Connell Street, where thousands of people had gathered to cheer Bill and Hillary. The rain was coming down in sheets that morning, but just as the president's motorcade pulled up to the stage, a ray of sunlight poked through the downpour, followed by a glorious cascade of

119

light. The rain stopped as the president and the first lady rose to the stage to meet the Mayor of Limerick. As political analyst Carl Cannon remembers it: 'Hillary looked up at the sky and then looked at her husband as if to say: this lucky bastard.' For the first time since the president's televised admission, they were a couple again. 'Their old political symbiosis seemed to be switched back on,' wrote Hillary's biographer Gail Sheehy after that day in Limerick. 'And when the two stood to take their bows, Hillary's arm, almost absently, slipped around her husband's back. As automatic as a turnstile his arm thrust out and circled her waist.'

Resurrecting the political partnership was the second stage of Bill Clinton's salvation. Within days of returning from Ireland, the president and his wife were back in the trenches, rallying their dispirited troops in preparation for the battle ahead. A trickle of public apologies, which began during a very awkward photo opportunity with Taoiseach Bertie Ahern in Dublin, turned into a torrent. It seemed that every time the president stood before an audience, he was struck by a frenzy of repentance. He could afford to confront his guilt because Hillary was back on his side. While her husband performed public penitence, the first lady was twisting arms in private, persuading wavering Democrats that they must stand by the president in the face of the approaching impeachment enquiry. One congressman on the receiving end of her appeals summed it up like this: 'If I was going to war, I'd want her covering my rear. She's never going to run from a fight.'

Just as Clinton's defining traits were learned in childhood, so were Hillary's, but they were very different childhoods. She grew up in Chicago in an atmosphere where love was earned through hard work and moral consistency. There was one special story Hillary's mother,

Dorothy, liked to tell about her daughter. When Hillary was four, the neighbourhood bully pushed her around. She ran to tell her mother but found little sympathy. 'There's no place in this house for cowards,' she was told. The next day, Hillary went back and punched the bully, ran home and exclaimed, 'I can play with the boys now.' Almost half a century later, she was standing up to bullies but her motives were not as clear. Exactly why was she standing by her man?

There is the Mills and Boon theory: that the Clinton marriage is a remarkable bond forged out of immortal love. The marriage does have some elements of a paperback romance. The couple met at law school where an uncharacteristically shy Bill Clinton would not approach a young and studious Hillary Rodham. Eventually she confronted him: 'Look, if you're going to keep staring at me and I'm going to keep staring back, we should at least introduce ourselves.' Over the years, close friends and advisers have complained of uncomfortable moments when Bill and Hillary would cuddle and kiss in their presence like love-struck teenagers. But the same aides talked of the purple rage of a *Clinton* versus *Clinton* row in which lamps were reportedly thrown across the room. They were witnesses to the doom-laden silences and heard the explosions of profanity from behind closed doors.

The Clinton partnership cannot be understood through the prism of any normal marriage. None of us can judge that relationship unless we have lived our entire adult lives in the white heat of political warfare and public scrutiny. We cannot understand it until we see this as a partnership in which adversity brings the couple together, instead of driving them apart. A recognisable form of love existed in that marriage, even in the worst of times, but what kept it together was the sense that one half could not succeed without the other half. To succeed, they needed his skills as a great political charmer, the man who is always looking for friends. To survive, they needed her instincts as a political street fighter, the woman who is always looking out for enemies. Hillary Clinton's elevation to the Senate and her husband's demotion to speechmaker-in-chief may have altered that dynamic, but it was a powerful force when they needed it most; the only force capable of keeping a bizarre union together in the most bizarre of circumstances.

To survive in the public eye, Bill and Hillary had to manipulate reality to cover up the dysfunction at the heart of their marriage, but the Clintons were blessed with their choice of enemies. During the Lewinsky scandal, they tried to persuade the public that the fault lay not with a philandering husband called Bill but with a fanatical independent counsel called Ken. Leading the righteous crusade against Ken Starr's enquiry was Hillary's way of rationalising her choice and retaining her dignity. Divorce was not an option then; Hillary Clinton knew that the ultimate victory for that 'vast right-wing conspiracy' was the self-destruction of her marriage. After a quarter of a century of struggle, she couldn't accept that defeat. Only by standing by her man would she find freedom from Monica Lewinsky, Paula Jones, Gennifer Flowers and all the other rumoured mistresses.

The bargain at the centre of Bill and Hillary's partnership was vitally important but so was the bargain that Bill Clinton struck with the American people when he was first elected president. It was not so much a formal contract but one of those subconscious understandings that had protected Clinton since his Hot Springs childhood. It is hard to put into words, but in late January 1998 it was captured by a series of incredible images. More than 100,000 people had crammed into a sports stadium in St Louis to share mass with the Pope. At times, it looked and sounded like a rock concert. 'John Paul Two, we love you,' chanted the younger members of the crowd. President Clinton shared in the overwhelming mood of celebration that day when he officially welcomed the Pope. He stood by the pontiff and soaked up the warmth of the cheering crowd. He needed these moments like others need food and water.

In St Louis, this troubled, and troubling, politician got to bask in the reflected glory of virtue personified. Yet the Pope stood for everything that Bill Clinton did not. John Paul II preached against the death penalty, while Bill Clinton actively supported it. John Paul preached against abortion; Bill Clinton fought harder to keep abortion legal than any president of modern times. John Paul was a man revered for his simplicity, consistency and purity; Bill Clinton was the man they put on trial for sex, lies and the abuse of power.

The audacious coupling of the president and the Pope should have prompted a loud collective intake of breath, but it did not. The lack of outrage speaks volumes about the inconsistencies of the American public. Americans may love the Pope but they have learned to pick and choose from the credo he offers. Many of the faithful who turned up in St Louis were 'Cafeteria Catholics'. They love that pro-life message, but prefer to leave that anti-death penalty stuff at the side of the plate. Bill Clinton was the ultimate à la carte believer: a deeply religious southern Baptist who strongly believes in law and order and personal responsibility, he is also a child of Hot Springs, the Sixties, the Vapors Club, Oxford and the days when he smoked pot but didn't inhale. While his life experience and his views on society put him well to the left of many Americans, the ambiguity that is Bill Clinton suited the United States during his presidency.

The American people cheered John Paul II as a man who rises above the cynicism and materialism of daily life. One celebrant at the mass in St Louis put it like this: 'He's a beautiful old man who won't lie to you, won't ask for your vote and won't try and sell you something you don't need.' People like this see in the Pope what they would like to be. They see in Bill Clinton what they are: the personification of the daily struggle between what's right and what is. Shortly after I observed that crowd, I read an opinion poll in one of the news magazines. It asked who was the public figure Americans most admired, and the answer was Bill Clinton. The Pope was way down the list.

The Pope might personify virtue but Bill Clinton personifies optimism, and optimism defines American politics. Ronald Reagan seduced voters with his 'shining city on the hill', George Bush had his 'thousand points of light', and Bill Clinton rallied the people towards his 'bridge to the twenty-first century'. What made Clinton remarkable was that people endorsed his optimism even when they knew he was deeply flawed. In many ways, his imperfections helped him to sell his brand of optimism. He was human, and in a political culture defined by cynicism and alienation, that made him easier to identify with. If there is a defining characteristic of the Clinton era it is not grand idealism but practical self-interest. A majority of the American people pledged to ignore the fact that their president was a man of limited personal virtue, as long as he continued to do a good job for them, as long as he remained one of them. Clinton kept his side of the bargain and the American people kept theirs, even when they were confronted by the most blatant lies.

If you came from Hot Springs and knew the atmosphere that surrounded young Billy when he was growing up, you had a unique understanding of why the broader public adopted this flawed individual. The people of that complicated southern town always knew that they could not wipe away the seediness of their history with a fresh coat of paint on the Arlington Hotel, but it would certainly help to cover it up for a while. In the same way, they would try to ignore the contradictions that threatened to destroy their favourite son. Once the American people got to know Bill Clinton, they too would begin thinking the Hot Springs way.

When Clinton rose and wagged his finger and told the world he did not have sex with that woman Monica Lewinsky, he might have well been arguing with his mother about the mysterious disappearance of those cookies. Just like Virginia, the public saw the crumbs on his lips, but they chose to ignore the bad in a person who made them feel good.

# Nine

## Live Free or Die

The small commuter plane taxied towards the terminal at Des Moines airport and bounced along the shiny lumps of frozen snow strewn along the edge of the runway. It was January 1996 and a presidential election campaign was getting underway in Iowa. I knew it would be cold, but I had no idea just how cold. I walked to the doorway of the plane and flinched as a wall of freezing air slammed against my face. My eyes widened as I made my way gingerly down the steps of the aircraft, and a dull ache crept into the muscles of my hands. The hairs in my nostrils were freezing. It felt like my nose was lined with a toilet brush. The warm glow of the terminal building beckoned just fifty yards away, but I was not sure that I could make it that far. I feared that if I moved too fast one of my limbs might freeze solid and fall off. I knew that temperatures like this existed in theory, but this was not the polar ice cap. This was the American heartland, and there was supposed to be an election campaign going on. In Des Moines, I found the international press corps huddled in the hotel bars talking frostbite, not sound-bites. A cameraman for one of the international news agencies was sent out to chase a rumour that cows' ears were freezing and falling off.

Those first couple of days in the tundra raised a lot more questions than answers. How does one conduct a political campaign in these temperatures? Why is Iowa the first state to cast ballots in the presidential process? Why not Hawaii? Why do the corn-bred, hog-rearing, God-fearing, overall-wearing citizens of this Midwestern state have such a disproportionate say in who the next American president will be? And why pick a state with so few distinguishing features? Iowa is flat. Look at Iowa on a map. It looks like a sloppily drawn square. There are no bends in the highways. You could fall asleep at the wheel and wake up an hour later and still be on the right side of the road. Close neighbours drive an hour to borrow a cup of sugar. In the five years I spent in America, I never met anybody who was from Iowa. Except, of course, the people I met in Iowa. John Wayne was born there, as was Buffalo Bill. Clint Eastwood and Meryl Streep snogged among the Bridges of Madison County. Kevin Costner built his baseball field there in *Field of Dreams*. Travel writer Bill Bryson is perhaps the only major literary figure to emerge from Iowa, and he became famous only by leaving. Ronald Reagan had a brief career as a sports announcer in Des Moines. Buddy Holly, Richie Valens and the Big Bopper died when their plane crashed into a cornfield outside Mason City. But that is pretty much the history of Iowa as it affects the rest of the world. Iowans don't even have an accent to make them different. No elongated vowels, no nasal twang, and no musical cadence at all. People in this state are so literal that the name of their state song is 'The Song of Iowa'.

Despite this determined mediocrity, there are good reasons why the voters of Iowa are the first in the nation to cast ballots in the presidential election process. People in this state take politics seriously. There is still a sense of purpose on the campaign trail, as it winds its way along

soulless politician trying to be a real human being, and failing miserably. Iowa also gives you that exhilarating feeling that politics has a pulse. But Iowa also demonstrates a contradiction at the heart of the American election process: voters will applaud sincerity and flirt with the underdog but, more often than not, they will plump for the establishment candidate. That's just what Iowa did when it was presented with a candidate called George W. Bush.

Governor Bush, as he was then, had his first major campaign rally in the summer of 1999 during the World Pork Expo at the State Fairgrounds in Des Moines. The Expo is a celebration of pigs: equipment for pigs, food for pigs, medicine for pigs, houses for pigs, stuff to get maximum yield out of pigs, and, of course, there are the pigs. There are live ones and dead ones, little bitty piglets running around amusing the children, big fat sows at the centre of intense haggling between weather-beaten far-mers, and succulent dead pigs, sliced and diced, broiled and barbecued, seasoned and sauced up and stretched out on tables along a half-mile stretch under the ferris wheels and kiddy rides.

In the midst of this vegetarian's nightmare, there were also Republican candidates for president of the United States. The main stage at the Fairgrounds had been set aside for the candidates to make their pitch to the pork producers and consumers of Iowa. My favourite was Elizabeth Dole. She was so polite, you got a sugar rush just from looking at her. Liddy was a true southern lady. She was so pleased to be with you – head nods slowly. She couldn't tell you how wonderful it was to be at the Pork Expo – hands clasped as if in prayer – to meet all those wonderful people – shows both rows of perfect teeth – and see all that absolutely delicious 'bar-bah-kooo' – leans over to stroke piglet. Liddy Dole never actually spoke the phrase 'thank you'; she lovingly exhaled it. If honey slipping from a spoon made a sound, it would be the sound of Liddy Dole leaving a room. There was a chance her campaign would catch fire but then George W. Bush, aka Dubya, came along. There wasn't room for two southern stereotypes in the same race.

That day at the Pork Expo, Bush didn't have to make an appearance on the main stage along with the losers. He got top billing at a fundraising dinner in a massive barn near the gates to the Fairgrounds. At the appointed time, a big man with an ear-piece pulled back the curtain on the left side of the stage and, like a prize stallion, Dubya bounded out to begin his campaign for the presidency. It was a masterful performance. Bush plunged straight into the warm embrace of the crowd, winking, pointing, hugging and joking his way across the barn. With the cameras trained on his every move, he sat down at a predetermined space at a trestle table just a few feet in front of the media platform and tucked into his corn on the cob. I immediately gave him some brownie points for that. Corn on the cob is up there with doner kebabs and spaghetti bolognese as a food you cannot eat while you are trying to impress your dinner partner, let alone the American electorate. Yet, with the cameras waiting for a soggy kernel of corn to lodge in the gap between his teeth, Dubya kept eating and talking.

The man on show that day looked like the coolest kid in school. He wore a rumpled shirt, with rolled up sleeves and loosened tie, and winked out to his new mates in the audience. When a big bald-headed blowhard grabbed the microphone to sing a painful operatic version of the 'Star-Spangled Banner', you could see the suppressed mirth in Dubya's cheeks. I think I even caught him rolling his eyes. Beside him sat his wife Laura, and every now and then he would lean in and whisper something to her as if they were alone. As someone later observed: 'He's just so comfortable in his skin.' He was comfortable until he rose to speak. Armed with political clichés that had obviously been written by some back-room committee, he talked of a foreign policy 'with a touch of iron, driven by American values and American interests'. He told the audience he was running 'so our party can match a conservative mind with a compass-ionate heart'. It was not Jack Kennedy but it would do. Bush left the stage to thunderous applause and even the media agreed that we had probably heard from the next president of the United States.

There would be serious problems along the road to the White House. Bush's victory in the Iowa caucuses in January 2000 was less than convincing, and as the campaign moved on to New Hampshire there were frayed nerves among his closest supporters. New Hampshire is just as unrepresentative as Iowa. Less than two million people live in this state. That is about four-tenths of one per cent of the American population. Yet New Hampshire has done more to chart the course of American politics in the last 30 years than any one of the biggest states in the union. The first thing you notice as you drive from Massachusetts into New Hampshire is the slogan on the licence plate: 'Live Free or Die.' 'Piss off back to Washington' would more accurately capture the feelings of the voters of the Granite State.

In New Hampshire, George W. Bush decided that he could win the Republican primary by meeting voters in the most ridiculous settings allowed by law. One day, Bush had held an impromptu press conference on the back of a snowmobile. He went round in circles a couple of times with a big childish grin on his face as the photographers huffed and puffed in an effort to keep up. My favourite photo opportunity of the primary season was the inflatable tube ride. With the media circus in tow, Bush trekked to the top of a snow-covered hill to meet a couple of teenage girls. They invited him to join them on a tube ride down the slope. With the young girls wrapped around him, he slid down the hill with his dignity shaken but intact. What message this was supposed to convey remains a mystery to me. Maybe the message was that Bill Clinton could never have got away with such a stunt. Imagine him bouncing down a snowy hill with two pretty young women in his lap. His campaign would have been over before you could say the words 'White House intern'.

Bush had fallen into a trap. He had wrongly assumed that he could win in places like New Hampshire and Iowa by goofing about in front of the cameras and limiting his public utterances to ghost-written platitudes at expensive rallies. That strategy would work when the campaign went national, but it was incompatible with the proud, contrarian spirit of voters in Iowa and New Hampshire. The people of these states knew they were being spun by the Bush campaign and they resented it. Bush won in Iowa because there was no compelling alternative candidate. In New Hampshire, there was Senator John McCain.

I first met McCain in South Carolina in October 1999, when he was still the longest of long shots. The McCain entourage consisted of two other reporters, two campaign staffers, the candidate and me. We all fitted into a small van. McCain kept up a relentless stream of consciousness about life, the universe and everything. It had the feel of a political joyride. 'I know I'm following a risky strategy,' he told me. 'But do I fear losing? No.' Even the members of McCain's staff were fun. Both of them, a man and a woman, had agreed which parts of their respective bodies they would eat first if they were stranded alone on a desert island after a plane crash. Predictably, he planned to eat 'her ass'.

When McCain arrived at his first stop, a Republican state convention, he was greeted by warm and respectful applause. The small crowd seemed a little detached at first but the candidate asked them to move closer to him, and then embarked on an intimate little monologue. He talked about issues with a practised confidence, and alluded to his heroic service in the Vietnam War with references to the veterans in the audience. He rocked on his heels as he gleefully ran through a list of well-practised one-liners, beginning every riff with the words 'My dear friends'. He slagged off his campaign staff: 'I got most of them on a work-release programme from the local prison.'

Back on the bus, McCain just kept talking until there was nothing more to talk about. He did not care what was on and what was off the record. The things he said would have rebounded badly on any other politician. When talking about some minor diplomatic confrontation, he blurted out, 'That's just one of the many reasons why I hate the French.' On another bus ride, he recalled his days in a Hanoi prison camp, referring to the North Vietnamese as 'Gooks'. His aides would blanche, the reporters would scribble furiously in their notebooks, but McCain never got into serious trouble because the media were falling in love with him. The emerging love affair even had a name: 'The McCain Swoon'.

That day in October, I got so much access I ran out of questions to ask. Those were the good old days when McCain, in the words of one reporter, 'was easier to get access to than a Hong Kong hooker'. Things started to change after the New Hampshire primary in February 2000. McCain defeated George Bush by a margin of 19 points. The scale of the victory made McCain a real contender for the Republican nomination for president, and it punctured the air of invincibility surrounding Dubya. Everything was set for a showdown in South Carolina where the next big primary would take place. The good news was: this election was now a real contest instead of a coronation. The bad news was: I would never get near John McCain again.

One rainy Monday in February 2000, I travelled to see McCain in Anderson, South Carolina. When I pulled into the car park of the cheap hotel where McCain was staying, my heart sank. A few months before, McCain had travelled in a single mini-bus. Now his expanded entourage filled four coaches. I approached the polite young woman who was doling out seats on McCain's bus. I asked if I could sit with the candidate on the way to the first campaign event. She responded with a tired smile and said, 'I'll see what we can do.' That was the last time she talked to me. Meanwhile, my friend Lisa, of the *Detroit News*, was squeezed on board McCain's bus, modestly named the 'Straight Talk Express', where she remained for the rest of the day. Lisa writes for the biggest newspaper in Michigan and can help deliver votes in the next big primary. I am a waste of space.

A little disappointed, we travelled to McCain's first event. It was still only eight in the morning, but hundreds of people had crowded into a recreation centre on the outskirts of town. The sign on the wall read 'No smoking and no profanity'. These were conservative and devout people from South Carolina's 'Up Country', a region first settled by Scots-Irish farmers during the revolutionary war. The land was tough and the farms small. Today, new industries are transforming the region, but you cannot ignore the white poverty along the back roads, and the rough edge of the greeting you get from locals.

This should have been a tough audience, not prone to

outbursts of any kind, but there was excitement in the fetid air of the recreation hall that rainy morning. McCain won the crowd over the moment he said 'hello'. The look in the eyes of those people was a mixture of adoration and awe. The reporters at the back of the hall looked on with practised cynicism. We were trying to keep our crush on McCain's secret. Sarcastically, we mouthed the punch lines of his jokes because we had heard them a hundred times. 'They're thinking of making a movie about my life,' he told the crowd. We were a punch line ahead of him: 'I think Tom Cruise should play me, but my kids want Danny DeVito.'

Despite the media's affected cynicism, there was a genuine emotional bond between McCain and his audience. A lot of questions at this meeting came from veterans of past wars. McCain thanked them for serving their country and dropped some subtle references to his own war record, but nothing too explicit. He stopped short of offering a detailed description of the horror and squalor he had faced in a Vietnamese prison camp. McCain's story was all the more powerful because so much was left unsaid. It hung in the air like a ghostly presence, simultaneously comforting and unsettling. One young man stood up and declared, 'I know you have suffered pain in your life and I know that means you can feel the pain of the common man.' McCain looked genuinely touched as the young man continued with a tremor in his voice, 'I know you will bring balance to the White House when you're elected president.' After almost an hour and a half of shared emotion, McCain wrapped up the meeting and ran into the crowd to shake hands, sign autographs and pose for photos. 15 minutes later, the 'Straight Talk Express' was back on the road.

By the time I left Anderson, the morning fog had lifted and the sun was shining. I noticed, for the first time, the slogan on the licence plate read 'Smiling Faces and Beautiful Places'. It was a nice change from New Hampshire and 'Live Free or Die'. As I travelled down the back roads, I reconciled myself to my exclusion from McCain's immediate presence and began to feel much better. The car raced along, past the trailer parks and stores selling fishing bait and ammunition, past the small towns with funny names: Calhoun Falls, Fork Shoals, Ninety Six, Due West, Honea Path and Plum Branch. As I followed the pick-up trucks and the occasional eighteen-wheeler, a thought began to form in my mind: Behind all the fluff and the photo opportunities, this is a battle that could change American politics and produce a new kind of leader, someone elected with more than just the passive acceptance of voters. John McCain will catapult out of this state with unstoppable momentum. He will do it because the people of South Carolina will vote for what is real and not manufactured. Within days, I would realise this was just a daydream – a dream that would end when the unstoppable force that is John McCain met the immovable object that is the Republican establishment.

George Bush was devastated by his loss to McCain in New Hampshire, but by the time he arrived in South Carolina, he was just angry. There was a new combative spirit in the Bush campaign as it flew down to South Carolina. At a rally in the town of Saluda, Dubya was all fired up, triple-espresso fired up. 'I'm here to ask for your vote,' he screamed. Dubya was so close to the microphone you could almost hear him grinding his teeth with excitement and aggression. He stretched out his hands around the microphone as if he was hugging three people at the one time. He stayed like this for the rest of the event, occasionally tiring and dropping his hands to his side for a few seconds. The speech slipped over a range of topics without regard to logic, grammar or decibel level.

'Faith is my priority,' Dubya yelled into the microphone. 'Family is my priority.' His hands dropped for a moment, as did his voice, and then he let out a little nasal laugh. You could almost hear his brain shouting: 'Next topic. What the fuck is my next topic?' The candidate knows that what people are looking for are not reasons to vote for him but reasons not to vote for his opponent. He is the candidate of the Republican Party establishment and these are the voters of the Republican Party establishment. He wants their vote. Right now. Gimme. Gimme that last cookie. I want it. I need it. Vote for me or I will scream again.

In the end, Bush's desperate appeal to conservative Republicans helped him to victory in the South Carolina primary. As the make-or-break Super Tuesday primaries approached, I could see the writing on the wall: Dubya was going to beat McCain and become the Republican nominee for president. On the Saturday before the crucial primaries, he travelled to Binghamton, New York, to walk with the Knights of Columbus, local firemen and the NYPD pipe band in the annual St Patrick's Day parade. This was my last chance to get a moment alone.

When Dubya arrived, he was wearing the compulsory green tie. His wife looked splendid in her green suit, but wearing green would not be enough to win over this sceptical crowd. He had come to walk more than a mile between two rows of Catholic Americans, not his natural constituency. The going was tough. Bush had just left St Mary's Church when the first boos were heard. Outside the first bar along the route, three young men in Irish soccer jerseys yelled abuse at the Texan Governor. The candidate was protected by a group of young staffers who tried to outshout the protesters and obscure them from view with posters reading 'Viva Bush' and 'Irish for Bush'. Most of the 25,000 people who lined the parade route seemed pleased to see Dubya, and some of the kids in the crowd treated him like a teen idol, screaming his name as he passed. Dubya was 'some kind of fired up' when he arrived at a local hotel for a press conference. The national media had been excluded and there were just a handful of local reporters waiting there. I had sneaked in with my cameraman early and no one had kicked me out.

The press conference began and I asked Bush if he thought there was a role for the United States in the Irish peace process. With a brittle smile, he launched into an awkward response. He had obviously been briefed at some stage about Ireland and was visibly striving to remember what he had heard. 'It's important that peace be brought to this very important part of the region ...' Eventually, a light seemed to come on above his head. The rambling stopped; he produced a fairly intelligent analysis of the peace process and said America had to be patient.

When the press conference was over, Dubya shook a few hands and then turned to me. I complimented him on his green tie and he asked me where I was from.

'Ireland,' I said.

'Really,' he replied, with cheerful sarcasm.

'Dublin,' I added quickly.

He came right up close, turned his head slightly, as if we were sharing a secret, and asked me if the peace process would survive. I was not prepared for the question, but leaned forward and said something about the people wanting peace. I'd hardly finished when he said emphatically: 'You're right.' He turned his head and fixed me with a stare, as if to underline his words. Then he winked, turned and walked away.

I had felt this way before. I had been seduced by the reflex intimacy of a skilled politician. I had felt the same way with Bill Clinton. I knew Dubya was no Bill Clinton, but the same raw intuitive skill was there. At that moment in Binghamton, it seemed inevitable to me that George W. Bush would be the next American president, and for a split second it did not seem like a bad proposition. Like millions of American voters, I believed Bush was not the best candidate for the most important job in the world, but at a crucial moment I couldn't help feeling he was not the worst. And in the last tortured months of election 2000, that would be the secret of Dubya's eventual success.

# Ten

## Retail Cynicism

There is no way I could ever have known just how grasping and cynical Al Gore is unless I had witnessed him up close on the campaign trail. It was a couple of weeks before the New Hampshire primary and I had been told that Gore was going to speak at a rally of Irish-Americans in a high school near the state capital, Concord. His supporters assured me that he would make a substantial reference to the Irish peace process in his speech. We arrived in New Hampshire on one of those glorious New England winter mornings where the biting cold is overwhelmed by the razzle-dazzle of a cloudless blue sky. We drove out of Manchester, past the old mills that line the banks of the Merrimack River, and within minutes were in Concord. If Concord were situated in Ireland, it would win tidy town of the year every year, without fail. The reflected glow of the golden dome on top of the capitol building lit up Main Street, which was spookily clean and blemish-free. The sunlight bounced off the bright white spires of the churches as the locals braved the cold, under multiple layers, to window shop in the elegant storefronts. It was all far too perfect for my liking.

After passing through Concord, we reached the high

school gym where Gore was due to rally his Irish supporters. Two musicians were setting up their gear on a small stage on the left side of the hall. They had identical perms and moustaches. It was the kind of look popularised by English soccer players during the Seventies. They raised their guitars and began singing 'Molly Malone'. The crowd was just starting to trickle in and I spotted the busload of Irish-Americans taking their place at the back of the hall. As the Kevin Keegan look-alike musicians played away and the hall filled up, I realised we'd been had.

The Gore people were shameless. They had brought the Irish-Americans and put them at the back of the hall, and left them to peer out from behind the 'Union Members for Gore' and 'Families for Gore' who, in turn, were transfixed by the 'Cheerleaders for Gore'. The bright young things of the cheerleading squad entertained the crowd on one side of the hall as the Kevin Keegan duo ran through their repertoire of Irish standards. They launched into the 'Boys of the Old Brigade' just as three cheerleaders with short skirts, tight knickers and indelible smiles were launched into the air. The boys kept singing about the IRA as these young women flipped, flopped, danced, clapped, twirled and swirled. The rumbling sound I heard that day was Ireland's dead patriots turning in their graves.

The Gore people had mixed their metaphors and exposed their desperation. They needed votes from wherever they could get them. Al Gore needed those votes. Please vote for him. We'll sing you a rebel song. Al Gore loves rebel songs. He's got all the Wolfe Tones' albums. He'll give you pretty girls if you want. They'll dance; he'll sing the 'Broad Black Brimmer'. Just please, give us your vote. We'll make you happy. We'll be Irish for a day. We'll talk about unions. We'll join your union.

The union forever. You want to know about Al Gore and families. He's for families. He's got a family. He'll take care of families. Your family. He'll come over and babysit. You're black. Al Gore is black. Deep down, I swear, he's black. He's black and he's proud.

Al Gore bounded through the door of that hall like an accidental nudist running for cover. In preparation for the campaign, he had slimmed down and was flaunting his girlish figure, 'perky pecs', earth tones and tight polo shirts. He flung his body at selected members of the crowd and gave consecutive bear hugs to Irish-American leader Brian O'Dwyer and Congressman Richard Neal. They looked momentarily stunned at this surprisingly intimate gesture, as if they did not know whether to hug him back or slap his face. Before they could decide, Gore had moved on to the podium and was poised to speak.

The speech was part magic act and part margarine commercial. Gore had been tested with consumers, his weaknesses discarded and his strengths exposed. He was the big mac without the gherkin. Where he was lacking, he had learned to substitute. Gore had no natural presence, so he picked up some basic political conjuring tricks. Like a modern-day alchemist, he turned bullshit into gold with a studied gesture. He 'did' gravitas particularly well. He grabbed the microphone with two hands, laid his chin on his chest, dropped his voice by an octave and turned his head at a slight angle. 'I want to fight for you.' It sounded just like he meant it.

On the Sunday before the New Hampshire primary, I followed Gore for an entire day. This time, I decided to travel inside the media bubble that surrounded the candidate. At this stage of the campaign, you had to travel with the convoy to really get a close look. Turning up at an event does not cut it anymore; you are just another punter with an obstructed view. Travelling on the press bus with a candidate makes you feel you are on some thrilling school trip, but with Gore, things were different. There was none of the usual warmth. Just that whiff of overwhelming cynicism.

Early that Sunday morning, I arrived at the Sheraton Hotel in Nashua to join Gore's entourage. I found a member of the campaign staff who immediately informed me I could not get on the main bus. 'The next event is a retail,' he explained. I was totally confused, but nodded my head in fake understanding, turned to another reporter and quietly asked, 'What's a retail?' It turned out to be a small, carefully controlled walkabout with 'real' people. Just a handful of press people was allowed and they were kept at a respectful distance away from the candidate. It was manipulative and cynical but everybody I talked to accepted it as a fact of campaign life. It was part of a new lexicon I would pick up from the Gore people as they categorised different events. I was in a twilight zone, where nothing was real and no event was simply an event. It was 'a retail', 'an OTR' or, my particular favourite, 'a spontaneous'.

I stood there in the lobby of the hotel and considered making a dash for it, driving away before anyone noticed I was taking a day off. But there were just two days to the New Hampshire primary and I had to see Gore up close. The bus-driver lost his way as we looked for the candidate's big event of the day. I didn't care anymore. I lay back and looked out of the window at the beauty of this New Hampshire winter. We passed over ice-covered lakes and rivers, past hillsides covered in a blanket of shiny snow. Snowmobile tracks were carved into the whiteness like a child's doodle. As we drove east, we approached the ocean. In the clear sunshine you could see the light dancing on the waves for miles out to sea. I was roused from my catatonic state when the bus pulled up at the Hilltop Equestrian Centre near Somersworth, New Hampshire. There was a thin film of liquid mud across the car park and the vague smell of horseshit. Inside the show jumping arena, there were thousands of people who seemed genuinely enthusiastic about Al Gore. It was the first innocent excitement I had seen all day. But everything else about the event was staged. There was an old horse-drawn cart on stage with bales of hay arranged around it. There was the ubiquitous oversized Stars and Stripes and country music band at the corner of the arena. The lights were set and the soundman was just finishing the sound check. 'Two, two, two...' It was time for Al Gore to sell some snake oil.

The campaign bus pulled up at the back of the hall. It was parked in such a way that the front door of the bus was in line with the back door of the hall, allowing Gore to walk from one hermetically sealed environment to another without seeing anything but friendly faces. It was like watching some agoraphobic rock star. Ready to greet him inside the hall were Ted Kennedy and a couple of members of Congress. They stood on either side of Gore as he was escorted up to the stage. He was wearing a brown leather jacket, denim shirt and skin-tight jeans that revealed far more of the candidate than we really wanted to see. Standing beside Ted Kennedy, Gore looked positively anorexic.

Kennedy began the warm up speech and the sweat stains under his arms spread rapidly down his sides and across his chest. Before long, his chinos and casual check shirt were speckled with ever-widening patches of wetness. When the time came for Gore to speak, he was in fighting form. You knew when he was angry because he started reading from a prepared script, just in case he couldn't remember why he was angry. The theme of the day was that opponent Bill Bradley was a good for the back roads of Iowa. In no other place have I heard ordinary people talk of duty, honour, patriotism and politics, all in one conversation. In a nation where political activity is only slightly more respectable than alcoholism, Iowa is the one place where you can see and feel the poetry of American politics. While the campaign lasts, one Iowa voter in three will meet a presidential candidate and one in four will meet the candidate they planned to vote for. According to a local joke told during the last election, one Iowan turns to another and asks, 'What do you think of Al Gore?' 'I don't know yet,' replies the other. 'I've only met him three times.'

During the last presidential campaign I travelled to the town of Indianola, just south of the state capital, Des Moines. The town's mayor Jerry Kelley agreed to meet me for lunch at Crouse's restaurant, just off the main square. Mayor Kelley sat in a chair at the back of the room as I went around bothering diners with questions about the presidential candidates. Everyone else seemed perfectly pleased with all the attention, at least in that reserved Iowa kind of way. One of the old-timers casually mentioned that every presidential candidate in each campaign since 1976 had passed through Crouse's looking for votes.

'We've broken a lot of hearts here in Iowa; the hearts of men who think they're going to impress Iowans,' the mayor told me. 'If you're sitting in Crouse's enjoying a piece of pie, and George W. Bush walks in, the only thing that's really going to impress you is a better piece of pie. The people here are looking for someone like them, only a lot smarter. They know their limitations and they want someone who doesn't have those limitations.'

Iowans have a way of catching out the real phonies. They reward sincerity and punish dishonesty. One of the greatest sights in American politics is a smarmy and

Students' Union days at Trinity College Dublin, 1988,
in politically correct attire of the time.

My first winter in Washington – the blizzard of '96.
(*Inset*) Exile on M Street. My apartment in Foggy Bottom was just to the right of the Union Jack flag.

*(Above)* First 'grip and grin' at Dublin Castle 1995; the beginning of a spate of unsatisfying meetings with President Clinton.

*"The Guinness in me wanted to say, 'Mother of Divine Jesus, you will not believe how glad I am to shake your big, fat paw.' Instead, I burbled, 'Hello, it's great to meet you.'"*

*(Below)* At the White House party, St Patrick's Day, 1997.

# Who gives a flying fuck who you are...your illegally parked you potato sucking moron

An array of souvenirs from the Washingrton years, including the note that put paid to any notions I had about my status as an Irishman in Boston.

Presidential inauguration, 1997, with Tara.

*(Above)* With my daughter Sorcha, New York, 2000.
*(Below)* With Tara at the wedding of our friends Bill Owens and
Helena Fernandez in Seville, Spain, August 2000.

(*Above*) Jalozai refugee camp, Pakistan, April 2001.
(*Below*) On the road to Kabul, Afghanistan, April 2001.

*(Top)* Hacks on the beach, Santa Monica, the morning after the
Academy Awards ceremony, 2000.
*(Above)* Last night with friends at the Red Tomato, Washington,
December 2000.

nothing sack of shit. Of course, Gore never quite said those words, but outside the arena there were plenty of people willing to do so.

It was the last thing I expected to see but there was a bad-tempered shouting match going on as we left the hall. Two of Bill Bradley's most prominent supporters were there, waiting to counter Gore's attacks on their candidate, and they were anxious to brief the media. Some of Gore's supporters had told them to leave, and things were getting ugly. When I arrived on the scene, Bradley supporter Congressman Jerry Nadler was telling a reporter that Gore 'is a fucking liar'. Senator Bob Kerrey of Nebraska was standing just a few feet away in front of a forest of microphones. He was supporting Bill Bradley and was standing side by side with Senator Tom Harkin of Iowa, who was supporting Al Gore. The two men stood in the muck, trading jibes and good-natured insults like two old friends at the bar. It was great entertainment until Bob Kerrey got ready to leave and the Gore supporters followed him to his car shouting slogans in his ear. The mud was now splashing all over the place as the excitable crowd formed an unfriendly cordon around the senator. Kerrey had a streak of mud all down his back as he finally reached his car.

That little row outside the arena made the day for the reporters on the bus. They settled in for the long ride back to the hotel and pulled out their mobile phones, selling the minor drama to their editors back at base while they munched away on the remnants of the particularly fine lunch the Gore people had provided. The newspaper reporters gathered together to check their quotes. They were all excited because the candidates were moving into attack mode. They read their notes back to each other and debated the source of all that mud on Bob Kerrey's back. 'Did someone throw it?' 'Nah. It was accidental.' The rest of us sat back and watched *Austin Powers 2*, which was playing on the bus's entertainment system. 'This is a rare day,' a TV producer said. 'We get grilled chicken, a story and a movie on the bus.'

About the only thing we did not get was the candidate. Other than the small group of reporters on the main bus; the 'tight pool', we never got within 40 feet of Al Gore. For all the food, drink and well-informed gossip, I may as well have stayed at home and watched television. Al Gore's people had removed all spontaneity from the campaign. They had sealed their candidate away from the world and would produce him only when they could completely control his immediate environment. The media could never be completely controlled, so they must be contained and kept well away from the candidate. We never got to know Al Gore, so the only thing we could write about and broadcast was the freshly minted persona he presented at those rallies and 'retails'.

Gore really had no choice because he was up against a real candidate, someone who made a career out of idealism and authenticity. Bill Bradley was a former basketball star and New Jersey senator who had entered the presidential election campaign with a splash. Just months before New Hampshire, as Al Gore was struggling with his new identity, Bill Bradley was walking on water. I first saw him on the boardwalk of a resort town in the part of New Jersey they call the 'Irish Riviera'. It was September 1999, the last Sunday of summer, and Bradley was walking the beaches and meeting the people. He wore a golf shirt, long shorts, long basketball socks and a pair of battered old runners. Instead of the politician's smile, he wore a smirk that occasionally gave way to a ready laugh. When he met someone he was interested in, he would stop and utter his trademark: 'Tell me your story.' If that story interested him, he would stay and listen for what seemed like an eternity, but if he got bored, he would abruptly wrap up the conversation and seek out new stories.

When he met the media, he was sucking a Hall's Defender Vitamin C sweet and a smirk that said, 'I don't really give a shit what you think.' He was dressed like an awkward kid, but he had the bearing of the neighbourhood tough guy. There were no fake smiles, no hamming it up for the camera, and occasionally he would answer with a simple yes or no. When he decided to really answer a question, there was a lyrical quality to his rhetoric, a grounded idealism that sounded like the foreword to a really good book of essays. All the while, he kept sucking that sweet.

From the beginning, it was clear that Bradley was brutally authentic, the kind of man it is easy to respect but hard to like. He had no trouble persuading the world he was devoted to principle. He simply asked them to take a look at his life. He talked a lot about his childhood in Crystal City, Missouri, and the slow birth of his lifelong obsession with basketball. He talked, with vaguely erotic overtones, of the feel of the leather ball in his hands and the squeak of his shoes on the floor of the school gymnasium. He spoke of the endless self-imposed practice sessions and the nights he would not go home until he had dropped the ball into the basket 25 times in a row from every position on the court. This is Bill Bradley: the boy from the small town with a little talent and an obsessive desire to be better.

In September 1999, Bradley had established a lead over Gore in the key state of New Hampshire. Bradley was a serious contender, but we would also find out that he could be a serious arsehole. It was not that Bradley was pompous or vain. He had no need for vanity because he had tremendous self-confidence, but that self-confidence came across as arrogance. He could inspire real idealism in people and then would mock that very idealism. He had a ready wit, but it could also be cutting and cold.

I still really wanted him to do well, if only because I was starting to develop an unhealthy and obsessive dislike of Al Gore, but by the Iowa caucuses I could see Bradley had screwed up any chance of beating Gore. I saw him on the eve of the caucuses at a rally in a basketball arena at Drake University in Des Moines. The last minute opinion polls reported bad news for Bradley, but he still packed out the hall. Most of the 800 people at that rally were students, and they had the air of true believers. I met two friends of mine from Washington who had travelled, at their own expense, to campaign for Bradley in places they had never heard of. They were typical of this crowd.

The posters on the wall featured a colour image of Bill Bradley as a basketball player and the slogan 'Athlete, scholar, presidential candidate – basically the guy you hated at school.' Another poster read: 'Remember your favourite teacher at high school – now he's running for President.' This may not be belly-laugh humour, but you learn to appreciate even the slightest evidence of wit on the campaign trial, because it does not come along very often. Taking the piss out of yourself or your candidate is something you do not do. But Bradley's supporters had lives. They were sceptical enough not to take themselves or others too seriously, and yet they were not afraid to show passion and idealism. However, they were still political animals, and so was their candidate.

He arrived without warning at that rally at Drake University, and went straight to the balcony of the hall, where an ABC television crew had set up for an interview. Bradley seemed a little disconcerted as the cheering from the crowd below held up the interview. An anal-retentive staffer with an acid frown tried to keep the audience quiet, but the crowd was having none of it. Finally, Bradley himself turned to the crowd and flapped his arm up and down. The wave of noise subsided for a few minutes. Then it became clear the interview was running over. The blow-dried anchorman just wouldn't stop asking questions and Bradley was getting visibly irritated. One of his aides spotted this and signalled frantically to the crowd to raise the noise level again. The interview came to an abrupt end as cheers filled every corner of the hall.

Bradley was introduced by a local student leader with apple-pie good looks and bouncy-castle enthusiasm. 'O-mi-god.' This was just the best day of her life. 'I can't handle it. I'm so excited. My heart is about to burst.' She had wrapped one leg around the other as if she was going to wet herself and she kept sweeping her hair off her hyperventilating face with sudden violent motions. I was seriously worried she was going to spontaneously com-bust. As she turned away from the podium at the end of her speech, Bill Bradley rose from his seat and gave her a hug. It was all he could do to prevent her collapsing in a heap from excitement.

I wondered how anyone could follow that, when Dr Cornel West came to speak. The young woman had introduced him as 'the foremost African-American scholar in the country, if not the world'. West had been at the forefront of black intellectual life for three decades, and with his trademark Afro goatee and thick-rimmed glasses, he was a captivating sight. He spoke with slow determination at first, building up like every great preacher, stretching his audience as he went. 'To be a great president, you need gra-vi-tas.' He savoured every syllable as if it was a truffle. 'To be a great president, you need ver-i-tas.' With a pregnant pause, he wound himself for the final line. 'And to be a great president, you need car-i-tas.' Half the audience had no idea why they were cheering, but they could not stop themselves. They were all under his spell and they willed him to talk forever.

The crowd gave Cornel West a thunderous response at the end of his speech, and was still cheering when Minnesota senator Paul Wellstone came to the microphone. He screamed, ranted and raved for ten minutes in the most endearing way. He was short and balding and had no obvious signs of charisma, but when his finger started pointing and his voice became strained by the flood of fire and brimstone, he was a powerful man. If I had been Bill Bradley that night, I would have taken the microphone, said, 'Thank you for coming,' and left the stage. After West and Wellstone, I would have been far too intimidated to speak. Yet, Bradley languidly rose to shake Wellstone's hand, then slipped the microphone from its fixed position on the podium and began strolling to and fro across the stage.

'I'm just a jock, what do I know about all of this stuff?'

Bradley proceeded to poke fun at himself and everyone else on the podium. 'Wellstone, Wellstone, Wellstone, Wellstone.' His voice rose to a crescendo as he delivered a merciless imitation of his friend. There was an edge to his slagging, but Wellstone and everyone else rocked with laughter as Bradley delivered the first minute of his speech à la Wellstone. Everything about Bradley's speech was the usual political formula, with that extra inspiring twist. He praised his wife, Ernestine, and not just with the usual 'isn't she a great girl?' shtick. There was true respect in his tone, real admiration. He was not slow to tell us about his exploits as a sports star, but the story he chose to tell us did not necessarily reflect well on Bradley. When he captained the US basketball team in an Olympic final against the Soviets, he learned some Russian in order to intimidate the player marking him. He likes the story and if you don't like it, tough shit.

Bradley is just absolutely not Al Gore. Being in that hall was like an antidote to all the cynicism I had waded through on the campaign trail. As Bradley reached the end of his speech, I was feeling the buzz again. There was an infectious pride in the hall that night. The people there may not have warmed to Bill Bradley as a person, but they had basked in the reflected glow of a politician they respected and admired, and not many people can say that.

Yet, reality was not far from the minds of these people or their candidate. Bradley was going to lose to Al Gore in the Iowa caucuses the next day. The commentators were already saying that Bill Bradley's campaign was effectively over. At this rally, Bradley refused to accept defeat, and rolled out the usual sporting metaphors to justify his flickering optimism. Then he said something sad. Maybe I was the only person in the hall who thought it was sad. 'This campaign is based on the radical premise that you can go out and tell people what you really believe and still win.' It sounded so sad because I thought that under the right conditions it was true. Maybe it will be, someday, but not now. Not in American presidential politics at the beginning of the twenty-first century.

# Eleven

# The Suburban President

Since 1823, when America's white pioneers kicked the Tamali Indians off their land, Tallahassee has been Florida's capital city. It is far from the polyglot beach culture of South Beach or the antiseptic trickery of Orlando's theme parks, but in so many ways it is the real Florida. Life revolves around processed food, religion and football. Perfection in Tallahassee is the pre-football prayer at a Gators home game at Florida State University and extra cheese on your nachos.

By Tallahassee standards, the Florida Supreme Court building is a thing of beauty. In November 2000, the court played a central role in choosing America's forty-third president; ruling that Florida's endless recount should be kept alive until the votes of all the people were counted. It was a worthy principle. However, principle had no part in the electoral farce that overwhelmed Florida. I joined the media vigil on the day the court was due to deliver another 'vital' ruling. It was either 'vital' or 'crucial' or 'key' at that stage of the election saga. Journalism had become the repetitive use of a handful of clichés. I had hoped I would feel some sense of history in the making, but Tallahassee seemed to kill any profound emotion before it was fully formed.

From my vantage-point at the foot of the Capitol Building, I watched the zealots gather on the steps of the Supreme Court. A handful of cheerful Democrats stood out in a crowd dominated by right-wing rednecks. One Bush supporter, in the white trash uniform of baseball cap and mullet hairstyle, had travelled all the way from Indiana with a placard that read: 'Gore – commander in thief.' His brother had adapted the official 'Gore–Lieberman' poster to read: 'Sore Loserman.' But their lacklustre chants were drowned out by the duelling accordions of Angelina the Polka Queen, and her partner, King Ira. The weirdest presidential election in history was coming to an end with a pathetic whimper.

In truth, the election ended long before Tallahassee. It ended when John McCain lost the South Carolina primary. That was the day we knew with some certainty that the big political parties would nominate brand names, not candidates, for the highest political job in the land. The horse race was only beginning but the election was over when John McCain no longer mattered. Former New York Governor Mario Cuomo once said, 'You campaign in poetry. You govern in prose.' When McCain paid his respects to the American people and left the race, the poetry was replaced with advertising copy and marketing buzzwords. Mario Cuomo's idealistic assessment of American elections was outdated.

The true political zeitgeist was summed up by one of the most combative politicians in modern American history. Newt Gingrich led the Republican takeover of the US Congress in 1994, and yet four years later he was defeated and disgraced at the hands of Bill Clinton and the Democratic Party. In a rare moment of clarity, Gingrich once said, 'In every election in American history both parties have their clichés, and the party that has the clichés that ring true wins.' Republicans had the clichés, and they had the money to make them ring true.

Republicans have traditionally had the edge in attracting the hundreds of millions of dollars necessary to run in presidential elections. But competition for campaign funds was tough in the year 2000, as both major parties upped the stakes in the fundraising war. By the end of the election cycle in November 2000, candidates for president and congress had raised and spent about three billion dollars, almost one-third more than was raised and spent in the 1996 campaign.

The fundraising war reached its peak during the party conventions in the summer of 2000, and Republicans were remarkably honest about their desperate drive for cash when they gathered in Philadelphia. In the old days, the conventions were real events, with real issues and real people. They even smelled different. Back in 1948, one newspaper reporter said you could conjure up the feel of the Republican convention by 'swallowing a snort of bourbon, lighting a cigarette, putting scented talcum powder on a damp baby and inhaling.' In the year 2000, you could get a sense of the convention by scooping up a handful of ten-dollar bills and sniffing very hard. Everything about the conventions screamed 'big money'.

When you walked through the security cordon around the First Union Centre in Philadelphia you got the feeling you had walked into a vast political shopping mall. But what the Republicans were selling was influence, not ideas. Inside that cordon, on an old railway line, the luxury carriages of an ancient steam train had been set aside for some of the countless parties hosted by corporate sponsors. The real work at these parties was done by the lobbyists. They promoted a wide range of vested interests by helping senators and congressmen raise the money they needed to fight for re-election. Back in Washington they showered the politicians with hard cash, but in Philadelphia they came bearing *filet mignon* and fine wines; perks for the Republican establishment at play.

Looking at the television pictures out of Philadelphia you would have sworn that the crowd in the hall was a multicultural mix of ordinary Americans. The efforts by the Republican leadership to woo ethnic minorities were almost comical. Every second speaker at the podium was either black, Latino or in some way disadvantaged by American society. It was all fiction. The *New York Times* reported that one in five delegates was a millionaire and 83 per cent were white. Less than four per cent were black, and fewer African-Americans attended this Republican convention than the one 90 years ago.

I had no reason to believe the Democratic Convention in Los Angeles would be any more egalitarian, but there were some differences. At the Republican convention in Philadelphia, they served up free cheese steaks and warm pretzels. In Los Angeles, you were offered a complimentary massage and a free cup of Paraguayan tea: 'Guaranteed to leave you balanced, relaxed, happy and clear.' Besides the fancy tea, there were more substantial differences between the two conventions. The Democrats who gathered in Los Angeles looked like they had been plucked off the streets of an average American city and not the fairways of an exclusive country club in the suburbs. Black and white, and every other shade of diversity were represented in the crowd, and the leadership of the Democratic Party never let you forget it. Occasionally it went a little too far; I spotted a middle-aged man holding a poster with the slogan: 'Lesbians for Gore'. I never got a chance to ask him what part of Lesbia he came from. The Democratic convention was just as slick and stage-managed as its Republican counterpart. When we got a copy of the speech from Joe Lieberman's wife, Hadassah, the first word on the script was 'Wow', just in case she would forget to be amazed at the warmth of the reception she would receive.

There was a taste of the good old days at these events, when icons of the Democratic Party like Jesse Jackson and Ted Kennedy roared about the injustices of modern America, but they were the exceptions. The Democratic and Republican conventions were stripped of the principled conflict that should drive parties with proud traditions. In that sense, the conventions were symbols of the 2000 election season. There was no pride or principle behind the faux optimism of those campaign slogans. This was a battle between personalities, but not competing philosophies. This election was about nothing but fear of failure.

If there was one moment that captured the emptiness at the heart of the campaign, it came the night that Bill Clinton made his last address as president to the Democrats. I sat and watched his entrance in a trailer behind the hall and marvelled at the audacity of the organisers. They had a camera follow Clinton as he strode purposefully through the bowels of this modern basketball arena, onwards towards the stage. By the time he reached the podium, there were tears in the eyes of many delegates; tears broadcast live on the jumbo screens inside the hall and into our stuffy little trailer. On cue, Bill Clinton endorsed Vice President Gore with another audacious coupling: 'Forty years ago Los Angeles launched John Kennedy and the New Frontier. Now, Los Angeles is launching the first president of the new century: Al Gore.'

I watched Clinton on a television screen split into four parts. One showed the head shot of the president's speech, a second provided 'cutaways' of the president's profile and the crowd's reaction, and the last two quadrants of the screen showed aerial and close-up views of protesters outside the convention centre. After watching Clinton for a few minutes, my eye was drawn to the protests. I had heard the helicopters overhead for some time, but now I could see the police on horseback moving in to disperse a large crowd of demonstrators. As Clinton spoke inside the hall, there was mounting chaos and violence outside. And it was all taking place at the same time on the split screen in that small trailer.

As Clinton thanked the audience for giving him the chance to serve, the police began the first of many baton charges against the protestors. They were armed with specially adapted shotguns and rifles, and fired tear gas, pellets and little beanbags (a low impact alternative to rubber bullets). I watched one protester fall under the hooves of a police horse. As he lay unconscious, a few hundred yards away Bill Clinton thanked delegates for 'supporting the New Democratic agenda that has taken our country to new heights of prosperity, progress and peace'.

All of a sudden, Clinton seemed irrelevant. I left the trailer to see what was happening on the streets. I got to the wire fence surrounding the media trailers just as a line of policemen in riot gear fired another salvo of projectiles at the disparate group of young people ranged across the roadway in front of them. Other police officers had blocked off the main gates to the convention complex. Protestors could not get in, journalists and photographers could not get out. As we raced to another exit, more LAPD officers obstructed us, insisting they had to keep the way clear for President Clinton's departing motorcade. By the time we made it on to the streets, the protestors were well out of earshot of the convention centre. There was nowhere to go but back to the split screen to watch Bill Clinton urge on the Democratic faithful: 'Remember, keep putting people first. Keep building those bridges and don't stop thinking about tomorrow.'

The colourful celebration inside the convention hall in the wake of Clinton's speech provided the images the Democratic Party wanted to plant in the minds of voters. The last thing they wanted was television footage of angry young people outside. When those protestors were forced back by teargas and beanbags, the last audible signs of dissent from real people were being driven from the presidential election campaign.

The only remaining irritation for the political establishment came from the Green Party candidate Ralph Nader. The veteran consumer activist was an engaging presence, if only because he was the real optimist in this race, refusing to believe the American people were as apathetic as the statistics showed they were. He reminded me of Howard Beal, the fictional newscaster turned prophet in the movie *Network* who urged viewers to stick their head out of the window and scream, 'I'm mad as hell and I'm not going to take it anymore.' The problem was the American people were not mad as hell. On election night, Nader emerged with just three per cent of the popular vote. Some Democrats believed that three per cent denied Al Gore victory, but it was still just three per cent; by no means a sign of a popular uprising against the powers that be.

I looked hard for signs of that popular uprising, or at least some vague sense of collective discontent. A few weeks before polling day, I climbed into a jeep with RTÉ producer Angela Daly, and film crewmen Cedric Culliton and Cormac Duffy, and drove one thousand miles from Washington to St Louis. Our first stop was West Virginia, where a third-party candidate was stirring things up in the race for governor of the state. Denise Giardina was running on behalf of the Mountain Party. An award-winning novelist and lay preacher, she was born in the coal mining camp of Black Wolf. Among her books was a fictional account of the Coal Wars of the 1920s, one of the bloodiest episodes in American labour history. By the 2000 elections, she had become deeply involved in the battle to preserve the local environment from the most destructive form of coal mining: mountain top removal. Coal companies were lopping off the tops of mountains, like they were boiled eggs, to extract fuel from their insides.

For Denise Giardina, this was intensely personal. Her Italian immigrant family had suffered deeply at the hands of the coal industry and her political manifesto was based on this challenge to 'King Coal': 'You are flattening our mountains and filling our hollows and this is the last evil you will do.' We met her at a public debate in Elkins, a college town in the Allegheny Mountains. She addressed the audience with a calm, modulated tone but her message was direct enough: 'My grandfather was a slave of the coal industry. His whole family were slaves of the coal industry.' Giardina told the students they were also slaves of the coal industry. The industry still dominates politics in West Virginia, and candidates for state office still need its financial support. While it may be a waning power in strictly economic terms, it still owns a huge amount of land across West Virginia. 'In various ways it is still a colonising force,' said Denise Giardina.

I expected some reaction from the student audience, but apart from a polite round of applause, what I witnessed was boredom. As the Mountain Party candidate pleaded for the people to challenge the coal industry, one student made paper aeroplanes in the back row while his girlfriend slept soundly in the seat beside him. I found out later that most of the students had attended the debate because their lecturer had told them it was part of their coursework. After the debate, I met the lecturer in the campus bar. Dr David Turner was the head of the college's History and Politics Department, and had his own theory about the absence of idealism. As he tried to explain the obvious boredom of the audience that night he had to strain to make himself heard above the sound of a squealing guitar riff, blaring from the jukebox: 'Listen, these kids don't need to care about politics. They've done a deal with the devil: if the politicians keep the prosperity going, they can do pretty much what they like.'

As a member of Ireland's most complacent generation, I was not surprised by the absence of angst among these students. What really depressed me on that road trip to St Louis was the lack of anger from those who had been excluded from America's prolonged economic boom. Towards the end of our journey, we stopped off in Cairo, Illinois. The town was built at the meeting point of the Ohio and Mississippi rivers, on the unofficial boundary between North and South. During the Civil War, Cairo was a refuge for escaped slaves fleeing from the bordering states of Kentucky, Arkansas and Tennessee. The town was also a thriving commercial centre in the days when riverboats plied the length of the Mississippi. But the river commerce eventually died away, and the merchants abandoned Cairo. By the late 1960s, the town was racked by race riots as the civil rights struggle pitted poor Whites against even poorer Blacks. Today, Cairo is at the bottom of almost every social index, although the mayor of the city James Wilson, was trying to revive the town's downtown business district.

We arrived in Wilson's office just as the Chief of Police was briefing him about a shootout between rival gangs. By the window in the office hung a portrait of John F. Kennedy, and above the conference table was a photo of the mayor with Bill Clinton and Al Gore. The president and vice president kicked off their 1996 campaign in Cairo, but four years on, this loyal Democrat was considering a vote for George W. Bush. Wilson had been disgusted by Clinton and he believed Gore was guilty by association. He did not fear Bush, because he thought a Republican in the White House and a Democratic Congress might bring some measure of balance back to American politics. The mayor spoke without any trace of rancour, until he started to talk about the apathy of the community he represented. Cairo's initial decline was caused by commercial failure, but the town's complete disintegration stemmed from political neglect. Still, that neglect seemed to provoke nothing more than a fatalistic shrug from the town's citizens. 'They don't even know who their political representatives are,' Wilson said. 'I did a little test recently. I went into four different diners and asked the people working there who was the governor of their state. No one knew the answer, and these are the people that are supposed to choose the next president.'

On the road from Washington to St Louis, I began to understand the parallels between the apathy of a poor town and the complacency of those contented young students. The common denominator is consumption. The single-parent family in Cairo consumes to survive, and finding the money to consume overwhelms everything else in life, including outrage. Consumption provides some measure of dignity and status for the children of that family. There may be no earned income in the house and nothing in the bank, but the eldest child plays basketball in a pair of Air Jordan boots. In this world, hopes and dreams are channelled into the pursuit of the best footwear for the kids.

The middle-class kids consume because that is the defining pursuit of their generation. In their world, Gap and Nike are far more meaningful labels than Democrat and Republican. The corporate advertising campaigns offer them images of youth and contentment; they are mirrors to their branded souls. Political activism, on the other hand, is no choice. It implies there is some void in the life of these contented young adults, something flawed in the small but perfectly formed world they inhabit. The radical politics of Denise Giardina and Ralph Nader no longer suggests liberation; the word they conjure up is 'loser'.

The majority of the poor and the young in America are united in their belief that nothing will change, and so they have no interest in the outcome of a presidential election. Since they are unlikely even to cast a ballot, the candidates can safely ignore them. Instead, Democrats and Republicans concentrate their efforts in the vast, generic expanse of suburbia: the beating heart of modern American politics. Suburban voters have been the dominant force in American politics for decades, but it is only in the last ten years that a definable suburban political philosophy has emerged.

That philosophy has evolved alongside the development of standardised consumption patterns. Whether you live in Kentucky or Florida, the suburban shopping experience never seems to vary; the names on the shops are the same, the design of the mall almost never changes, the background music is a constant, the food courts are identical, and even the vehicles in the car parks are remarkably similar. On that trip from Washington to St Louis, the conformity along the side of the highways was breathtaking. When you stand in the forecourt of your motel and look out at the endless generic spectacle of suburbia, the only clue to your location is the weather. This generic reality of consumption in the suburbs has translated into a generic approach to politics.

One of the telling observations about the political might of the suburbs came from Canadian sociologists Arthur Croker, Marilouise Croker and David Cook, in their book *Panic Encyclopedia*: 'The future of America may or may not bring forth a black president, a woman president, a Jewish president, but it most certainly always will have a suburban president. A president whose senses have been defined by the suburbs, where lakes and public baths mutate into back yards and freeways, where walking means driving, where talking means telephoning, where watching means TV and where living means real, imitation life.'

The 'real, imitation life' of the suburbs is fairly sedate and the suburban political philosophy essentially moderate. As a rule, suburban voters are not angry. Anger and extremism will not be tolerated among friends and neighbours, and so will not be tolerated in politics. In an era of sustained affluence, suburban Americans have a considerable degree of security, so there is no great desire for radical economic change. They have long-term concerns about their retirement, and so pensions and social security are among the issues at the top of their political agenda. But what concerns them most is the safety of their children and the quality of the education they receive.

The great flaw in this safe, suburban philosophy is that there is no space for real debate. A candidate cannot afford to wander away from the centre at any time, and so it becomes almost impossible to distinguish one candidate from the other. Presidential contenders are forced to stage the political equivalent of pillow fights. There is no danger either side will be seriously injured, but there is a chance one candidate will lose his footing and slip out of the safe, suburban centre. In the 2000 presidential election, the last such pillow fight took place in St Louis, at the end of our thousand-mile road trip.

The last televised presidential debate of the campaign was inside a university lecture hall in the suburbs of St Louis. From the beginning it was like a school production of *West Side Story*, burdened down by stage-managed aggression. George Bush had just started explaining his health-care proposals to the invited audience when, without warning, Al Gore rose from his stool and unbuttoned his jacket. He walked forward with a sarcastic smile on his face and stopped just short of his opponent. It looked like he was about to throw a punch. Bush turned, paused briefly and cocked his head back in mock horror. There was a roar of laughter from the hundreds of reporters watching the debate in the college gymnasium. Exactly what message this macho moment was supposed to convey was never made clear, but it was obvious that this election was no longer about issues. This had descended into petty rivalry for the affections of the suburban voter.

The raw aggression of the Gore campaign intensified as the debate drew to a close. Even before the host wrapped up the debate, 'The Parade of Surrogates' assembled outside the press centre. The surrogates are the candidates' prominent supporters, sent in to spin the media right after the debate. That night in St Louis, they did that job on a small cramped basketball court, nicknamed 'Spin Alley'. It's easy to find out who's who; the names and affiliation of the surrogates are written in bright red letters on placards held up by young campaign volunteers. From high above Spin Alley, members of the public crowded around a window to look down on the spinners and spinnees, as if they were exhibits in a zoo.

It all sounds absurd but there was a desperate logic driving the spin machine as the election drew to an uncertain close. At that late stage of the campaign, George Bush and Al Gore were locked in trench warfare, fighting state by state, city by city, suburb by suburb. In a campaign where a tiny number of votes would make the difference, Al Gore's theatrical aggression and the absurdities of Spin Alley made perfect sense.

The debacle in Florida was perhaps a fitting end to the 2000 presidential election campaign. After more than one hundred million votes had been cast, it all came down to a few hundred ballots of elderly suburbanites in Palm Beach. The closest presidential election in American history would be decided by a flawed recount, a legal wrangle and a public relations battle. Shortly before the end of the drama, I found myself on the North Lawn of the White House, waiting for Sinn Féin's Martin McGuinness to emerge from a meeting with officials of the National Security Council. It was a bitterly cold December night, and my fingers began to freeze. I slipped into the Briefing Room just as Vice President Al Gore began his televised response to the latest legal ruling in the recount saga. He had fixed the time of his speech to coincide with the evening news, guaranteeing his remarks would be carried live. He read from a teleprompter, knowing it would end up just out of shot. Over his left shoulder, some clever aide had placed a photograph of the vice president and his eldest daughter with big grins on their faces. To the prime-time audience he had hijacked, Gore was spontaneous and sincere; at least in the spooky patronising manner that defines Al Gore.

'Our goal,' the vice president said, 'must be what is right for America.'

'Let it go,' moaned one of the cameramen, slouched in the briefing room.

In that smelly room in the West Wing, with the Rose Garden out one door and the Oval Office a few yards away, I couldn't help feeling sorry for Al Gore. He was about to lose his bid to become president, but he was still fighting for the affection of those suburban voters. I had spent the campaign loathing him, but of the two candidates in this race, it was clear he was the real fighter, the suburban warrior who had never quite managed to make the political theatrics look real.

Later the same night, I watched George Bush deliver a similar address to the nation. The Bush advisers styled the Governor's speech on those Oval Office addresses that herald the beginning or end of an international crisis. They wanted their man to look like Ronald Reagan. All I could see was Dan Quayle. Yet while Al Gore had to work hard to manufacture his connection to the voters, Bush had a raw unprepared quality that was quite endearing. That night he captured the mood of the suburbs with a single line: 'This process must have a point of conclusion, a moment when America and the world know who is the next president.' By that stage, the majority of Americans really didn't care which one of the political brands occupied the Oval Office. Just finish the lawsuits and the hand counts, they said, give us a big finale and let us all go home to sleep.

This was a response entirely consistent with the public mood throughout the 2000 presidential campaign. Partisan conflict is out of line with the soporific pace of life in the American suburbs and so it had to end. It was time for 'closure'. When it was all over, the American people walked sleepily from the Clinton era into the Bush era, not quite sure how they would differ, but confident those differences would never really matter. After all, in an age of affluence, they are all suburban presidents.

# Twelve

# Flights of Fancy

Before that day in September, the skies above the United States were a source of wonder. Today they inspire dread. There is no way back to the age of hassled innocence that defined air travel before those planes and their hijackers ripped a hole in the American psyche. The face that defined air travel for me in the wake of September 11 was no longer that of a bubbly young flight attendant, but that of a National Guardsman with a blank stare and an M-16, on duty outside the airport Burger King. Rather than reassure me, the heightened security at the departure gate merely stoked up my unspoken fear. There was something profoundly depressing about boarding a plane and watching the eyes of my fellow passengers dart about in search of ethnic and religious difference.

This was not the way it used to be. This was not flying as I knew it. During my five years in the United States, air travel had become more than a means of transport; it had become a pathway leading me through the complex dynamics of American society. It was not always pleasant, and it was never relaxed, but there was an odd charm about life inside the parallel universe of air transport. The charm was most apparent during my frequent journeys from Washington to New York, especially on the return flight. Every time I climbed aboard the Delta Shuttle at La Guardia airport I knew exactly what was in store for me, and in the unchanging routine I found something inspiring. Every hour, on the half-hour, the shuttle lumbered gracelessly away from its gate at the Marine Air Terminal, moved towards the end of runway 31, turned a full 180 degrees, and paused. In a matter of seconds, the rising whine of the engine brought forward movement. The shuttle charged towards the end of the runway, lifted off over Jamaica Bay and climbed into the sky over the sprawling prison complex on Rikers Island. As it continued to climb, the plane banked gently above the Bronx, passed over the sacred triangle of Yankee Stadium and the upper reaches of the island of Manhattan, before crossing the Hudson River into New Jersey airspace. Just when you thought you had left New York behind, the plane swung left and the Manhattan skyline reappeared in miniature. In the middle distance were the Statue of Liberty and the twin towers of the World Trade Centre. Beyond were Brooklyn and Coney Island, then nothing, until Ireland.

When the plane reached cruising altitude, the baseball diamonds and cemeteries were the only identifiable landmarks in the vast anonymous expanse of suburbia stretched out below. But as your eye lingered on the peculiar geometry of American life, there was method to be found in the madness. The poorest lived in sprawling neighbourhoods, drawn and quartered by the restrictive grid of numbered blocks, while the rich found space for their homes, pools and tennis courts under the ample canopy of suburban greenery. Bridging the gap were the gentle curves of the roads and highways, filled with the tail-lights and headlights of a million cars; America's blood-stream pulsing red and white in the dim evening light.

At the right time, on the right evening, the shuttle took

you over the Chesapeake just as the sun sank into the ocean and lit up the meandering rivers and streams that fed the bay. You glided over Delaware and into Virginia and a few minutes later the plane banked and descended rapidly, like some lumbering dive-bomber, into the strictly controlled airspace around the nation's capital. The shuttle followed the course of the Potomac and its wings rose and fell to adjust to the gentle curves of the river. Suburb turned into city, revealing the tree-lined streets of Georgetown, the right angles of the Kennedy Centre and the curves of the Watergate building. As the plane swung low over the Lincoln Memorial, the symbols of power were so close you could almost reach out of the window and touch them. But there was only time for a fleeting glimpse. There were just seconds to locate the White House, the State Department and the Capitol Building, before it all disappeared behind the dome of the Jefferson Memorial. The plane flew fast and close over the surface of the tidal basin before a final bounce on the runway at Washington's Ronald Reagan National Airport.

I took the shuttle trip twice, maybe three times, a month and I always looked forward to that return journey with childlike anticipation. The shuttle service was flying, as it should be, fast, friendly and full of the simple thrills and frills that once made air travel a glamorous activity. But it was also the exception that proved the immutable rule: for most people, air travel is misery. Back in 1965, when air hostesses served real food on real plates with real smiles, about 85 million people travelled by air inside the United States. By 1999, when flight attendants with plastic smiles were serving peanuts in plastic bags, 582 million were taking domestic flights in the United States. Bus travel had become more glamorous than air travel in America. Think about it. You take a look at the sleek,

169

silver Greyhound bus pulling out of the station and easing on to the highway, there is still the promise of freedom, the vaguest hint of Kerouac, *Easy Rider* and Route 66. In the middle seat of an overbooked Boeing 727 on a hot day at LAX, surrounded by the vaguest hint of body odour, there is nothing but suppressed rage and a new element of fear.

The air traveller in America lives in a world of frightening conformity. Every morning, the hotel room looks the same, whether it's in Des Moines or Dallas. The shuttle bus to the airport is about as close as you will get to the outside world. Once inside the airport, the land-marks never change. Turn left at Pizza Hut, right at Starbucks and there's your gate. Even the airline staff begin to look and sound the same. Their vocabulary is limited to a series of carefully selected greetings, warn-ings and apologies. Before long, life is distilled into one simple organising principle: 'Please make sure your tray table is in the upright and locked position.'

By my rough estimate, I sat through nearly 800 aeroplane take-offs between September 1995 and Decem-ber 2000. Of course, I was a novice compared to some of the people I encountered in airports across America. I envied their inner peace, their superhuman levels of endurance and stamina, and their ability to scam an upgrade. The logistics of travel took the lustre off what was, by any standards, a charmed life. Anyone watching my travels must have envied the regular visits to Miami, New York and Los Angeles, but my life was increasingly dominated by the fear of middle seats, delayed flights and missed connections.

Mass transit can make you feel unbearably hassled. It can also make you feel vulnerable. No matter how many times you climb aboard an aircraft, you can never be certain you will make it out alive. You would think that with so much of my life spent inside a plane, I would have completely conquered my fear of flying. Yet even after years of constant travel, my palms would still sweat as the plane dropped towards the ground. There was nothing rational about it, but I still felt the risk that I would die in a fireball increase with every successive flight.

On one flight to Spokane, Washington, I was horrified when a huge overdressed African-American woman across the aisle began to read loudly from a bible. I wanted to yell, 'Put the bible away!' But that is not a clever thing to say 25,000 feet above the American heartland. Still, something in my gut told me she was inviting disaster. As we descended towards the airport, the right wing of the plane lurched upwards and the nose dipped sharply. The shrill voice of 'Bible Woman' filled my ears and my heart filled my throat. The plane righted itself but we were still falling faster than normal. Moments after we spotted the runway lights there was an enormous shuddering thud followed by a bounce and a final jolt which set the oxygen masks loose in the cabin. Bible Woman moaned loudly as the rest of us made our way off the plane in silent, single file.

I knew the statistics better than most. I was safer in a plane than in a car. But then how many people are driven to read from the Bible every time they get into a taxi? I resented Bible Woman, not because of her fear but for her loud unwanted reminder that we were both doing something terribly unnatural. Show me a person who is truly comfortable with manned flight and I will show you a person with no understanding of their own mortality. This is a heavy metal tube packed with lots of people, hurtling across entire continents at hundreds of miles an hour, tens of thousands of feet above the ground. It is not natural. No matter how many times we travel by air, we should never forget that it should not work, even if it does. Every time I fly, there is always a moment when I look out of that window and wonder what freak of nature allows me to view humanity from this distance.

Once, as I pondered this concept over the Kansas plains, the thought struck me: air travel is a metaphor for the United States. You can travel thousands of miles and still feel you are in the same place. There is plenty of friendliness but a peculiar lack of permanence. There is incredible conformity, but there is also a dizzying array of choice. And like air travel, the United States should not work and yet it does. It is too bulky and cumbersome to exist as one country, and yet it remains the world's remaining superpower. What keeps Americans sane and civil is what keeps passengers on an airliner sane and civil: belief. The passengers believe the plane will fly, even if it shouldn't, while Americans believe their future will be better than their past, even though there is no evidence to back up their irrepressible optimism. On my travels through the United States, I found that belief was the answer to every mystery in American life. Other countries live within the boundaries of logic, physics and geography, but not the United States. Every person has a dream, and no matter how ridiculous the dream, they have a moral obligation to pursue it.

While everyone I met on my travels through America needed to believe in something, it was only on very rare occasions that I shared their desire to believe. One of those rare occasions was a sunny day at the Kennedy Space Centre in May 1998. Along with another 4000 journalists I stood in a field and watched NASA send one of the pioneers of the space programme back into orbit aboard Shuttle Mission STS-95. John Glenn was part of the original Mercury team of astronauts, and had gone on to represent his home state of Ohio in the US Senate. The older he got, the more determined he was to go back into space. NASA caved in to political pressure and invented a reason for sending Glenn on one more mission. As launch date approached, VIPs and journalists descended on Cape Canaveral. Some of the more experienced reporters must have had an idea of the sheer majesty of the sight we were about to witness, but they didn't tell us novices.

The sound of the voice leading the countdown faded into the background as my gaze was drawn to the bottom of the launch tower. A small bright light had erupted silently with the blinding white intensity of a magnesium flare. Like a fast-forward version of an approaching storm, I saw the clouds of smoke around the now yellowing fireball expanding at great speed. The space shuttle began to creep up the side of the launch pad and then clear it. In those first few seconds there was silence. But a wave of rolling thunder was racing across the swamp that separated me from the launch site, and was about to engulf me.

The ground beneath my feet started to tremble and the shallow rumble got deeper and deeper until I instinctively put my hands to my ears. For a few seconds the sound changed. It became a sharp and shallow crackle, like hot oil in a frying pan, before getting deeper and louder once again as the shuttle picked up speed and began to break free of gravity. All the time I stood rooted to the spot. At the moment I felt I could move again, the shuttle was just a speck of light at the top of a zigzag column of vapour, suspended in the clear, blue Florida sky. As I became aware of the cheers and the applause and the tears of joy, I knew that, as long as I lived, this would be one of my most powerful memories.

The central compound of the Kennedy Space Centre on launch day was like a waiting room in a maternity hospital. There was a combination of heightened expectation and unspoken fear. The quirky rituals of the final countdown were kind of morbid: the final breakfast for the astronauts, the suiting up procedure and the last goodbye from the technicians as they sealed the hatches. The launch is a sight that overpowers all the senses, like a visual orgasm. The emotions you feel will last for a lifetime, but a small part of you wonders how much of this is simply spectacle.

John Glenn's last mission brought an element of farce to Florida's Space Coast. Near Cape Canaveral, Fat Boys' Barbeque proudly displayed a sign offering free food to astronauts over 65. Among the shops, restaurants and bars wishing 'Godspeed to John Glenn' were the numerous strip clubs along Highway One. But despite the odd lapse into bad taste, I am convinced something special happened that day. It was something peculiarly American. In no other country is there so much innocence in public discourse. You can mock it, but the innocence also means there is purity in the emotions that are unleashed by events such as John Glenn's last mission. This was an event that brought Americans together in celebration, an event that provoked uncomplicated and simple pleasure in the achievement of another human being, an event that gave a dysfunctional community something to believe in.

An intense bout of nostalgia played a part in the John Glenn effect. For those Americans old enough to remember, Glenn was the square-jawed, clean marine with 'the right stuff' who restored American confidence in the depths of the Cold War. However, a younger generation looked at John Glenn's final mission in a less reverential way, at least initially. To Americans who grew up in the Eighties and Nineties, the space programme was never a source of great inspiration. While their parents remember John Glenn's first orbit, these Americans remember the explosion of the Space Shuttle Challenger in 1985. While older Americans sat glued to television reports of early space shots, their kids were only vaguely aware that NASA was still launching space shuttles from Cape Canaveral. But that seemed to change, at least temporarily, thanks to John Glenn. It was as if this grandfather had helped a new generation to discover a sense of wonder about space flight. He gave them the essence of the American dream: a fantasy fulfilled.

America seems to have a love affair with such high-tech fairy stories. They are an expression of the deep desire to believe the impossible is possible. The space race was a healthy and patriotic outlet, but some place their faith in more perverse science fiction. The flip side of the coin that carried John Glenn's face is the side that carries the big bulbous eyes of ET. One in ten Americans believes there have been alien abductions, and in one survey 80 per cent of Americans said their military knew more about extra-terrestrials than it had chosen to admit. To the true UFO believers, New Mexico is their spiritual home.

On a spring morning in 1947, a farmer discovered pieces of what he thought was a flying saucer in a field outside the town of Roswell, New Mexico. In truth, the wreckage was probably just the remains of a weather balloon launched from a nearby Air Force base. There are different versions of the story, but most include reports of alien casualties among the debris. One local undertaker told me he was summoned to the air base to provide child-size coffins for the dead aliens. In Roswell, as in every other great American conspiracy, the myth was turned into legend because of government ineptitude and cover up. Today, Roswell's alien encounter has spawned an industry with its own very profitable brand name.

Roswell's elders have decided to cash in on their town's dubious fame. In May 1997, they held a festival commemorating the fiftieth anniversary of the 'alien arrival'. As I drove into town on the night before the festival, I spotted a billboard outside a seafood restaurant that read: 'They came for the fish.' A bridal shop off the highway had a bug-eyed, life-sized alien mannequin modelling one of its wedding dresses. A disused cinema had been turned into the festival headquarters and housed a museum featuring an interactive alien autopsy. Everything in the place was for sale, from alien dolls to an impressive range of paranoid bumper stickers. I bought two. One advertised the dream presidential ticket of 'Nixon–Presley in 2000' and another summed up my growing sense of paranoia: 'Trust no one, Roswell 97'.

Not everyone was happy to see the UFO circus come to town. Walking down Main Street, I overheard a young woman tell her friend that when she travels she lies about where she is from because the response is always the same: 'You're from the place where the aliens landed.' If the aliens did land near this small New Mexico town you have to ask why. Roswell has bright sunshine, friendly people and the largest mozzarella plant in the world. It was also the childhood home of actress Demi Moore. Otherwise, it is a drab little town with the usual procession of fast-food joints and discount supermarkets jostling for attention along the main drag. The unrelenting sunshine, dry air and cheap housing attract senior citizens looking for a retirement home, but for Roswell's young people there is nothing but the highway out of town. Roswell was this boring half a century ago. Back in 1947, the day the local paper reported the discovery of the flying saucer, its front page was dominated by the following headlines: 'Dairy farmers of area to hear lecture series.' and 'Cotton acreage is above 1946.' Roswell is nothing without those aliens.

I went to the site of the 'alien landing' with Sky News correspondent Jonathan Hunt. What we discovered was an extra-terrestrial theme park. The owners of the land had turned the small slice of desert into a place of pilgrimage. The site of the 'crash' looks like a set from a 1950s' B-movie – all tumbleweed and barbed wire. It's the perfect starting point for an alien invasion, and the appropriate site for a memorial to the victims of this first documented inter-galactic space tragedy. Two American flags were planted at discreet intervals on a rock face in the desert. We joined a tour party of ten people. All of them spoke in hushed tones. They had come to pay their respects at a place more sacred than the grassy knoll on Dealey Plaza in Dallas, or Elvis's bathroom in Graceland. One man, who stood apart from the group, broke his silence when he heard we were journalists. He had a story to tell. President Harry Truman actually met one of the aliens that crash-landed at Roswell. The alien was brought to the White House where he concluded an interplanetary peace agreement with Truman. The man was not a raving loony, despite his story. In every other respect he seemed sane and sensible. He was like most of the people I met in Roswell that week. They were all slightly off centre, some in very endearing ways, and they were convinced the rest of us – the unbelievers – were the insane ones. I had come to Roswell expecting to feel pity for these people. Instead, I was the one receiving the sympathy.

By the end of the festival I could feel my skin prickle with all their sincerity and unblinking belief. I snuck away to the corner of the only decent steakhouse in Roswell, with Jonathan and my cameraman Duane Empey, and we got completely hammered. After a brace of Martinis, served up by a sceptical waitress called Doreen, we performed an alien autopsy on a bread roll. The bread roll was brought back to our motel and placed on the hood of my car. Next day, I took great pleasure in driving out of

Roswell with the 'corpse' of the bread-roll alien burning to a crisp on the bonnet of my rental Lincoln. That was my kind of alien abduction.

The line between fantasy and reality is easily blurred in a culture that celebrates imitation, and no country celebrates imitation like the United States. The American philosopher Eric Hoffer believed this was an unfortunate by-product of unlimited freedom: 'When people are free to do as they like, they usually imitate each other.' Europeans look down their noses at America's desire to imitate, and yet they spend millions on Hollywood's dodgy historical epics and American-style theme parks. We laugh at America's obsession with fantasy yet our television schedules are filled with sexed-up science fiction shows from the United States; Roswell is no longer a town in New Mexico, it's a teen drama wedged in between *Buffy* and *X-Files*. Europeans mistakenly believe the cult of imitation is a sign of a gullible public. But the reality is that Americans do understand the difference between reality and replica. It's just that many of them prefer the copy to the original.

Getting to grips with Las Vegas gave me fresh insight into this. I was prepared to loathe everything about this city. I was actually looking forward to being repelled by its falsity. My first impressions were not good. Between the arrival gate at the airport and the baggage claim there are slot machines at every turn. You could gamble yourself penniless before you even got to your hotel room. There are signs of emptiness everywhere. The owners of the hotels in Las Vegas have made sure there is nothing to keep you in your room – even the most palatial suite has no minibar or even free coffee. Everything I wanted to hate about Las Vegas was confirmed to me within an hour of my arrival, but within the next three days I would begin to think differently.

Las Vegas has changed from the city of sin into the city of family values. It is a curious set of family values, placing kiddy-friendly theme parks alongside bigger and better casinos and persistent pockets of vice. But Las Vegas, according to the *National Geographic*, is 'a cruise ship on a sea of sand'. By the end of 2000, the city had 11 of the world's 12 largest hotels. Along the Strip, there were more than 120,000 hotel rooms – twice as many as New York City. It's not just the tourists who are coming. At the beginning of this century, Las Vegas and its suburbs were among the fastest-growing metropolitan regions in the US, with 75,000 new residents moving in each year. What amazed me was that all these people were flocking to a city which is styled on other cities. The massive Bellagio Hotel, with its gondolas and imitiation Venetian canals, is not fooling anyone. No one mistakes the fake Eiffel Tower on the street for the real thing. The Manhattan skyline of the New York, New York Hotel is clearly a replica, and the pirate ship outside Treasure Island is just another show. The whole city is a show, a 24-hour revue in which everyone has a part. For that brief holiday in Las Vegas, you can forget about the line between fantasy and reality, and embrace the grandeur of imitation.

There is a dark side to that innocent premise, and you see it in the casinos. In the grand gambling halls of Las Vegas, the addictive fantasy can be contained within the confines of a short holiday. But in other less grand casinos in America, the line between real and imagined disappears. One of the most depressing places I have been to in my life is Atlantic City. Just a few hours outside New York, it is a pale replica of the ultimate replica city, Las Vegas. I was covering a story a few miles down the coast of New Jersey and decided to spend a night in Atlantic City on the assumption that it could not be as awful as everyone says. It was.

At five in the morning, after a long night on the town, I was back in my hotel. I could not sleep. I decided to go for a walk down by the casinos, which were still open. I walked up the steps to one gambling hall and stood at the top of this enormous room with my mouth open. There were lights everywhere, producing a dull form of daylight at five o'clock on a winter morning. The air conditioning made it feel pleasant, even balmy, while outside it was freezing. The card tables were empty, but there were still a few croupiers standing about. Now and again, from behind the rows of slot machines, an occasional figure would walk briefly into the aisle before disappearing again. As I walked farther into the enormous room, I saw there were people spread out behind rows and rows of machines. Nobody seemed to be with anyone else, but the loud noise and bright lights removed any need for loneliness.

The manufactured feeling of comfort and belonging is replicated in every American casino I visited, although in the smaller casinos it is harder to manufacture. On our road trip along the Ohio and Mississippi rivers before the 2000 election, the team stopped for a night in the riverside town of Paducah, Kentucky. We were looking forward to a nice meal with a bottle of wine, so we strolled over to a steakhouse a few hundred yards from our motel. There were Budweiser signs in the windows and I was confident we could at least get a cheap bottle of Californian plonk. 'Today's Sunday,' the waitress told us, 'and the law says I can't serve y'all alcohol.' She said the only place we could get a drink was on a riverboat casino moored on the Illinois side of the Ohio River. We drove blindly across the state line, pleading for directions at each gas station. Just as we were about to give up, we spotted the ornate twin smoke stacks of an old riverboat.

The car park was full of spaces for disabled drivers.

Inside, there was a terrible feeling of decay. There were bright lights, loud noises and bars on every level, but there were no smiles. I sat down at one of the bars beside a doll-like old woman, playing a tabletop slot machine. She was dressed in a white vinyl pantsuit. Her tiny face was dwarfed by a huge pair of spectacles and a bouffant hair do. Underneath a second skin of make-up she was skeletal, like a macabre little child, perched up on her stool, smoking a long menthol cigarette. As she prepared to move on to another slot machine, she reached over to a little bucket of coins, sitting on the edge of the machine. The caption on the bucket read: 'Are you ready to party?' The old woman scooped the money out of the machine with one hand, as the other hand supported her stick-thin wrist. Like a crane she moved her hand over to the bucket and dropped in the coins. The whole operation took about a minute. Then she clambered off the stool and moved away. In the ten minutes I sat observing her, I didn't see a flicker of emotion in her empty eyes.

America led the world beyond the confines of earth and its gravity because it had heroes worth believing in. America is still the world's greatest power because every American believes they too can be that hero, that John Glenn. But the self-confidence also brings a deep hunger for fantasy and fairy stories. Many Americans find themselves caught in a twilight world, where distinctions between real and imagined are blurred. In a world of growing uncertainty, a compelling fiction is sometimes much easier to live with than fact, especially if that fiction makes you feel you are in control. Belief can make your life better, and can inspire a nation to greatness. But unless belief springs from reality, it is artifice and will lead you to darkness, whether you live among the bright lights of Las Vegas or by the banks of the Ohio River.

# Thirteen

## The Tragedy Business

One of the things that depressed me most about the aftermath of September 11 was the predictable scramble for words and images that would neatly define the horror of that day. It was not possible but the media tried anyway. In an effort to understand America today, you could learn as much from the reaction to the massacre as from the massacre itself. Every time the United States is shaken by a momentous event, it turns into a frantic, babbling chat room, gushing forth opinion like a broken water main. It has the appearance of chaos, as it did in the wake of the most momentous event of modern American history, but there is always method to the madness. The methodical exploitation of tragedy is no longer an American phenomenon. In my experience, it never was.

On 8 August 1994 an off-duty member of the Royal Irish Regiment called Trelford Withers was shot dead in his butcher's shop in the village of Crossgar, County Down. He was the IRA's last victim before the organisation called a ceasefire three weeks later. More than 3500 people had lost their lives in the Northern Ireland conflict and many had died in more horrifying circumstances, but the death of Trelford Withers will stay with me forever because it was the first time I truly understood the perverse relationship between my profession and the suffering of others.

Trelford Withers was buried on a glorious day at the Kilmore Presbyterian Church in a small wooded valley in the County Down countryside. I was sent to cover the funeral for RTÉ and regarded it as just another tragic event in a violent summer. But the grief of the dead man's widow, Jean, had gone beyond the bounds of any grief I had ever witnessed. She appeared to be in a trance and there was an almost serene expression on her face. When the mourners reached the church, the camera crew and I retreated to the top of a hill overlooking the graveyard. Jean Withers seemed oblivious of her surroundings. Once the coffin was lowered into the ground, she walked forward, sat down on the grass beside the grave and started to move her lips as if communicating with her dead husband.

I believe the Withers family would have resented my presence at that moment, if they had been aware of it. I was sharing a moment of unspeakable loss with a woman I did not know, and, even worse, I planned to broadcast this heart-rending scene into hundreds of thousands of homes on the evening news. Then, as now, I realised there was a very good reason for my presence at the funeral that day. My report might well have forced at least some viewers to sit up and take notice of the human cost of violence in Northern Ireland. That possibility alone justified my intrusion at the Kilmore Presbyterian Church. But the funeral of Trelford Withers confronted me with a doubt that haunts all journalists caught in the midst of tragedy. At some point, we have to ask if our words and pictures are merely another recreational drug for the TV generation, a Class-A narcotic that provides an initial thrilling shock but eventually numbs the viewers' senses to the complexity of what we are trying to describe.

Jean Withers died two years after her husband. She now shares his grave in that green valley in County Down. I have thought about her many times over the years. I could not help but think about her during my five years in the United States. The doubt that crept into my brain during the funeral service at the Kilmore Presbyterian Church never seemed to be far from my thoughts as I criss-crossed America in pursuit of tragedy. I thought about Jean Withers late one night in April 1998 as my plane climbed out of Washington National Airport bound for Denver. I was on the way to cover an act of mass murder, another unspeakable act of violence that I would spend days speaking about. 15 students and teachers had been killed inside a high school in the Denver suburb of Littleton. The two teenage gunmen were students at the school. Dylan Klebold and Eric Harris used pistols, automatic rifles and home-made bombs to murder their fellow pupils, and at the end of their rampage they killed themselves. Even after a rash of school shootings, this massacre was beyond comprehension. Of course, in the age of 24-hour news, nothing is beyond comprehension.

I pulled up at the entrance to the school's car park at around four in the morning. Local police officers were directing the fleet of media cars and satellite trucks with an oddly jovial, stage-struck air. Journalists and camera crews from all over the world were beginning to gather at the marquees pitched by the big television networks at the perimeter of the school grounds. As dawn broke, survivors and victims began to mingle with reporters in the muddy field by the car park. In full view of the cameras, teenage friends were meeting for the first time since the tragedy. The sound of terror came tumbling from their mouths: explosions in the canteen, bullets thumping into school walls and the sickening worry over missing friends. As the day wore on, the field filled up with scores more reporters and teenagers. Every tear, every expression of emotion was scrutinised for its news value. A young woman raced past me. She was followed by a group of friends, who were in turn followed by two middle-aged grief counsellors. Bringing up the rear were five or six cameramen. Fifty feet beyond me, the young woman fell to the ground in a lifeless heap, as if the air had been sucked out of her body. Within seconds her friends had caught up and thrown themselves on her limp form. Then came the grief counsellors, photographers and cameramen, jostling for position around a heaving, sobbing mound of teenage girls.

By lunchtime, the crowd outside the school was enormous and there was an air of macabre theatre in the field. Every few minutes I witnessed another scene of utter desolation as some teenager was overcome by the enormity of what had happened. As I walked past the car park after lunch, I saw a deeply distressed young woman with her cheek pressed flat against the roof of a red car, her hands stretched out and her fingernails pressed down hard on the cold metal, as if she was afraid of being dragged away. The car was parked amid the satellite trucks and was hardly noticed at first by the reporters who had made this base camp. When I came back a couple of hours later, the car was covered in flowers and a crowd of young women sat cross-legged in front of it. Some were chanting their school motto, others sobbed into their hands, and occasionally someone screamed at the cameramen to go away. The car belonged to one of their friends. The previous morning, she had driven to school, attended class, taken an early lunchbreak and died in a hail of gunfire and shrapnel.

I stood and watched in silence as a steady stream of young people carried flowers and other tributes to the police lines in front of Columbine High School. A British reporter I knew from Washington joined me. We stood together and stared for a few moments at this tableau of collective grief. Then, as he turned to leave, he whispered to me, 'It's just like when Diana died.' I thought the comment was simplistic and heartless. These people did not lose some distant icon. They lost brother and sister, friend and classmate, in the most senseless and shocking way. But with hindsight, I think my friend had a point. During the following two weeks, public discourse was transformed into a hyperventilated panic attack. The Columbine killings were gruesome, but so was the subsequent national debate, a debate characterised by voyeurism, paranoia and recrimination. Voyeurism inspired the television marathon of funerals and public mourning; paranoia prompted a majority of Americans to conclude it could happen in their local school; and recrimination characterised the response of politicians as they rounded up the usual suspects. After Columbine, cable news channels saw their ratings jump by up to 400 per cent as they broadcast a daily round of memorial services and tearful interviews with the people of Littleton. The coverage of Columbine was self-sustaining because it inspired other newsworthy events. The week after the tragedy, talk of hit lists and violent threats closed schools, caused bomb scares and prompted arrests in Texas, New Jersey, California and Illinois. One school superintendent in California said, 'We have to react to every little thing because we can't separate the real from the imagined.' And the reality, despite televised paranoia, was that the fifty million students in the American school system were relatively safe. Less than one per cent of schools across the country experienced a violent death in the 1990s. It's no wonder the public felt there was something terribly wrong with this generation of

American teenagers, when the only statistics promoted in the post-Columbine debate were those that promoted fear.

The more television stations are forced to compete, the more they need melodrama to engage the viewing public. News can provide that compelling narrative, but only if it stresses those aspects of reality that provoke a reflexive response from viewers and plays down events that the public will tire of quickly. In America, as television companies fight harder for ratings, crime has become the daily staple of television news, even though crime rates have fallen dramatically. In the United States, the total number of murder stories featured on the three main evening network newscasts in the United States increased by 633 per cent in the last decade of the twentieth century; there were 80 such stories in 1990 and 587 in 1999. Yet over the same period, the national murder rate was almost halved.

The most compelling criminal acts are random, rather than systematic. A crazed killer bludgeoning a passing stranger is a far more gripping tale than the killing of yet another Palestinian militant by Israeli security forces. In a similar fashion, crime that is motivated by an uncontrolled human impulse, like greed, desire or jealousy, delivers high ratings because we are all prone to those emotions. It does not just happen in the United States. In Ireland, over 30 years of conflict, the daily litany of violent images from the North became the equivalent of visual wallpaper for those not directly affected by the Troubles. The sheer repetitive nature of the unfolding death and destruction led to 'compassion fatigue', and if you grew up in the safety of the Republic of Ireland the violence was distant and ultimately inexplicable. In comparison, the cops and robbers drama emerging from gangland was box-office material. 'Ordinary decent criminals' with mythical names like the General, the Monk or the Penguin were far more interesting than the self-styled freedom fighters up north.

Television is a business that thrives on tragedy, but the most important principle in this business is that tragedy is relative. Death is important when it is compelling and not necessarily when it is significant. It can, of course, be both, as September 11 proved beyond doubt. But barring an epoch-changing tragedy, drama will almost always trump significance. For example, Princess Diana's death unleashed a tidal wave of grief around the world and even the death of Mother Teresa, a few days later, was swamped. During her life, Mother Teresa improved the lives of countless people and inspired millions, but Diana made the cover of *People* magazine a record 43 times (Liz Taylor came a distant second place with 14 covers). The coverage of Diana's death was entirely consistent with the coverage of her life. That's the simple logic at the heart of the dark art of 'necrojournalism'.

I spent much of my time in America as a travelling salesman for the tragedy business. Some of the human drama I covered had real significance, like the killings at Columbine High School. Other tragedies were driven by celebrity values but also had real meaning to millions of Americans; when John F. Kennedy Junior died in a plane crash in July 1999, the United States lost a symbol of all that was good in America's most celebrated political dynasty. What began to worry me about the melodrama was that for all the grief shared, there was no outcome. Unlike other events that capture the collective imagination, televised tragedy leads to no change in the way audiences view the world. For a couple of days, we are united by grief, but when it is all over nothing has changed. In *Bowling Alone,* a brilliant analysis of the collapse of social solidarity in the United States, sociologist

Robert Putnam describes the emptiness of the televised tragedy: 'The bonds nurtured by these common experiences are psychologically compelling ... but they are generally not sociologically compelling, in the sense of leading to action.' Like a child having a good cry, we feel better afterwards, even though the problem has not gone away. In fact, the events that provoke the greatest outpouring of emotion are seldom related to the greatest sources of pain in our society.

On my travels around the United States, I began to understand how the real tragedies often go unreported because they raise too many uncomfortable questions. It struck me most forcefully on a visit to a well-tended graveyard in the Badlands of South Dakota. The graveyard sits on a hillside overlooking Wounded Knee Creek, the place where the American Indians suffered their deepest wound on a winter's day in 1890. On that day, 300 men, women and children of the Lakota Sioux tribe died at the hands of the US Seventh Cavalry. Today their names are etched on a simple monument in the graveyard and their memory is burned into the consciousness of every living Native American. The site of the Wounded Knee massacre lies in the heart of Pine Ridge reservation, home of the Oglala Lakota nation. Despite their rich heritage, they also have the dubious distinction of being the poorest community in the United States; effectively a Third World country in the heartland of the most developed nation on earth.

During my visit in 1998, unemployment among the 28,000 residents of the reservation stood at around 90 per cent. Almost 65 per cent lived below the poverty line and the average person in Pine Ridge did not live beyond the age of 60. Suicide rates were double the national average and tribal leaders estimated that about half their people suffered from alcoholism. Diabetes had reached epidemic proportions, the result of a diet made up almost exclusively of processed foods, and widespread alcohol abuse. The human cost of this crushing poverty was brought home to me by the story of Geraldine Bluebird. Despite her health problems, she cared for 30 members of her extended family in three rundown shacks. They had no running water and their drinking water came from the cistern of one shared toilet. Geraldine's children would no longer sleep in the bedroom of the main house because that is where a young friend of the family had recently shot himself dead. Geraldine Bluebird and her family were not exceptional. Pine Ridge was a community almost completely dependent on meagre handouts from the federal government. Against this backdrop, the rare sign of self-sufficiency stood out like a lighthouse. They had just built a brand new hospital, and several new community groups were tending to the needs of the very poorest. But what provided the most hope was the rebirth of the old Lakota traditions. The slow death of the native language had been halted and an upcoming generation was learning about its heritage in the reservation schools. However, the drive to renew the Pine Ridge reservation faced daunting obstacles. Even the most basic improvements in the quality of life were stunted by bureaucratic struggles between the tribal government and federal agencies like the Bureau of Indian Affairs. Efforts to create local enterprises faltered in the isolation of this unforgiving South Dakota landscape.

What offended the people of Pine Ridge most was the indifference of outsiders. It had taken more than a century for the world to begin to wake up to the suffering inflicted on the Lakota Sioux at Wounded Knee. But that tragedy had been packaged as an epic historical drama. Just like good melodrama, the story of the Native American is expressed without the awkward nuances that define reality. The conflict between Cowboys and Indians has become a metaphor for the struggle between good and evil, but Hollywood got the bad guys and the good guys mixed up and so created a tragic parody of the truth. That has prevented the world from coming to terms with the suffering that was inflicted upon the Lakota Sioux at the end of the nineteenth century, and a hundred years later the continued debasement of that proud-warrior nation falls outside the narrow priorities of the tragedy business.

Indeed, some of the most significant political challenges facing the United States – including inner-city decay and the abuse of the environment – fall outside mainstream political debate because they fall outside television definitions of tragedy. It's hard to generate box-office interest in an issue which is not easily resolved within the confines of a 90-second news report. As a consequence, such issues become virtually invisible to the millions of people who rely on television to define the boundaries of their world.

Where significant issues are brought centre-stage they are generally presented without context. Crime, for example, is now debated almost without reference to the administration of justice. On television the crime story has three interesting aspects: the criminal act, catching the criminal, and punishing the criminal. But the broader issues that used to define the debate about the criminal justice system have fallen off the public agenda, as television does its best to stir up public fears.

In the last two decades of the twentieth century, the US prison population quadrupled to approximately 1.8 million people: 455 prisoners for every 100,000 citizens. The federal government predicts that one in every eleven men will be imprisoned during his lifetime. If you are black, the odds rise to one in four. The rising levels of incarceration coincided with the breakdown of the old liberal consensus on law and order in America. When Democratic presidential candidate Michael Dukakis lost the 1988 election to George Bush, it was partly because he was perceived as being soft on crime. As the crime statistics rose, conservatives hijacked public paranoia to such an extent that liberals rolled over and died. In this new age, being soft on crime means electoral defeat. 'There are no more liberals,' joked criminologist James Q. Wilson. 'They have all been mugged.'

The old liberal consensus collapsed because it no longer matched the public mood. But today it is hard to tell if Americans are fully aware of just how draconian their criminal justice system has become. The media obsession with crime provides little room for debate about the severity and scale of punishment meted out on a daily basis. There has been a shift in the public mood in states such as Illinois, where citizens are taking a closer look at the application of the death penalty. But in Texas it is business as usual. The number of prison inmates in Texas rose in the 1990s by 173 per cent. Texas also led the way in the number of legal killings. During George W. Bush's four-year reign as Texas governor, 152 executions were carried out. To see the reality behind the death penalty, I went to Texas in December 1997, shortly before Texas stopped allowing foreign media to peer inside the execution machine.

Death Row is situated a half-hour drive from the city of Huntsville. It's a single storey, ranch-style building at the side of a bigger prison complex. Once you have passed through the prison gates, and met an escort inside the waiting area, you enter a long bright corridor, full of noise and men in white jumpsuits. Each one is a convicted murderer and has been condemned to die. My guide that day was a brusque prison spokesman who had met too many cynical European journalists to be pleasant. He did, however, trade wisecracks and small talk with the inmates. After sharing a joke with one prisoner, he turned and said, 'That's Gonzales. Shot a young woman in the head at a stop light because he wanted her car.'

Out in the recreation yard, a group of young men were playing a fast and furious game of basketball. One of the other inmates stood with me, watching the game: 'Those guys are known around here as the "the little rascals",' he said. One was a skinhead convicted of a racist killing; on the basketball court he was the only white player. Inside the segregation unit, I was allowed to look through the wire mesh into the darkness of a cell. At first I could see nothing. Then I began to see a shape: a young man crouched silently on the floor, his eyes staring blankly through the thick black rims of his spectacles.

After a while, the proximity to these 'dead men walking' forces the sense of dread out of your head. You slowly begin to realise that the most pressing concern for these condemned prisoners is just how drab and boring everyday life has become. The 530 inmates on Death Row during my visit would spend an average of ten years waiting for execution. During 1997 the state had cranked up the execution machine and 36 men had been put to death. Michael Lee Lockhart was about to become the thirty-seventy.

In 1988, Lockhart was sentenced to die for killing a police officer in Texas and for murdering and mutilating two teenage girls in Indiana and Florida. A week before he was due to be taken to the death house and injected with a lethal cocktail of drugs, I spoke to him through the wire mesh of the prison waiting room. He was serene in an affected sort of way. He had found God in prison and declared himself a reformed character. In these circumstances, he had chosen 'calm' as the most appropriate tone, even in the face of my questions about his impending death. 'I done walked that last walk a thousand times,' he told me. 'I don't fear death because I am going to a better place where there's no more pain, no more suffering.' A few minutes into our interview, the serenity was replaced by anger, as Lockhart railed against the death penalty. He did not say it, but the anger seemed to be a symptom of desperation. He knew that as he talked about imperfect remedies and inadequate deterrence, nobody was listening.

Once Lockhart's execution would have been national news. In 1997 it was recorded with a few lines in the local paper and a short dispatch on the American news wires. Part of the reason death in Huntsville is no longer a source of pained debate is that the whole process has become just another industrial procedure, carried out behind anonymous walls in a company town. Huntsville has a population of 35,000 people and about half is employed directly by the Texas Department of Criminal Justice. Right by the Dairy Queen at the edge of town is the Walls Unit of Huntsville Correctional Facility. Behind the administration block is a long redbrick wall, behind the wall is a small garden, and by the garden is the Death House.

A prison warden brought me into the cell where Michael Lockhart would eat his last meal. He had the dull, rehearsed air of a tour guide who is long past caring about his bizarre surroundings. Even when he opened the heavy door of the death chamber, he showed no sign of awe. The bright lime-green room was dominated by a padded couch, with arm-rests pointing out towards mirrored glass on either side. Behind one window, the witnesses would assemble. Behind the other, the executioner would work the machine that would end Michael Lockhart's life. 'We will insert two IVs, one in either arm,' the warden told me. 'We will announce the death by announcing the time of death.' He could have been giving me directions out of town for all the emotion in his voice. Modern science and good public relations had turned a once grisly spectacle into a sanitised routine, notable for its efficiency and not its result.

Lawmakers in Texas realised that outrage about violent crime was not enough to guarantee continued majority public approval of the death penalty. The people needed to feel that the ultimate sanction was being applied in the most efficient and least troubling manner. So the death penalty no longer has to be a moral dilemma; it is just a fact of life. As long as execution is carried out 'humanely', public interest wanes, as does public debate. The execution industry has separated tragedy from the story, and so the tragedy disappears. For my money, the real tragedy was not that Michael Lockhart died. It was that nobody cared, either way. The tragedy of the murders he committed was forgotten. The moral questions raised by his execution were ignored. Death has become a relative term in a society desensitised by the tragedy business.

# Fourteen

# Gay, Straight and European

Long before American bombs rained down on
Afghanistan and European pundits launched their verbal
counter-attack on America, there were all kinds of
dramatic transatlantic spats. They were not always rows
about foreign policy or trade; often it was the really
important things, like sport, sex and food, which
prompted controversy. It was in some of these rows that I
discovered the true nature of the chasm that separates the
United States and Europe.

In October 1999, US golfers won the Ryder Cup at The
Country Club in Brookline, Massachusetts. Justin
Leonard was the American hero, sinking a 45-foot putt
on the seventeenth green. The American team and their
supporters did a little victory dance around Leonard,
provoking howls of outrage from European players and
fans. The Europeans had complained all weekend about
the drunken, boorish behaviour of American fans at
Brookline. The US team's unsporting celebration on the
seventeenth green was simply too much for European
commentators.

'The United Slobs of America' said the *Daily Mirror*.
'American players and their fans belong in the gutter,'
said the *Sun*. The most spectacular verbal assault came

196

from Matthew Norman, a columnist at the *Evening Standard*, who insulted every living American: 'Let us be painfully honest about it. They are repulsive people, charmless, rude, cocky, mercenary, humourless, ugly, full of nauseating fake religiosity, and as odious in victory as they are in defeat.' US golfer Hal Sutton was compared to Adolf Hitler by one letter writer in the *Irish Times*: 'To see him lifting his arms, inciting the crowds to cheer and jeer was reminiscent of those Nazi rallies before the Second World War.'

When the anti-American tidal wave washed up on the shores of the United States it provoked an angry backlash: 'Now we know why the English talk like they're sucking lemons – sour grapes, to be precise,' said one Boston sports columnist. The Internet chat rooms were full of similar emotions. One American golf fan posted this message: 'If they can't handle getting beat by the greatest country in the world then go play mini-golf.' Just as the bad behaviour of American players and fans fits longstanding stereotypes of the Yanks, European reaction confirmed American assumptions about their cousins across the pond. *Boston Herald* columnist Steve Marantz broadened the scope of the debate with this line: 'The Europeans choked because deep down, they hate one another and place silly things like health care and education above golf.' Explaining the rowdy behaviour at Brookline, Marantz wrote: 'American fans tend to speak their minds because we have a custom Europe has long resisted, free speech.' This sporting controversy hit a nerve for Americans, sick of smug and ungrateful Eurotrash. On the Internet, one contributor complained: 'We're only the good guys when they want something.'

The Ryder Cup brought out into the open an emotion I had been trying to quantify ever since I had arrived in the United States. Americans are genuinely confused and hurt by Europe. They know why Islamic nations despise US dominance, they understand the Russian people's continued wariness of them and they've never really trusted the Chinese, but Europe is different. Americans are troubled by Europe's deep-seated antipathy. After all we have been through together, they say, after all we have done for you. That alienation is expressed repeatedly in political discourse in the United States. It is expressed in its most virulent form by isolationists like Republican Congressman Dick Armey, who once famously declared, 'I've been to Europe once. I don't have to go again.' Even in the mainstream, you detect the resentment. An American friend of mine would repeat the same line whenever we discussed transatlantic tensions: 'The only Americans the Europeans like are the ones buried in their military graveyards.'

Continually bashing the Yanks is like prescribing too many antibiotics for too long. After a while, they develop immunity. The more criticism Americans hear, the less they listen. Europeans might sound eloquent and persuasive to their own ears, but by the time their well-formed criticism reaches the shores of the United States it is simply 'Blah, Blah, Blah!' At a cocktail party in Washington one night, I stood listening to a friend of mine, a prominent American magazine writer, debate the death penalty with a group of indignant European diplomats. Later, I asked him if he really cared what they thought: 'For every one person who cares about what they say, there's another red-blooded American who says, "My father lost a limb during the Second World War trying to save those bastards".' Americans do like Europeans but their friendship should never be taken as an invitation to give advice. British actor Patrick Stewart is loved by a legion of young science fiction fans in the United States for his starring role in one of the modern

*Star Trek* series. But he made the mistake of attacking the United States for its 'bullying and insular attitude'. In response, a *Washington Post* columnist warned him to '... put a lid on it baldy, or we'll break your nose.'

That is one of the assumptions that most annoys Americans: that they are insular. There are clear limits to American general knowledge about the rest of the world. Al Capone once said, 'I don't even know what street Canada is on.' And he was not alone. One survey taken by a lecturer at the University of Michigan found 75 per cent of his class did not know who Stalin was, and just two per cent could name the prime minister of Canada and the president of Mexico. Yet Americans are starting to wonder how much Europeans know about their place in the world. Newspapers in the United States made big play of a Gallup poll of British people that showed that 40 per cent of those surveyed did not know Britain had lost the American War of Independence. Another survey taken at the end of 2001 found that 24 per cent of Britons did not know their country was a member of the European Union.

The reality is that as European attitudes to America remain fixed in time, the United States is becoming less insular and less provincial. In 1999, 25 million Americans travelled overseas, another 35 million visited Mexico and Canada, and about ten per cent of all bachelor's degree candidates in the United States had studied abroad. Even before September 11, there was a growing awareness in the American heartland that the rest of the world matters. This growth in awareness is driven, to some extent, by trade; imports and exports now account for a quarter of the US Gross National Product. Even Hollywood, that great symbol of American cultural imperialism, could not survive without 'them damn for'ners'; American movies earn 60 per cent of their box-office receipts in other countries.

The great irony is that the more Americans get to know about the rest of the world, the less they like what they see. This manifests itself on various different levels, not all of them profound. Europeans tend to have a very simplistic image of what an average American should look and sound like. They are generally big, sometimes enormous. They are loud, sometimes unbearably loud. In response, young Americans have developed very specific clichés about Europeans, in addition to the classic assumptions about specific nationalities (British people have bad teeth, the French are rude and Irish people fight and drink). My American girlfriend is well educated and well travelled, and so are her friends. One of the first secrets Tara shared with me was the American woman's rule of thumb about men: 'They come in three types: gay, straight and European.' She meant this as a compliment, a comment on how European men are less aggressively macho. 'It's about the shiny shoes and the way they wear trousers, but it's also about a different sensibility,' she explained. 'For example, few American men would ever dream of saying the word "lovely".'

But not every American woman is as charitable. Among the most telling comments on US–Europe relations came from the 15-year-old daughter of the former American Ambassador to Britain, Phil Lader. Mary-Catherine Lader told *Tatler* magazine that British guys were 'scrawny, pale and unhealthy-looking' and tended to wear their trousers too tight: 'While Tony Blair and my father wax lyrical about the special relationship between the UK and the US, it does not apply to teenage British boys and American girls.'

There is far more to all this than a bad dose of teenage angst. During the past decade, the fault lines in the relationship between Europe and the United States have opened up on subjects far more important than tight trousers and golf. The transatlantic trade relationship accounts for almost half the world's exports, yet it is overshadowed by apparently intractable disputes. The European Union blocks US beef treated with hormones, objects to dumping by American steel companies and is hostile to genetically modified agriculture. The United States contests European restrictions on banana imports, condemns the protection of European aircraft manufacturers and protests about EU regulations on aircraft noise abatement. Washington likes to think of itself as the champion of free trade, while Brussels sees itself as the defender of civilised standards of behaviour.

Even more contentious is the effort to create an equitable balance of power between Europe and the United States as the Cold War fades into memory and the US-led 'war on terror' dominates world affairs. The emergence of the United States as the lone superpower worries European leaders. You hear eloquent objections from the French, who talk about the United States being the 'Hyperpower'. French President Jacques Chirac says Europe's 'ever closer union' is a necessary balance to America's 'attempt at domination in world affairs'.

It is worth asking whether the Americans really do want to dominate. On the face of it, they do have an elevated sense of their own importance. Even under the relatively benign vision of Bill Clinton, US diplomats regularly employed rhetoric full of majestic arrogance. This ranged from former Secretary of State Madeline Albright's oft-repeated assertion that the United States was 'the indispensable force for peace' in the world, to the campaign rhetoric of Democratic presidential candidate Al Gore, who, during one of his televised debates with Republican George W. Bush, said that America 'is now looked on by peoples on every other continent, and the peoples from every part of this earth, as a kind of model for what the future could be'. Such egotism, although it fuels European resentment, does not accurately reflect where American sentiment and policy are heading in the wake of the Cold War.

Before the horror of the World Trade Centre attacks, there was a powerful trend for disengagement in the United States. The same night Al Gore made his flowery claims about American leadership, George W. Bush presented a far more accurate reflection of the mood of the voters who would elect him president. 'We cannot be all things to all people,' he declared. 'Nor should we walk into a country and say, "We do it this way, so should you".' The Bush doctrine, if such a thing existed, reflected a growing uncertainty among Americans. They believed in the pre-eminence of their values and felt that if other countries behaved rationally they would choose to live by those values. But that did not mean they were responsible for solving the world's problems. America's leading conservative satirist, P.J. O'Rourke, put it this way: 'America is the world's policeman all right – a big, dumb, mick flat-foot in the middle of the one thing cops dread most, a domestic disturbance.' Most Americans do not want to be involved in long-running family arguments between people with names they cannot pronounce, in places they cannot locate on the map. They may have nodded in agreement when politicians like Bill Clinton talked about fighting for American values in Kosovo, but their long-term views were better expressed by politicians like Pat Buchanan, who said, 'Our world war, the Cold War, is over. It's time for America to come home.'

Of course, Osama bin Laden showed that 'home' is no longer the safe place it once was. Defending American interests in the era of transnational terrorism means taking sides in disputes between people with unpronounceable names. It also means coming to terms with the failure of past US policies, such as unthinking support for the extremes of Afghanistan's Mujaheedin during the years of Soviet occupation, and it means constructing a US foreign policy in which the search for allies is at least as important as the search for enemies. It seems to me that these realities were grasped by a large number of ordinary Americans in the immediate aftermath of the terrorist attacks. New thinking also seemed to inform President Bush's action in the immediate aftermath of September 11. As he appeared to move away from his unilateralist instincts, his critics were quick to offer backhanded compliments. 'President Bush is strongly supported by the American people,' explained former Senator George Mitchell, 'in part because he has discarded almost everything he said on foreign policy prior to September 11.'

Unfortunately, the unilateralists within the Bush administration took a different meaning from the public's continued support of the president and his war on terror. After the destruction of the Taliban the hawks were clearly back in control and, as far as they were concerned, the United States had liberated Afghanistan without any real help from their supposed 'allies' (save the Brits). The United States had achieved success only by dictating the pace and scale of the response to September 11. Unilateralism 'is the driving motif of the Bush foreign policy,' wrote conservative columnist Charles Krauthammer, 'and that is the reason it is so successful.'

To many Europeans this was the worst possible conclusion. Bush's bellicose rhetoric against an 'axis of evil' and pledges to boost military spending appeared to signify a return to the bad old days, and a legion of indignant commentators across Europe were quick to condemn American warmongering. However, the critics missed two important realities. First, instead of weakening America's unilateralist tendencies, European criticism strengthened the hawks. Second, in spite of all the flag-waving, America is not a warrior nation.

War is not a natural state of affairs even for the massed ranks of the US military. Before President Bush declared his *jihad* on terror, America's military commanders were struggling to work out the role in a world where there was no rival superpower. The year before the attacks on America, I discovered these men and women bore no relationship to the clichés I had grown up with. There are no Dr Strangeloves left in the American military leadership, no Curtis Le Mays urging a nuclear strike against Cuba. There are men like Colonel Evans 'Hoops' Hoapili. His official title is Operations Group Commander for the 91st Space Wing of the US Air Force, which means he is the man who controls the nuclear missiles. I met him during a trip to Minot Air Force in North Dakota in October 2000. The base is the only US military installation used as headquarters for both heavy bombers and land-based intercontinental ballistic missiles, two-thirds of America's 'strategic triad'.

Colonel Hoapili let me sit in on a regular morning briefing for the men and women of the Space Wing. They call themselves the 'Rough Riders', and for 24 hours a day, 365 days of each of the last 30 years, they have sat in their assigned silos, spread out across 8000 square miles of North Dakota prairie, and waited for nuclear war. I had expected to see a group of square-jawed zealots, but instead I found myself sitting with a group of skinny whiz kids in flight suits. Gathered in front of their computer screens, these men, and women looked like the smartest students in a university maths class. Even as their commander talked of Defcon five and terrorist threats, I was struck by how old-fashioned this all was. Beside me, at the back of the briefing room, was a replica of one the original missile launch systems. It looked like an old telephone switchboard, complete with a bulky handset and rotary dial-pad. On this nuclear-age antique, the board lights up to reveal phrases like 'warhead alarm' and 'missile away'. For most of that day at Minot, I felt trapped inside some museum of the apocalypse.

I don't know what I expected when they led me through the low-slung belly of the B-52, but I certainly didn't expect things to be so cramped. The plane was built to transport about 70,000 pounds of bombs, mines and missiles and enough fuel to carry it more than 8000 miles without pause. 'The plane is nothing but bombs and gas' is how one crewman put it. Of course, he is not a crewman; he is a 'crew dog'. The language of the US Air Force is a limitless collection of cute words and phrases describing deadly realities. For example, the crew dog does not call it a B-52; it's a BUFF. A polite young public affairs officer tells me that stands for Big Ugly Flying Fellow. I assume the last word of that phrase changes depending on whom you are talking to. On the split-level flight deck of the B-52, the navigator proudly points out that some of the flight gauges are of Second World War vintage and he turns to open an ashtray that's still moulded into the wall. As I listen to the crew dog telling me all this, I can't take my eyes off the dull grey metal switches that arm and release the plane's cargo.

The men and women who fly the B-52 talk about it like a lovable old Volkswagen Beetle. They proudly tell you the plane was built in 1960 and, thanks to regular overhauls, it has another 40 years of service to go, but during my visit to Minot the unspoken question was whether the bombs on that B-52 and the missiles in the prairie around Minot would still be around in 40 years time. As the crew dogs and 'missileers' at Minot continued their daily preparations for a war they had already won, their commanders struggled with the uncomfortable truth that they were of another era. The days of Mutually Assured Destruction are over, and the US military is no longer an imperial force that might one day destroy the world in order to save it. America's warriors know this and, more importantly, the people they protect know it too.

Watching the TV pictures of B-52s pounding Afghanistan, you could easily assume that this was the expression of a new American quest for domination through military means, but moral objections to the conduct of that war should not blind Europeans to more complicated realities. After September 11, the demand for a powerful military among ordinary Americans is stronger than it has been for years, but that does not mean that the people have shifted back to the aggressive paranoia that informed Cold War foreign policy. The draft is gone and citizens are no longer compelled to fight for their country. The wounds from September 11 are still deep and raw, but terrorism is a vague and faceless enemy in comparison to the Soviet Union. George Bush may talk about the threat from 'rogue states' like Iraq, but Saddam Hussein does not seem to pose the same apocalyptic challenge that a succession of Soviet leaders once did.

You cannot understand America's search for a new role in the world unless you understand the changes in the American psyche. General George 'Blood and Guts' Patton once said, 'All real Americans love the sting and clash of battle.' That may have been true once, but not anymore. Political leaders in the United States know there are clear limits to what Americans will endure. War is not a natural state of affairs for the citizens of this country. The United States has not had a war on its soil for more than a hundred years. In the twentieth century, half a million Americans died in battle, but in the same period ten million Russians were killed defending their country. For Americans born in the last 30 years, war is not even a memory; war is stories from parents and grandparents or it is images on a screen. War is *Saving Private Ryan* or *Black Hawk Down*.

The hawks have been able to win the debate in Washington not because there is a fundamental shift in American attitudes to war, or a new-found desire to impose American values around the world, but because they have won the battle of perceptions. Images of al Qaeda detainees in Guantanamo Bay played badly in Europe but very well 'back home', providing at least circumstantial evidence that a stinging blow had been struck against the terrorist network. The images from the battlefield in Afghanistan were calibrated to fit the national mood, and so did nothing to challenge the presumption that the US-led war was both clean and godly. It also meant that there was no great debate inside the United States about the number of ordinary Afghans who were killed by American bombs.

Ironically, the storm of criticism from abroad has made it easier for the unilateralists to argue that the United States is on its own in the war on terror. They could quite persuasively argue that reliance on a coalition bloated with anti-American bile was pointless. These messages filtered back down through every level of American society. By the time I returned to New York at Christmas 2001, I could not get over the seething resentment among my friends. 'If Europeans have a problem with this,' I was told, 'we'll do it ourselves.' It all comes back to that old familiar sense of bewilderment. Europeans saw what happened to the people of New York and Washington on September 11, so why don't they get this? Not for the first time, I wondered if Americans and Europeans were living on the same planet.

If Europeans really want to influence public policy in the United States we should adopt a more balanced approach, spend more time changing people's views and less time slagging them off. European pressure groups should forge links with progressive organisations that have deep roots in the mainstream of American society, such as trade unions and farm groups. At the same time, European politicians should reach out to rising stars in the Republican Party, to try and check the growing isolationist trend among American conservatives. If we spent half as much time promoting our common interests as we do complaining about our differences, we would have a far more profound and productive relationship with the people of the United States. The goal in this process must be the creation of popular support for change on issues of universal concern, and not a European-led overhaul of the way America runs its own affairs.

There are two big challenges for any European who wants to come to a better understanding of the United States. The first is to see the American psyche as an organic entity that is constantly developing and changing, and which is open to the right kind of influences. The second is to understand that relentless self-righteousness and persistent use of the same negative clichés play right into the hands of the most regressive elements of American society. You do not get more regressive than Senator Jesse Helms of North Carolina. He held up compromise on America's outstanding debt to the United Nations, and used criticism of the United States as a 'deadbeat nation' to justify his actions. 'The American people hear all of this and they resent it,' he told the UN Security Council in January 2000. 'And I think they have grown increasingly frustrated at what they feel is a lack of gratitude.'

The likes of Jesse Helms should be reminded that other countries have paid a terrible price for the mistakes of America's Cold War foreign policy, from Vietnam to El Salvador, from Indonesia to Afghanistan, but the Cold War is over, and now is the time for Europe to help the United States find a new more constructive role in a rapidly changing world. So far, there is too much complacency and smugness in European capitals. The European Union may soon have a military capability to rival the Americans, but it would be a mistake to think Europe no longer needs the United States on its side, just as it would be a mistake for the American people to think they can retreat behind their well-fortified borders. As *New York Times* foreign affairs columnist, Thomas Friedman warned: 'The greatest danger is if America is no longer ready to play America – the benign superpower that pays a disproportionate price to maintain the system of which it is the biggest beneficiary.'

Europeans want to forge a common foreign policy that is, at the very least, independent of American influence and yet they still depend on the US military might to fight their common battles. Europeans want to rein in the American tendency to respond to crises without international consultation, but they fail to come up with any coherent responses to those crises. European public-opinion-makers seem almost blind to these contradictions, possibly because American foreign policy is such an easy target; as long as this 'big flat-footed mick' keeps sticking its nose in, we Europeans never have to feel guilty about our own indifference or inaction.

The hypocrisy struck me forcefully when I travelled to Afghanistan in April 2001. This country, once described by the great Indian poet Iqbal as the 'heart of Asia', was rotting alive. Of the 25 million people who lived in Afghanistan, 70 per cent were malnourished. The country had one of the world's highest rates of infant mortality and the average adult male could not expect to live beyond the age of 40. After more than 20 years of war and three successive years of drought, a million people were at risk of starvation, according to the United Nations, and millions more had been forced to abandon their homes. Yet the world averted its gaze. The United Nations was urgently seeking 250 million dollars to pay for emergency aid in 2001. By May of that year, they had received pledges of less than $50 million from the international community.

Near the border between Afghanistan and Pakistan was Jalozai, a makeshift camp inhabited by 80,000 Afghan refugees. When we visited, four or five people were dying at the camp every day and there was rising desperation among the living. Whenever we turned our cameras on a family, we were cursed. 'You come and film us and promise us help,' one woman screamed. 'But nothing happens. Where is the help?' As we prepared to leave, a tribal elder turned to the translator in our group and asked him, in Pashtu, if we would all stay and have lunch at Jalozai. The thought of taking food from these people was obscene, so we politely declined. 'Next time,' I said. Before my words had been translated into Pashtu, I heard a voice from the back of the crowd say in perfect English: 'Next time we will be dead.' I don't know what happened to the people of Jalozai, just as I don't know what happened to the people I met in Kabul and Jalabad. All I know is that we in the West, we in Europe, we in Ireland, all failed them.

Hundreds of thousands of Afghans have been killed, maimed and starved during two decades of civil war, a war started and sustained by outside powers, and yet we have hardly raised an eyebrow. It was only when American bombs began falling that we applied moral outrage to the plight of 25 million Afghans. European indifference had helped create the mess that spawned the Taliban and fostered al Qaeda. Yet this was all forgotten when the Americans acted. We never had to ask what role we played in prolonging the suffering of the Afghans because the Americans were to blame for everything.

Unless we in Europe finally work out what values are worth fighting for, we shall continue to devalue our valid criticism of the United States. Unless Europeans jettison their own out-dated clichés, confront their own hypocrisy and find a more positive script with which to engage the United States, they risk elevating the isolationists and xenophobes in successive American generations. That would be the worst possible outcome for people on both sides of the Atlantic, and the worst possible outcome for the people I met in Jalozai.

# Fifteen

## The Colombian Connection

If Europe and the United States want a project on which they can unite with maximum effect then Colombia is that project. So far, however, there is no sign the world has taken Colombia's plight seriously. In Ireland, in August 2001, we became temporarily expert in the affairs of this tragic Latin-American nation when three Irish citizens were arrested on suspicion of training members of the FARC guerrilla group. For a couple of weeks, we debated the provenance of Colombia's leftist revolutionaries, the relative threat of right-wing paramilitaries and the prospect of the collapse of the country's struggling peace process. But as summer turned to autumn, Colombia returned to the small print, only to resurface with the occasional mention of the humanitarian plight of those three Irish prisoners. I could not forget so easily. I have not been able to get Colombia out of my head since I travelled there in 1999. The country had fascinated me for years and I was determined that I would visit before the end of my posting as Washington correspondent. Within 24 hours of arriving, I would regret my determination.

My producer, Maria Ines, told me we should move quickly. The slums outside the city of Medellin were the property of urban militia loyal to the National Liberation

Army, better known by their Spanish initials ELN. They would know we were there very quickly. They knew faster than we expected. We had pulled up on a piece of waste ground overlooking the *barrio* of Viajuello. My cameraman Mauricio had started to film the shantytown below. I stood behind him and listened. The valley was a natural amphitheatre and the noise from the slum filled the air. It was the sound of kids, dogs, raised voices, music and motorbikes: the white noise of poverty.

From behind us, there was another noise, angry and threatening. A young man had joined us. He had a look of bleak determination on his face. His baseball cap bore the emblem of some American sports team and his shoes were fashionable Nikes. It was the urban chic of any North American city, but this was Colombia and the young man was armed with a pistol. He waved the gun in front of Maria Ines as she sat in the car. He turned to us and shouted something in Spanish. In response, Mauricio and our guide Eduardo raised their hands in the air. For a moment, it was just too silly. I was being ordered to 'stick 'em up', like some character out of a Jimmy Cagney movie.

The angry young man frisked Eduardo and Mauricio. He moved with a thorough professionalism that was both sinister and reassuring. He clearly knew what he was doing, but was he trying to show us who was in control or was he making preparations for something unpleasant? I had a money belt under my shirt and the pocket was tucked into the small of my back. I don't normally wear these things, but I had picked it up at the airport in Miami after reading some article on the plane about rampant street crime in Colombia. When the young man searched me, he passed his hand over the ominous bulge in my shirt. He tugged at the belt and shouted at me. I shouted back at him in pidgin Spanish, 'Passporta'.

I fumbled with the clip of the belt, unable to open it because the angry young man had pulled it tight against my stomach. I yanked at the belt frantically as he pulled it tighter, trying to rip it off. For the second time in a matter of minutes, I felt ridiculous. I finally got the belt off, pulled out the passport and handed it over. The young man pulled back the cover. My credit card and about 200 dollars in cash were tucked into the plastic jacket that covered the passport. I was convinced I would never see any of it again, but the angry young man just kept flicking through the document. Finally, he said 'Ireland', in a quiet, reverential tone, as if the word was some magic incantation. Then he lobbed the passport back to me without ceremony.

He turned to Mauricio and said something I could not understand. 'He wants to know what you think of the IRA,' Mauricio explained. I didn't know what to say. I assumed that, despite the Nikes and the baseball cap, our scary new friend was a member of the ELN and sympathetic to the IRA, so a quick blast of a rebel song might do the trick. But what if he was part of one of those paramilitary gangs I had been warned about? Many are linked to the military and all are fiercely right-wing. Any pro-IRA sentiment on my part could make a bad situation much worse. So I muttered a compromise: 'I've met some of the leaders of Sinn Féin.' It seemed to confuse the young man and he turned away to talk to our guide Eduardo. I was relieved, but Eduardo was not.

The young man ordered us to hunker down and form a little semi-circle in front of him. I listened hard, trying to comprehend the odd word of the rapid Spanish from the conversation. It sounded like things had calmed down but when I looked at Eduardo's face I could see the tension around his eyes. Eduardo worked for a government agency that helps refugees displaced by Colombia's civil war. More than a million people had been forced to flee the violence during the previous ten years and most were living in slums like this one. A few months before, he had been kidnapped by the ELN and held for two weeks. He had told us this casually in the jeep as we came in from the airport. Now I could see fear building in his face, fear that the nightmare was about to be repeated. When the young man walked away to consult with his superiors, Eduardo's head sank into his hands.

The few minutes he was gone passed in slow motion. There was no point in trying to run to our car. I don't think we would have got the key in the ignition. So we stayed close and talked quietly. I asked Mauricio to apologise to Eduardo for me. When the angry young man returned, he got down on one knee and we gathered around him once more. The anger was gone and I could make out the word *disculpe* in his first sentence. He told us he was sorry for what had happened, but he had feared we were a paramilitary death squad. Our white jeep was similar to a suspicious vehicle seen in the *barrio* a few days earlier. That was all I needed to know. We were not going to be kidnapped. We were free to go, the young man told us, but if we came back a few hours later we would get to meet his superiors in the militia. I shook his hand with a little too much warmth and thanked him profusely.

Two hours later, we arrived back at the same piece of waste ground. This time there were two old buses parked in the dried mud. Two men worked under the hood of one of the buses as a deafening combination of techno and salsa music exploded out of the driver's door. A wizened old dog walked by, oblivious to the sound of the radio and the screaming kids who sprinted up the hill in front of us. Inside the jeep there was silence. I was the only person in that car who really wanted this experience. I wondered what Mauricio, Eduardo and Maria Ines were thinking at that moment, as they risked their lives and freedom for the sake of a three-minute report on Irish television. And then I was forced to ask myself, 'What am I doing here?' It was a rhetorical question with just one answer: I am here because I am an addict and this is my drug of choice.

Not for the first time, I thought about just how perverse my life had become. I was enjoying this: sitting in a strange place with a shallow fear in my belly and a childish excitement clouding my brain. I did not know what was going to happen next but I was pretty sure that I was not in any immediate physical danger. If I could get the cameras rolling without really annoying someone, then I was going home with a great story. But if I left this place without the video, then it might as well not have happened. Some people go fishing and tell their mates in the pub about the one that got away. I come back from a strange place and tell my mates about the guerrilla interview that never was.

I did not have much time to savour this moment of self-realisation. Out of nowhere, a man in a white T-shirt had appeared at the driver's window of the jeep. He was thin, but muscular, and sported a crew cut. He looked like one of the off-duty US Marines who drink in the downtown bars back in Washington. He politely told us to follow him. We were led down a hillside, along the edge of a football field, where two teams were playing a fast-paced game of soccer in front of about 50 or 60 spectators. As we passed, every eye in the crowd turned in our direction. Then, almost in unison, they turned their attention back to the game. We continued down a steep dirt path that wound its way past a line of wooden shacks. There wasn't a brick or pane of glass to be seen anywhere. Everything was constructed of odd-shaped planks and tea chests. The walls on some of the houses still had shipping instructions on them.

After a few minutes, we came to the end of the path and the last house, which was perched precariously on stilts. Inside, it was dark and cramped and the walls seemed paper-thin. But it was neat and tidy and I felt the warmth of somebody's home. The woman of the house asked us to sit, before scurrying down a ladder that led to the hillside below. Our friendly Marine reappeared with a bottle of lemonade. We sat, drank and made small talk for a few minutes. I turned to Maria Ines and asked her quietly what was going on. Before she could answer, the door opened and two men walked in. They had T-shirts wrapped around their heads and their eyes poked out of the necklines. They were obviously trying to protect their identities, but the T-shirts made them comical and menacing in equal measure.

One of the men sat down in a chair and told me he would not allow us to film him, but he wanted to pass on a message to the Irish people. As he spoke, I made a mental note of the expensive Nike runners he was wearing. He talked with passionate sincerity about the plight of the people in this community, people living in grinding poverty. Through an interpreter, the young man told me that the state had forced many of these people to become refugees by exploiting their lands and serving the needs of the 'gringo' multinationals. 'Massacres don't only happen with bullets,' he said.

Through an interpreter, I asked him for a solution to his country's political and economic crisis. He said the only solution was dialogue, but that dialogue could begin in earnest only after the people had been armed. I asked him what he thought of the peace overtures Colombian president Andres Pastrana was making to the biggest guerilla group, FARC. 'This is not a peace plan,' the young man declared, 'it's a plan for war.' He pointed out that much of the international aid the president had been seeking was military aid. As he spoke, I tried to work out in my mind how I was going to persuade him to let us turn on our camera and start filming. I told him he needed to speak to the Irish people directly, through the camera and not through me. I made some joke about how he should not trust a journalist. Maria Ines nervously translated, and in the ensuing silence I understood this was not a time for irony. After some debate with his companion, the young man agreed to give us an on-camera statement. He instructed his friend to go and prepare it. Then he turned to Maria Ines and said something in Spanish.

'He wants to know if you want to see their guns?'

I don't believe I'm hearing this, I thought to myself. 'Sí,' I told our new guerrilla friend.

I sat back in my chair, thinking I was on the brink of an exclusive. The ELN had been getting some bad press after a series of high-profile kidnappings across Colombia, and their leaders were not granting interviews. I was ecstatic at the thought of my impending scoop, although I said nothing. While I tried to restrain a big grin, the young man took out a notebook and started to question Maria Ines and Mauricio. I asked Maria Ines what was going on and she told me he was taking their names and addresses. As Mauricio later explained: 'This is a mailing list you do not want to be on.' I told Maria Ines I would politely decline the interview and leave, if she felt uncomfortable. She shrugged and said, 'He's already taken my address.' I felt guilty and very ill at ease. Journalism in Colombia is a dangerous career. Every armed group has a problem with the media and they are not afraid to kill reporters who cross them. Eight Colombian journalists were kidnapped the week after we had our run in with the angry young man. I had put my companions at risk of a reprisal, and I felt ashamed of the gormless excitement I had been feeling.

I felt even worse a few moments later when the second masked man reappeared. He had a brief message for his colleague: 'The police are coming.' I heard this and pushed the camera under the chair. The angry young man apologised and said he would have to leave. I was not going to get my exclusive. Our friendly urban guerilla adjusted the T-shirt around his head and got up from his seat. He ordered us to wait for 15 minutes before leaving the house. We shook hands and he was gone. I slumped back into the chair, and once again there was silence. We waited 15 minutes and then left the little wooden house to reclaim our car. On our way out of the barrio, we were stopped at an army checkpoint. The gloomy look on the face of the soldier reflected my mood. I could not wait to be away from this place and back in the safety and comfort of my room at the hotel in Bogotá, with room service, a stiff drink and a bath.

The next morning, before daybreak, Maria Ines, Mauricio and I were back at the airport for a flight to the city of Cali. There we were to be picked up by a colonel in the elite anti-narcotic division of the National Police and flown by helicopter to the town of Popyan, in the southern province of Cauca. Not for the first time during my trip to Colombia, and not for the last, my expectations were to prove completely inadequate.

The helicopter landed at Cali airport and off jumped Colonel Gilberto Villar and what looked like a detachment of bodyguards. Heavily armed does not even begin to describe these men. The colonel invited us for coffee and off we went, walking through the airport with his squad. They were dressed in jungle fatigues and had bandoliers full of bullets strapped across their bodies.

All of them carried automatic rifles and one man shouldered a heavy machine gun he had nicknamed, 'La Niña'.

We sat in a coffee shop with the colonel and talked about his work. I had met American cops involved in high-risk drug work and they had lived up to all the stereotypes. They walked with a swagger, talked with loud arrogance and exuded moral superiority. The colonel was different. He spoke quietly, and repeatedly flashed an innocent smile. He had the face of a young, idealistic parish priest, although this was a parish priest with an armalite by his side and a handgun tucked into his vest. Colonel Villar was small, but there was no doubting his physical strength. The colonel was a Llanero, a native of the Llanos Orientales region of Colombia. 'He's what the Americans would call a cowboy,' Mauricio explained. The Llaneros were warriors as far back as the early nineteenth century, when Simón Bolívar recruited them to fight the Spanish. They are known for their physical prowess, forged on their sprawling farms, the Hatos. As the colonel told us about his childhood, spent taming horses and herding bulls, a nostalgic grin spread across his face. Today, this Llanero is trying to tame a more sinister opponent, and it is a struggle that could cost him his life.

The colonel told me that every morning he leaves his house, his family says a prayer that they will see him again. They have good reason to pray. More than 3000 policemen have been killed in the last decade in the fight against the drug cartels. Now the real enemy is the guerillas who control most of the drug-producing areas of Colombia. Most days, Colonel Villar and the 150 men under his command work behind enemy lines.

We finally left Cali airport for the 45-minute helicopter ride to Popyan. We flew in an ageing Huey helicopter that the colonel told us used to take seven passengers. Now it could carry only five because of the weight of the armour plating fitted to the floor. That would protect us from guerrilla gunfire from the ground, the colonel told us. It sounded like Spanish for: 'You won't get your bollocks shot off.' As an added precaution, the helicopter had two heavy machine-guns trained on the ground below. I suppose this should have made me feel more secure, but all I could think about was the anonymous, hidden enemy in the fertile mountain valley below me. 24 hours earlier I had sat in a shack in the slums of Medellin and drunk lemonade with that hidden enemy.

Our helicopter touched down at the airfield at Popyan, where the rest of the colonel's squad was waiting to move out. Their target was a poppy field high in the mountains, in an area controlled by FARC guerrillas. The plan was that a small detachment would be sent up to secure the area and then we would be flown in to witness the destruction of the poppies. But a fog had closed in around the target and we were stuck in Popyan for the night.

We booked into the best hotel in town, a converted monastery, and were surprised to find we were the only guests. The phones did not work but the rooms were clean, the staff was friendly and the quiet courtyard in the middle of this once sacred place was a welcome retreat from the noisy chaos of the streets outside. I lay down in my room and tried to sleep. I was exhausted, but also disorientated, and the knot in my stomach kept me wide-awake. I could hear the helicopters from the nearby military base take off and land. I went out on the patio to look. The hazy evening sun warmed my face as I sat there, but I felt completely alone. I was cut off from every-thing except the sense of menace and foreboding all around me.

It was in Popyan that I had my first real near-death

experience. A local journalist called Adolfo invited us for dinner and offered to drive us to the town's best restaurant. Even by Colombian standards, he drove like a maniac. He ignored red lights, pedestrians and oncoming trucks, swerving at the moment before impact. It was almost impossible to concentrate on his never-ending monologue about adventures with the rebels, the cops and the drug-traffickers, a monologue delivered with sound-effects and too many violent gestures for my liking. I suddenly realised how much safer I had been sitting on top of that armour plating, beside the heavy machine-gun. We were at the restaurant before I discovered that I had not been wearing my seatbelt. I think I impressed our host.

Having survived a night on the town with Adolfo, I was well prepared for the next day, which started early at the Popyan airfield. Police helicopters swept across the runway at dawn to pick up Colonel Villar's men. The advance team waited in silence with their legs apart, automatic rifles strapped to their backs and machetes dangling from their fingers. They took the first helicopter, Mauricio and I took the second. As the aircraft picked up speed and altitude, out of the corner of my eye I saw Mauricio bless himself. I also realised that everyone else on the helicopter was wearing a flak jacket. As we flew higher into the Colombian Andes, I gazed at the early morning beauty passing below me and the fear slipped back into my subconscious. Shadow and light played along the wooded ridges as the mist rose to meet the helicopter. I found myself breathless and light-headed and I thought it might be the adrenaline coursing through my body. It was the altitude, and by the time we made the sharp turn into the target area, I was panting in time with the repetitive thump of the rotors.

We jumped out of the helicopter and were met by one

of Colonel Villar's men, who made us sprint to the top of the hill. As Mauricio caught up with me, I thought he said the word 'guerrilla' but I could not be sure, we were running so fast. We crossed the top of the ridge under the watchful gaze of three young police officers who had their eyes and weapons trained on the surrounding hillsides. We continued down the other side of the mountain, slipping and sliding along a steep, muddy track. Then, just as I felt the altitude sickness and exhaustion begin to overwhelm me, we stopped abruptly. Our guide pulled a purple flower off the end of a row of plants and ground it between his fingers for the benefit of our camera. It was a poppy, and all around me was the raw material for heroin.

The destruction of the field took 20 minutes. Colonel Villar's men hacked away at the poppies and then joined us at the edge of the field as an aeroplane swooped down from the ridge, trailing a fine chemical mist. The pilot made repeated sweeps across the field and the chemical floated towards us on the wind. We were dusted with herbicide, covered with mud and still wary of an encounter with the guerrillas. It seemed like a good time for us to go. I followed our guide back up the mountain at what seemed like a right angle. My thighs would hurt for days after that climb back to the helicopter. Every breath felt like sandpaper, as the oxygen forced its way into my heaving chest. I collapsed in a heap, falling into a trench at the top of the ridge. At that moment, I couldn't decide which was worse, the pain of the climb or the prospect of a well-aimed guerrilla bullet.

Safely back on the helicopter, I felt a rush of excitement and satisfaction. I had found the heart of the story: the fusion of Colombia's drug war and civil war. I had flown into danger with a group of men who put their lives on the line every day because they believe the risk is worth it. On the long journey back to Bogotá, I felt like a combat veteran returning to 'The World' to tell amazing tales of heroism and integrity.

The next day I would learn a valuable lesson in humility from Maria Jimena Duzan. She made a name for herself as a courageous young reporter, exposing the heart of darkness behind the drug-related chaos that had convulsed her country in the 1980s. She would suffer for that courage. She was almost killed in a bomb attack on her home. She had become a target for right-wing paramilitaries, angry at her reporting of the civil war, and was forced into exile for three years. A paramilitary group shot and killed her sister in a small town in the north of the country.

I met her at home in a fashionable neighbourhood of Bogotá. With some pride, I told her about my adventure in the mountains with Colonel Villar. I wanted her to know I had been blooded. She snorted in derision. 'It's a show,' she said, 'a show we've got to put on for an audience in the United States that doesn't understand this war and doesn't understand this country.' She was not being nasty. I think she assumed I knew. I felt stupid for letting my war correspondent fantasy overwhelm the truth behind my adventure. There was still no doubt in my mind that Colonel Villar and his men were dedicated and courageous, but everything about that raid was designed to create good public relations, even the frisson of danger I felt flying into the rebel-controlled area.

Maria Jimena helped me unload the other preconceptions I had built up in my determined effort to construct the unifying theory of Colombia. As a television journalist, you have so little time to really get to know a country that you try and soak it up like a sponge. Like a clever but lazy kid cramming for an exam, you read everything you can get your hands on, looking for the nuance and the anecdote that will capture the essence of the country. You hungrily consume every street scene, every piece of graffiti and the personality traits of every person you meet. But sometimes your judgement becomes clouded because you are having such a good time. If you get lucky, you meet someone who stops you in your tracks with the clarity of their insight, and you are forced to start all over again.

At first I tried hard to impress Maria Jimena with my deep and probing questions, but as we talked I began to understand there was something I had been missing about Colombia. It does not exist. It is not a country, but a collection of feuding gangs, who have jealously marked their territories and are caught up in a cycle of mutual deception and destruction. The war is fought on many overlapping fronts and between many connected enemies. There is war between the rebels and the government, the rebels and the paramilitaries, the paramilitaries and defenceless peasants, the government and the drug cartels, the drug cartels and the rebels. Inside each armed group there are fierce divisions and rivalries, between the factions there are some bizarre alliances. The easy money of the drug trade has helped the guerrillas and paramilitaries prosper amid this chaos. The poppy and the coca leaf did not cause the war but they were certainly prolonging it.

Maria Jimena described the country as if it were a car torn apart and sold for scrap. The government had the cities, the rebels and the paramilitaries laid claim to everything else. Not one person I met in Bogotá would consider travelling outside the city by road for fear of kidnap. 'As a result,' Maria Jimena explained, 'you feel like you're under siege, a prisoner of the city.' She reserved her deepest scorn for the powers that be in the United States, who see this purely as a war to stop drugs from leaving Colombia; the congressmen who demand 'the show' to make the folks back home feel a little bit more secure; the top brass who are prepared to ignore the human rights' abuses and the social inequality that helped create the war in the first place. She believes these people are prepared to forget that it is drug consumption on the streets of US cities that helps create drug production in the Colombian Andes. In *Death Beat*, her book about the drug war, Maria Jimena wrote that if the world does not grasp that last connection, Colombia will suffer the fate forecast by Gabriel García Márquez: 'We will rot alive, in a war that cannot be won, and the world will rot with it.'

That prediction is coming through in ways which most outsiders are unaware of. Only on rare occasions do we make the connections between the drug-fuelled war in Colombia and European countries like Ireland, but they are there. Colombia has become a wholesale market for the vast criminal conspiracy that floods our streets with heroin. There is also a very real threat of economic collapse and political instability spreading from Colombia through South America. In the event of a serious escalation of violence, there is the possibility of a broader regional war in which the United States would almost certainly become involved. You do not have to be a pessimist to see shades of South-East Asia in the early 1960s.

In the face of all of this, Europe has failed to meet its moral obligations. When Colombia first went to the international community looking for help, the European Union rejected the government's recovery plan as flawed, but refused to invest sufficient funds or political capital to create an alternative. Sooner or later, our complacency will catch up with us, but by the time we fully understand our obligations it may be too late. To the list that includes Rwanda, Bosnia, Afghanistan, the Congo and East Timor, we may soon have to add Colombia.

# Sixteen

# Home-grown Heroes

Imagine for a moment that Ireland had been struck by a major hurricane, a natural disaster like no other in its history. Just imagine. You find yourself in Dublin city centre when the sky clears and, within seconds, you know the city will never be the same again. You know the country will never fully recover.

You emerge from your hiding place at the north end of O'Connell Street, by the statue of Charles Stewart Parnell. The black, sticky mud that fills the street outside the Gresham Hotel is still deep enough to cover the cars that were flipped over by the powerful floods. Rescuers have not yet had time to check the cars for corpses. You find a way through the mess and pass by Clerys department store, now guarded by security men armed with shotguns and orders to fire on looters. You hurry toward the Liffey and the smell of rotting flesh becomes more powerful as you approach O'Connell Bridge. Of course, when you reach the river there is no O'Connell Bridge. The floodwaters took it away. You join a crowd of fellow citizens at Daniel O'Connell's statue. You can go no farther because in front of you is a newly created lake. The stagnant waters are filled with a toxic combination of human and animal remains. Some of the bodies have risen to the surface but most are still at the bottom of the new lake.

A third of Ireland's population has been made homeless, and travel between Galway and Dublin is impossible, except by helicopter. In small towns around the country, food supplies ran out more than a week ago. Water is rationed and a curfew prevents anyone from leaving home between 9 p.m. and 5 a.m. The pubs are closed because the sale of alcohol is banned. The Dáil, the Department of Finance and the Central Bank have been gutted. You cross the one bridge that is still standing and walk towards Trinity College. The university is now a shelter for some of the tens of thousands of people made homeless by the floods. The crowds that gather in Front Square have set up makeshift kitchens. The pots sit precariously on top of wood fires. Beans and rice are all that is on the menu and even they are in short supply. Someone is listening to a commentator on the short wave radio. Ireland's economic progress has been wiped out, the pundit declares; we have been sent back to the Fifties. Imagine all this and you get a sense of the appalling reality that confronted the people of Honduras in the wake of Hurricane Mitch in November 1998.

Even before the hurricane, Honduras and Nicaragua were among the poorest nations in the world. But the real tragedy of this disaster was that, after years of political violence, corruption and repression, the region was starting to enjoy the fruits of stable democracy and there were obvious signs of economic progress and social change. Democracy was well rooted and it survived the winds and floods, but everything else was wiped out in just a few hours.

A week after the floods, I stood by a river in an affluent neighbourhood of the capital city, Tegucigalpa, and watched a Mexican rescue team search for bodies. To get to the riverbank we had to walk through a ruined house. Mud had flooded the house, filled in every square inch of space and obliterated every detail of life. We had a brief and subdued conversation with one young member of the family that owned the property. He was a university student and spoke English. As he helped his grandmother climb through the debris, he told us that two of his neighbours were still missing. It was assumed their bodies would be found when they finally shovelled the mud out of their house. As we followed the Mexican rescue team, we stopped to watch the sniffer dog scout around the mud for the bodies of the dead. As the dog's head bobbed around the roots of a fallen tree, I looked around the garden I was standing in. A young woman was kneeling by a swimming pool with a man who seemed to be her older brother. They were washing the mud off a collection of vinyl records. A few feet away, a Mexican soldier waded into the brown water of the river, prodding the riverbed in a silent search for corpses.

I went to look for a place to do my piece-to-camera. I climbed over a mound of bricks which turned out to be the remains of the back wall of one of the houses. The floodwaters had receded and I found a piece of riverbed dried out by the midday sun. I walked around in a circle trying to come up with a line to describe what I was seeing, but I was distracted. Across the river, a group of kids picked through a pile of dirt that had spilled out of a ruined warehouse. It looked as if they were picking vegetables, but this warehouse had stored coffee beans, and the people on that riverbank were salvaging what they could, a single bean at a time.

As I looked closer at my immediate surroundings, random objects began to take on a definite shape and one of those shapes was a bus. It did not look like a bus. The wheels had been stripped of their tires and the glass removed from the windows. It just lay there, on its side, propping up an uprooted tree. The floods had carried the bus from somewhere upriver to this final resting place. I assumed the rescue teams had searched the bus for bodies. I hoped they had searched the bus for bodies.

My guide that day was an Irish development worker who had come to Honduras to help this country prepare for the future, and try and stop it slipping into the past. Adrian Fitzgerald told me that during the day he was too busy to let the tragedy sink in but, one night, soon after the floods, he went home to his wife and bawled his eyes out. I was touched deeply by that sorrowful image but I also felt a strange sense of pride. In that place, amid all that tragedy, I was thankful I came from a country that had produced this man. And I was thankful for whatever force of nature had produced Sally O'Neill.

Sally was the charismatic bundle of energy who ran the Trócaire and Red Cross operation in Tegucigalpa. The day the rains came, she stood on a bridge and watched the floodwaters sweep by the city's prison. She looked on as nervous prison guards fired shotguns at convicts who were either trying to flee the approaching natural disaster or taking advantage of the fact that the prison walls were crumbling into the swollen river. What really scared Sally about the chaos that overtook Honduras in those first few days was that nobody from the outside world seemed to know what was going on. It took days for the international media to realise the scale of the tragedy in Honduras.

Sally invited me to join her and another Irish aid worker, Sorcha Fennell, on a trip to Choluteca, a town in southern Honduras that was almost destroyed by the floods that came with Hurricane Mitch. The road out of Tegucigalpa had just reopened and Sally was anxious to get a shipment of food and supplies to an isolated community near the Nicaraguan border, people on the verge of starvation. Some of the villagers would meet the Trócaire trucks at Choluteca and take the supplies by foot and by canoe back to their friends and families.

'It's like coming to a new place I've never been,' Sally told me as we rolled into Choluteca. She had visited the town just a few days before the swollen river that flows past the town had broken its banks and swept away entire communities. We made the delivery in the centre of town and then Sally turned the jeep around and drove to the edge of a flooded square, a couple of hundred feet from the river. The biggest house on the square was still structurally sound, but it was stuffed with mud and leaves and branches. We walked past the building and delicately made our way towards a flooded cemetery, slipping ankle deep into thick, black, sticky muck. Coffins had floated out of this cemetery at the height of the floods. I could only imagine the horror of local people as this terrible omen of death drifted by. And yet, as I pondered that horror, I was jolted by an image of joy. There on a patch of dried out mud were wedding pictures that had obviously come loose from a photo album. The faces of the happy couple stared out at me. They were so full of hope for the future. I do not know what happened to that young man and woman, but nothing could illustrate the tragedy of Honduras better than that vivid record of their happiness, lying in the midst of almost biblical devastation.

As we left Choluteca that evening, we made our way slowly across the only remaining bridge, past the lorries loaded with human cargo, past entire families loaded onto motorbikes, past old men loaded down with sacks of rice, and past dirty kids. Everywhere there were dirty kids. On the other side of the river, Sally stopped the jeep and told me to follow her. We walked by two young boys, who were taking turns with a single shovel, digging aimlessly at the thick brown earth. Behind them was a confusing warren of shallow ditches, littered with broken slates and all manner of household appliances. As I looked closer I realised we were walking across the roofs of houses. Eight hundred families had lived in this place, before a wall of mud came and ended life as they knew it.

The local people gathered round Sally O'Neill with what possessions they had rescued from the mud. Sally listened and took notes as they told their story. Their *barrio* had been destroyed and the people needed to be relocated to begin a new life, but that would take money the local authorities did not have or were unwilling to spend. Sally had heard countless other similar stories in the other Latin-American countries she had served in, but instead of being jaded or despairing, she radiated infectious energy.

Her brand of social justice did not seem to be deeply ideological, even though it put her on the side of Latin America's liberation movements. She had lived a life that comfortable middle-class lefties had merely talked about. She had been a good friend of Maurice Bishop, the socialist leader of Grenada, and had stayed with him in the days before US forces invaded the Caribbean island in 1980. Bishop was killed during the invasion and Sally and a friend were left wandering about a beach just as the US Marines swept in from the sea. 'Some of these guys didn't know where they were,' Sally recalled. 'They thought they were still somewhere in the United States.' Among the equipment they brought ashore was a Coke machine.

Sally told her stories without vanity or any great self-awareness. To watch her mop of curly hair bob along with her easy laugh, you would swear she was talking about a package tour to Majorca. The hours we spent in that jeep on the rocky road between Tegucigalpa and Choluteca were a real pleasure, even though it was disconcerting to be sitting in the jeep surrounded by the warm friendship of Sally and Sorcha, as scenes of unforgettable devastation passed by the window. But what is the correct etiquette during a natural disaster? Do you sit in hushed silence and shake your head with affected concern, or do you lighten the load of a tough job with humanity and humour? I thought of all the deeply unpleasant zealots I had known in my life; the people who have such ostentatious devotion to their cause that they never really understand the world around them. They can shag off. Give me Sally O'Neill any day.

And for that matter, give me Father Larry Finnegan. I met Father Larry in July 1997, when I travelled to the Caribbean island of Montserrat. Two weeks before, the Soufriere Hills volcano had ended four hundred years of slumber with an abrupt and deadly show of violence. The eruption claimed the lives of 30 people. The mountain was still active when I arrived in Montserrat. The unspoken fear was that it could blow up again at any time. On that first night in Montserrat, I woke in a panic. The rain was coming down in sheets outside and a thunderous rumble sent an electric chill down my spine. I ran to the window, half-expecting to see the orange glow of an unstoppable river of lava, but there was only pitch black. I was pretty sure this was just a storm, but the rolling thunder guaranteed I would not get back to sleep. The rain eased as daylight approached so I went outside and looked towards the mountain. The summit was shrouded in mist but the lower slopes were covered with the vivid green of tropical trees and plants. It was hard to believe such an abundance of life could surround this deadly force.

Later that day, I arranged to meet a local writer by the pool at the Vue Point Hotel. We had ordered some drinks and were setting up for the interview when the cameraman, Darryl, let out an excited yelp: 'Holy shit!' I turned towards the mountain and saw a huge mushroom cloud, filled with thousands of tons of volcanic ash, spew out of the crater of the volcano. It had appeared without a sound and gracefully filled the sky. A green valley that I had admired early that morning, on the left side of the mountain, was filling with a fast-moving cloud of super-heated gas and rocks: what the experts called a pyroclastic flow. Within minutes the cloud over the volcano had spread out across the sky and blocked the sun. Soon it released its cargo of ash, which drifted to earth like featherweight raindrops onto the beautiful landscape below. The local writer told me this incredible spectacle was nothing to worry about. This was just another day in the shadow of the volcano.

In the weeks since the big eruption, the people of Montserrat had been forced to abandon the southern part of their island. The capital, Plymouth, had been turned into a ghost town and few believed it would ever be habitable again. The airport and the seaport were closed down, and the island's administration was being run out of holiday homes in the north. Refugees crowded into makeshift shelters. More than half of the 12,000 people who lived on Montserrat had fled the island. The unspoken fear was that there might not be enough people to sustain a real community there any more. When I asked average Monserratians why they stayed, they told me it was for love of their country. Then, in a lower voice, some admitted they just could not afford to flee.

There was so much at stake in Montserrat. It is a unique nation, born out of adversity and built of a remarkable ethnic mix. Among the earliest settlers were Irish refugees. Some were wealthy landowners, but most were indentured servants driven out of Ireland by

Cromwell, or forced from other British colonies by religious intolerance. Over successive generations, they intermarried with the African slaves who had been brought to work the fertile land. The result, according to one local tour guide, is Ireland's only colony. The customs officer stamps a shamrock in your passport when you arrive and St Patrick's Day is a public holiday, although that has more to do with the fact that 17 March is also the anniversary of a slave rebellion. Among the most common names are Riley, Farrell, O'Gara, Ryan, Irish and Galway, and the locals speak in a patois laden down with an accent that is part Caribbean and part Clonakilty.

The rich heritage was shamelessly exploited by the Montserrat Tourist Board. The island once attracted wealthy visitors who built spectacular holiday homes. The locals called them 'snowbirds' because they went north in the summer and south in the winter. But the volcano forced the snowbirds to flee, the farms in the south were laid to waste and Montserrat's small but successful industries were under threat. All that was left was a spirit of independence, pride and Larry Finnegan. 'When I came here I used to tell people I had died and gone to heaven,' Father Larry told me. 'Then a couple of weeks ago, an old woman came up and asked me if I still thought I was living in heaven. Yeah, I told her, but when I look out the window I see a little piece of hell.'

Father Larry had thick glasses, a shock of grey hair and the mischievous air of a slightly awkward teenager. He had served with the Divine Word Missionaries in Kenya for six years. After a stint at home in Ireland, he had landed in Antigua and finally came to minister in neighbouring Montserrat. I first saw him in operation at Sunday mass, which now took place in the ballroom of the Vue Point Hotel. A group of local kids had come to celebrate their first Holy Communion in a glorious service full of music, singing and joy. But there was also menace. One little boy stood up and offered prayers for 'our scientists and politicians who are working to keep us safe from the volcano'. I wondered what was in the minds of the proud parents in the audience who looked upon their kids in all their finery. Could they guarantee a future for their children on this island? Could they say with any certainty that their island nation would outlive the next generation?

Father Larry began his sermon by gathering a few of the kids together in front of the altar. He picked a boy and told him to take the end of a rope he had taken from beside the makeshift altar. The boy tugged and tugged but could not dislodge the priest from the altar. Father Larry told the rest of the kids to take the rope and pull together. With one sharp yank, Father Larry fell off the altar and laughter filled the room. 'You see,' Father Larry said, 'when we all pull together we can do anything, and when the nation pulls together it can do great things.' It was contrived and it was simplistic but it was perfect.

After the ceremony, Father Larry brought me to see the sole remaining Catholic Church on the island, St Martin de Porres. It had been turned into a shelter for those made homeless by the volcanic eruptions. 'Just imagine if the entire population of Dublin was forced to leave their homes and move to Connemara,' Father Larry said. 'That's what's happened here.' Inside the church, the pews had been piled up in a corner to make way for mattresses and 64 refugees. Two little girls lay in the corner without the slightest emotion on their face. They stared at me and the TV camera for a few moments and then one little girl put her hands over her eyes and threw her head on the pillow. Her sister did not break her stare.

The desperation had not weakened the patriotism of the average Montserratian. For some, it was all they had left. 'No matter how small you are, you are still a Montserratian,' Father Larry told me. 'There is a determination that we're going to see this through.' He explained that the islanders had suffered before, during earthquakes, storms and slavery. Just a few years earlier, they had braved the awesome power of Hurricane Hugo and were still rebuilding when the volcano came alive. They stayed not because of the magnetic draw of the island, but because of the collective identity it had spawned. Father Larry had a uniquely optimistic take on it. 'This is home, but if we all have to leave the island we'll just have to get another island.' The territory might be rendered useless but the nation would survive. What better person to harness the positive power of nationalism than a proud Irishman like Larry Finnegan.

Father Larry confirmed what I had always known, but had been loathe to acknowledge when I was younger. Among the people who do most to promote social justice are members of the clergy, and Sister Miriam Mitchell was also living proof of that. When I met Sister Miriam she told me, 'The poor will always be in my heart.' She was originally from County Galway, and travelled to the United States in 1961 to work as a teacher in San Antonio, Texas. But teaching was not enough to satisfy her wanderlust. In the early 1970s she decided to move to southern Louisiana. It is home to some of the poorest communities in the United States, but it has also produced the rich cultural tradition of the Cajun people. Sister Miriam finally settled in Houma, about an hour's drive west of New Orleans. She ran the Catholic Social Services centre there, and helped co-ordinate prog-rammes assisting the poor in the parish of Lafourche. In March 1994, she heard something that would change her life and the life of a remarkable community called Grand Bois.

Grand Bois is not really a town, but a collection of a few extended families. Their ancestors fled Grand Isle, in the Mississippi Delta, after a huge storm at the end of the nineteenth century. They settled in the bayou where the Houma Indian tribe lived and these two distinct identities gradually merged to create something very special. R.J. Molinaire belongs to one of the most prominent families in Grand Bois. RJ's grandmother still doesn't speak a word of English and insists on talking to her family in the rough French dialect that used to be the first language of this corner of Louisiana. 'It's weird,' says RJ 'Half the town speaks French and the other half speaks English.'

RJ is one of those people who automatically make you feel physically inferior. I always harboured notions that I was the outdoors type, a friend of nature, and an adventure man, fuelled by fresh air and testosterone. But after meeting R.J. Molinaire I know I will always be a wimpy city boy who deserves to have sand kicked in his face. RJ is a muscle-bound arm-wrestling champion and proud owner of an enormous, gleaming Harley Davidson. He is also a devoted hunter who talks with great passion about the central importance of nature to generations of his family. Grand Bois could not exist without some mutual accommodation with the other forms of life that claim joint ownership of the thick, still waters of the bayou.

RJ and his brother had inherited more than 300 acres of land from their father. Part of it they use for hunting deer and rabbit, although there are strict rules for preserving the herds on his land. 'We don't kill anything we don't eat,' RJ said. 'Even if that means putting a lot of venison in the icebox.' A big section of the land is swamp, and it is home to some of the scariest creatures on God's green earth. As we drove our jeep into a little clearing by the marshes, we saw an alligator wake from its slumber on the mud flats and race back into the deeper water. We got out of the car and RJ told me to watch out for the water rats, or 'neutras', as they are known locally. Sure enough, a big furry creature, the size of a small dog, popped its head above the green water behind us.

Amid the constant bird noise there was a rhythmic comical belch that turned out to be the anthem of a single, unseen bullfrog. 'That's nothing,' RJ told me. 'You want to hear the alligators when they're mating – they sound likes bears.' With a casual tone, I asked him if there were any snakes about. RJ recited part of a very long list. 'Water moccasins, river snakes, copperheads and rattle snakes.' Despite my rising panic, the raw beauty of the bayou overwhelmed me. The evening sun was an orange flicker on the uneven surface of the water, and it took the edge off the unseasonal chill of this spring evening. RJ reminisced about the days when he would wade into the marsh up to his neck and spend days just wandering the land, fishing for crawfish and hunting for anything that could be eaten. Occasionally, RJ fell silent and stared out across the water, listening to the unrelenting chatter of the animals, like some Cajun Doctor Dolittle.

Imagine nature provides the frontiers of your life, the prism through which you look at the world and your spiritual underpinning. Then you imagine Grand Bois. Now imagine you are witness to the slow destruction of the alpha and omega of your existence and you also imagine Grand Bois.

It all began on a bright March morning in 1994 when locals were confronted by an overwhelming stench. They knew it came from a local waste facility owned by the Campbell Wells Company. The plant had been there for years and took in waste from oil companies all across America's southern states. The plant was known as 'The Pits'. It had always smelled bad, but this was different. In the weeks that followed, residents complained of a variety of minor ailments, including nosebleeds and nausea. They tracked down the cause of the stink to a shipment of waste that the Exxon Corporation had brought to The Pits from Alabama. It was the trigger for over six years of legal war in the Louisiana courts.

The driving force behind the court action was a small cadre of villagers led by R.J. Molinaire and his sister Clarice Lisoux. Clarice has the dark, beautiful features of her Indian ancestors and a deep, sensual voice that turns her Cajun accent into a love song. Sitting with her and her family on the porch of her house, I listened as she told the story of her town for the millionth time. She was clearly weary of the long battle, but as she talked she seemed to tap into a deep reserve of strength that was evident in every person I met in Grand Bois. Beside me sat Sister Miriam Mitchell. She was silent as Clarice paid her a deep and heartfelt compliment: 'When I was first given Sister's card, I looked at it and said, "What can this woman, Sister Miriam Mitchell of the diocese of Houma-Thibidoux, do for me except pray?" Well she did that, plus.'

Sister Miriam had heard about the strange goings on in Grand Bois from a nurse attending a meeting at the Catholic Social Services Centre. She went to visit the village and knew something was wrong the moment she reached Clarice's house. The smell was so bad she gagged. On her way home, her eyes burned and she thought, What is happening to people who have been exposed to this on a constant basis? Sister Miriam is a hero to the people of Grand Bois: 'They say they've adopted me.' She stood by them as they fought in the courts and fought in the media. They won some victories along the way. Residents forced Campbell Wells into a multi-million-dollar settlement and its plant was scaled back considerably. But some court rulings have gone against the locals and, when I met them, they were struggling to keep alive their legal action against Exxon. The company continues to maintain that the material it sent to Grand Bois was non-hazardous and could not have caused any health problems.

RJ and his neighbours did not believe this and they feared the worst was still to come. There has been a high incidence of certain cancers among young women and unexplained respiratory illness in some local children, and an independent study found warning signs of 'developing diseases'. Besides the health concerns, there was also anger at what the people of Grand Bois saw as the injustice of this case. They said the oil companies would never have dumped this waste in the heart of a white middle-class suburb, but it was acceptable when the community affected was a poor, rural blend of Indian and Cajun.

I heard real outrage when these people talked about the environment. Sit on the porch of that house in Grand Bois and you will hear about the days when RJ and his childhood friends trapped animals in the swamps and drank the clear water of the local rivers. Now, they say, their children have been denied those experiences. They blame pollution, they blame the waste facility and they blame Louisiana's lax environmental regulations. As I walked through the swamp with RJ, I heard the voice of a poor and isolated community struggling to challenge entrenched power and preserve the rough beauty of the bayou. They still have hope, and part of the reason for that is a Galway nun.

The people of Grand Bois will have no better friend than an Irishwoman called Miriam Mitchell, just as a desperate Caribbean nation will have no better friend than an Irishman called Larry Finnegan, and the down-trodden of Latin America will have no better friend than an Irishwoman called Sally O'Neill. In the reflected glory of these people, I find a pure sense of pride in my nation. With the rose-tinted glasses of the displaced Irishman, it seems to me their decency, courage and compassion are threads pulled from the rich fabric that is Ireland. I want to believe this because I want to believe that something fundamentally good defines us now, beneath the veneer of angst-ridden affluence. What truly matters to me about my homeland became clearer the longer and farther I travelled from its shores. It is in the hearts and minds of those homegrown heroes, as they toil away in the shadow of the volcano, in the receding floodwaters of the hurricane, and amid the animal chatter of the bayou.

# Seventeen

# Only Irish Need Apply

In June 1963, President John Fitzgerald Kennedy made a four-day visit to Ireland and became the first leader of a foreign state to deliver a joint address to the Dáil and Seanad. The speech was charming and somewhat patronising, with the president paying a tribute to the achievements of 'little five feet high' nations like Ireland. Still, the visit is remembered not for what was said but for what was seen. John F. Kennedy was the personification of the future and, for the first time since independence, the future had come to Ireland.

A black-and-white image from that visit figured prominently in my childhood. In the kitchen of our house my father proudly displayed a photograph of Kennedy crossing O'Connell Bridge in Dublin. The president is standing up on the passenger side of an open-topped limousine and behind him is a crowd of well-wishers, jammed together on the traffic island at the top of O'Connell Street. My father was in that crowd and he can identify himself from the photograph. He appears to be staring at the camera. Both my parents were at different locations on the streets of Dublin that day and they vividly recall the mood that this glamorous stranger brought to their city. For my mother and father, and many others of their generation, Kennedy was the living symbol of what lay beyond the horizon. He was Irish in the broadest sense, American in the most exhilarating sense, and in his tanned face was the promise that things would be different from now on. Yet to Kennedy, and the Irish-American dignitaries he brought with him, Ireland still signified the past; it was a country that looked remarkably like the place their ancestors had fled from. Like a devoted nephew with an ageing aunt, the president promised he would be back in the spring. By the end of the year he was dead.

Thirty-five years later, in September 1998, President Bill Clinton made his second visit to Ireland. Where Kennedy's historic journey was soaked in sentiment, the Clinton trip was remarkably practical. Ireland no longer needed a rich and charismatic relative, and Clinton sensed that. On the opening day of his visit, in the Waterfront Hall in Belfast, he hailed the Good Friday Agreement as a model for peacemakers around the world: 'The Gaelic term for America was Inis Fa'il, Island of Destiny. Today, Americans see you as Inis Fa'il and your destiny is peace. America is with you. The whole world is with you.' In Dublin the next day, Clinton met workers at the Gateway computer factory and declared them pioneers of the global economy. 'Ireland has assumed great responsibility,' he told the workers. 'May the nightmares stay gone, the dreams stay bright and the responsibility bear easily on your shoulder, because the future is yours.'

Ireland had become the place with no horizon, a country of limitless potential, a place you did not want to leave. But in the process, the connection between Ireland and the Irish in America had fractured. President Clinton now personified an ethnic identity that simply did not hold the same appeal for a younger generation. If this generation had a message for the visiting president it would have sounded something like this: 'We no longer need Irish-American success stories to give us hope. Not any more. This is no longer the "little five feet high" nation that JFK patronised. And while we're grateful for all the nice things you have said, we don't need a born-again Irish-American to tell us we are ten feet tall. We have seen the future, and it looks nothing like Irish America.'

Ironically, Clinton had come to Ireland in need of succour for his tortured soul. He was a damaged and potentially doomed politician; the continuing investigation of his relationship with Monica Lewinsky had placed a question mark over his future. His visit gave the Irish a chance to show public sympathy to a devoted friend, while cracking a million dirty jokes behind his back. Where my father and mother had looked to John F. Kennedy for a vision of the future, the next generation looked to Bill Clinton for juicy titbits about his past. 'Yeah, all that stuff about the Island of Destiny is lovely,' the rising generation said. 'But what we really want to know is: did you ride Monica?'

Those two visits by American presidents provide the opening and closing chapters of a remarkable story that we have all heard, but perhaps not fully understood. In the 35 years between my parents' encounter with Kennedy and my experience with Clinton, the relationship between Ireland and America has been turned on its head. With help from our rich Uncle Sam, we had sprinted from one era into the next, but the speed of our mad dash towards modernity had caused tensions within our extended family, leaving all of us slightly bewildered and disconnected. Today, when our American cousins come looking for their roots, they find it hard to see the family resemblance in the faces of the young people they meet, with all their swagger and self-belief. In turn, the successful Irish-Americans, who once provided an example to their backward homeland, look strangely outdated to those of us in the 'old country'. Yet beyond the discord and disconnection, there are deeper forces at play in the extended family. As we ponder the impact of radical change on our national psyche, we should think about getting reacquainted with our American cousins. We would be pleasantly surprised by the stories they have to tell.

While Ireland was charging towards the twenty-first century with all guns blazing, the Irish in America were enjoying a renaissance. Two key factors in this reawakening were the globalisation of Irish culture in the late 1990s and the positive energy unleashed by the peace process in Northern Ireland. But another vital component was the growing confidence of younger Irish-Americans, for whom identity did not begin with the maudlin sensibilities of the ethnic ghetto. These were the sons and daughters of the Irish-Americans who had moved from their safe enclaves in the big cities to the well-tended lawns of the suburbs and merged into the generic affluence of middle-class America.

Unlike recent waves of Latino, African and Asian immigrants, who had clear linguistic ties to their homeland, these Americans had no daily reminder of their roots. Besides, they had become a mongrel ethnic group. There were still families in which both parents had Irish names and talked not just of their ancestors' country of origin but their *county* of origin. However, there were many others who boasted that Irish was the most imposing branch of their family tree, even though their names were Cohen, Nielson or Parlante. At the end of the twentieth century, most young Americans who expressed their Irish heritage did so in terms of fractions.

In New York I worked with a sound technician called Sean who was half Irish, a quarter Mongolian and a quarter Polish. One Sunday morning in March 2000 we were covering the St Patrick's Day parade in Woodside in the New York borough of Queens. We had come to see Senate-hopeful Hillary Clinton march in a traditional Irish neighbourhood, but what we witnessed was a celebration of diversity on a scale neither of us expected. Near the front of the parade the Lesbian and Gay Big Apple Corps played tunes from Broadway musicals and cut a dash in crisp white uniforms adorned with a rainbow sash. A whole range of community groups followed, including the Korean Community Empowerment Association and staff of the Han Yang supermarket. Out of all the disparate groups that marched in that parade, the biggest single collection of people represented the Falun Gong spiritual movement. I watched all this in the company of my Israeli cameraman, Ya'ir, and an Irish-Mongolian-Polish-American called Sean. Neither saw anything particularly strange in that parade.

To young people like Sean, Irish-American was no longer simply an ethnic label passed down from a grandfather or grandmother; it had become a choice. Ireland's polished, modern image made it a far more positive option for an American young person seeking to define his or her place in the wider world. The explosion of interest in Irish Studies courses in American universities is a good indicator of that. Throughout my time in the United States, I met students who would embarrass me with the scope of their knowledge of all nuances of contemporary Ireland and expose my relative ignorance. Publications like the *Irish Voice* and the *Irish Echo* were fostering this new consciousness by promoting a self-confident and optimistic view of Ireland and Irish America. The increased popularity of Irish music and dance was another well-documented sign of the renaissance. It was not simply about the success of Ireland's cultural exports, but the accomplishment of Irish-American musicians like Eileen Ivers, Seamus Egan and Joanie Madden. Chris Byrne of New York band Black 47 put it this way: 'All these kids in my neighbourhood come up to me and they want to learn the tin whistle. It's like a watershed moment.'

In the slipstream of *Riverdance* was a spontaneous grassroots movement that provided a fresh alternative to the homogenous culture of the American suburbs. It brought dance, music and song that was familiar to the older Irish, but added an experimental touch that captured the imaginations of their sons and daughters. The Irish-American author Peter Quinn once joked that when he was growing up in the Bronx the kids who took the Irish dancing lessons were the ones who could not run faster than their parents. On my travels, I met the next generation of Irish kids and they were no longer running away. This is how Peter Quinn put it: 'A lot of Generation X kids are discovering their ethnicity and that it's not just white and boring and some kind of green sentimentality. It has an edge and authenticity.'

I was at America's biggest Irish festival in Milwaukee in August 1997. By late afternoon I was dying to get out. There was plenty of free beer but none of the bartenders would slow down long enough to pull a decent pint of Guinness. Every time I passed the main stage, there was another sad Irish comedian telling another mother-in-law joke. As I strolled towards the exit, I heard the opening bars of a song I liked called 'Tripping Billy' by The Dave Matthews Band. It's a catchy, fast-paced rock song but on that day in Milwaukee it was performed by a group led by two uilleann pipers. In front of them a group of dancers had moved to the centre of the stage and started a celebration.

The male dancers competed with each other as if they were staging some Celtic-rock version of *West Side Story*. As they duelled away at the front of the stage, the young women arranged themselves in a chorus line behind them, ready for the big finale. Their mile-wide grins and stunning good looks worked magic on the thousands of people in the audience. A group of thirty-somethings beside me had climbed up on a picnic table with their kids to get a better look. An elderly couple with matching T-shirts that read 'Himself' and 'Herself' were on their feet in the front row, clapping hands and jiving to a piece of music from their grandkids' generation. The rest of the crowd started to rise and cheer the dancers and the band. As I watched the suntanned faces and broad toothy smiles of those kids on stage, I could hear delighted squeals from a group of teenage girls in the front row. They were pumping the air as if they were at a Limp Bizkit concert. But it wasn't Limp Bizkit on stage that day. It was a group of Irish-American kids kicking aside the clichés and inventing their own private Irishness. An identity weighed down by 150 years of suffering and introspection had been reborn in the image of a hyperactive teenage girl.

There is always a danger of getting carried away by events like this. While there were invigorating moments like the one I experienced in Milwaukee, there was also considerable self-indulgent hype surrounding this renaissance. 'Perhaps the peculiarly Irish mix of boisterousness and melancholy, along with ineluctable music and rhythms, is well suited to the times,' wrote a *New York Times* reporter around the time of my visit to that Irish festival. The quack psychology was matched by the self-congratulation of affluent Irish-Americans who seemed anxious to cash in on the Irish boom. If I heard another establishment type tell another black tie charity event that 'Ireland is hot', I would have puked. For a couple of years at least, everyone wanted a piece of the Irish cultural boom in the United States. The fever first became apparent around the time Martin McDonagh's *Beauty Queen of Leenane* was taking Broadway by storm. It coincided with the runaway success of Thomas Cahill's *How the Irish Saved Civilisation* (which spent 67 weeks on the bestseller list) and it came in the midst of Michael Flatley's campaign for world domination, one stadium at a time.

The insatiable appetite for some piece of Ireland had a shallow, faddish aspect to it, despite the genuine undertow that was sweeping young Irish-Americans along. I also had my doubts about the new-found enthusiasm of some Americans for their Irish heritage. Older, conservative, white Americans were naturally drawn to a cultural movement that was European and expressed mainly through the English language. It was no accident that Irish culture reached the height of its popularity at a time when the United States was struggling with the most dramatic changes in its ethnic make-up in almost a century. By choosing to be Irish, white Americans get to retain some measure of definition and identity in a society that is increasingly influenced by non-European cultures. For example, Latin-American culture may soon become the single most powerful influence in American society, if only because of force of numbers. By late 2001, 35 million citizens of the United States were Hispanic, accounting for almost 13 per cent of the population. That's more than the total number of African-Americans, and almost as many as claim Irish ancestry. Those New York neighbourhoods that were traditionally Irish are now home to many new immigrant nationalities. In his office in Queens, local Congressman Joe Crowley told me that this Irish heartland had become 'the new Ellis Island'. Locals boast that more than a hundred languages are spoken by the children in the playgrounds of certain schools in Queens. To keep afloat on this rising tide of diversity, you must grab hold of a defined ethnic identity, even if you first have to rescue it from your family's distant past.

The increasing popularity of the Irish cultural identity has obscured some of the less wholesome realities of Irish America. While most Americans have a more discriminating view of Ireland and the Irish, the old clichés persist. Drinking and fighting were never too far from any conversation about the attributes of my nation. When Americans are describing a certain level of violence or anger, they often use 'Irish' phrases I have never heard of: 'Getting your Irish up' means becoming angry, which in turn could lead you to become involved in a 'Donnybrook', or a punch-up. I was mildly irritated by the reflex prejudice implied in the use of these phrases, but what really offended me was the amnesia of some members of the Irish-American establishment. Almost every week there was another ceremony honouring Irish-American achievement or celebrating the prosperity that swept the Irish from the ghettoes to the leafy suburbs. But you never heard a peep from the established groups about the ugly side of Irish America, the people and places that were not part of the official history.

One of the proudest ethnic neighbourhoods in the United States is South Boston. 'Southie' has a split personality that has been described beautifully by a young writer called Michael Patrick McDonald. He grew up in the Old Colony housing project during the 1970s and wrote a powerful memoir of his childhood called *All Souls*. McDonald describes the day his family moved to South Boston: 'My mother just kept smiling and waving at all our new neighbours. She pointed to all the shamrock graffiti and the IRA and "Irish Power" spray-painted everywhere, and said it looked just like Belfast and that we were in the best place in the world.'

Southie produced a string of political leaders who challenged Massachusetts' old liberal elite. William Bulger was arguably the dominant political character in Boston politics in the second half of the twentieth century, and he was intensely proud of the no-nonsense working-class values that defined South Boston, as he explained in his autobiography, *While the Music Lasts*: 'We washed our windows. We swept our sidewalks. We went to school and we went to church. Families were stable: a divorce was a whispered horror. We had our share of bars and bookies and sin, but the area then, as now, had the city's lowest rate of serious crime.' It was too good to be true. Bulger's idealised vision of South Boston ignored the death and decline that have ripped apart this Irish heartland.

In the summer of 1974, Southie's residents were accused of racism when they resisted the policy of 'bussing': the forced integration of white and black schools in Boston's poorest neighbourhoods. In the violent protests that followed, residents were portrayed as unreconstructed bigots. However in South Boston, the villains of the bussing saga were the rich, liberal elitists who blindly imposed an unworkable scheme on a tightly knit community. The result was Southie's further isolation from the rest of the world. In the years after the 'bussing' protests, South Boston began a slow, terminal decline. Gangsters like the infamous Whitey Bulger (William's brother) established a stranglehold over the neighbourhood, and drugs flooded the streets. By the early 1990s, Southie had the highest concentration of white poverty in America, and one of the highest rates of teen suicide. Of Michael Patrick McDonald's nine brothers and sisters, four died through crime and poverty. Yet friends and neighbours continued to ignore the sickness at the heart of Southie, deluding themselves into thinking that this was still the best place in the world: 'We were proud to be from here, as proud as we were to be Irish,' wrote McDonald. 'We didn't want to own the problems that took the lives of my brothers and of so many others like them: poverty, crime, drugs – these were black things that happened in the ghettoes of Roxbury.'

Self-delusion played a central role in the destruction of South Boston, but so did the disgust of outsiders. Southie was an embarrassment to the liberal elite and to many Irish-Americans who had successfully made the transition into the suburbs. As a result, the things that made South Boston a proud Irish outpost have largely been destroyed. Property developers have moved in to gentrify the nicer parts, while new waves of non-European migrants find themselves in the rundown housing estates of the Old Colony. IRA graffiti still greet visitors to the area, but the paintwork is faded and peeling. Like almost everything else in Southie, the slogans on the walls are just reminders of what used to be. Even Whitey Bulger is on the run.

Just as the more refined 'lace-curtain' Irish looked on Southie as an embarrassment, they also seem to have collective amnesia about other, less savoury aspects of their history. In the rags to riches version of Irish-American history, there seems to be no place for the persistent imperfections. You do not hear the assembled masses at those glittering dinners in New York's Waldorf Astoria talk of the racism that infected the Irish in the big cities during the great debate over the abolition of slavery. There's no mention of the shameful role of the Irish in the genocide of the American Indian. That is perhaps the omission that annoys me most, since the Irish were instrumental in the conquest of the Native Americans' nation. On my visit to Pine Ridge Indian Reservation in 1998, I made the mistake of telling a local community leader how the Irish had forged close bonds with the Choctaw Indian tribe during the Famine years (despite their own poverty, the Choctaws had sent money to the starving Irish). As we walked through a vast wheat field, the community leader stopped and pointed to a barbed wire fence. 'You see beyond that fence,' he said, 'That's Sheridan County, Nebraska.' I knew immediately what he was saying. General Philip H. Sheridan was one of the men who did most to subdue the Native Americans during the nineteenth century. He was also the source of the defining phrase of the Indian Wars: 'The only good Indians I ever saw were dead.' Philip Sheridan's parents had emigrated from County Cavan and now this county in the Nebraska panhandle was named after him. As I stood in that wheat field, I felt a moment of silent shame.

It would be wrong to argue that the Irish in America succeeded through the oppression of others, but there is a dark side to the Irish success story that many would rather forget. You can be certain that on all those lists of great Irish-Americans you won't find notorious criminals like 'Mad Dog' Coll, Owney Madden, Whitey Bulger, the Westies and all the other Irish gangsters who gave the Mafia a run for their money down the years. The Irish are quick to claim the progressive heroes of America's past like Mother Jones, Al Smith and Eugene McCarthy, but they would rather forget the blistering anti-Semitic rants of Father Charles Coughlin, the modern nativism of Pat Buchanan, or the viciousness of anti-Communist dema-gogue, Joe McCarthy (the Wisconsin senator's mother was born in Ireland).

The brutish element in Irish-American history is understandable; it was often a reflexive response to the poverty, desperation and intolerance that confronted the Irish down the years, but if there is to be a proper accounting of the virtues of the Irish in America, there must also be a proper accounting of their sins, because they both spring from the same source. When that accounting is complete, the celebration of this most recent Irish renaissance will have true meaning. Some discordant voices have pecked away at Irish America's cosy consensus. California politician and author Tom Hayden says the Irish have already forgotten the essence of their identity. 'We've made vaudeville Paddies of ourselves,' he wrote in a collection of essays called *Being Irish*. 'We've tried to wash off every trace of bog, even from our memory. We've done our best to ethnically cleanse our race.'

It is not that Irish-Americans refuse to talk about the poverty of the past. The problem is that suffering is cited in a self-serving way, to prove just how unique and successful the Irish really are. Make no mistake: the scale of the Irish odyssey in America can never be underestimated. Just over a century ago, the *Chicago Post* wrote: 'Scratch a convict or a pauper, and the chances are that you tickle the skin of an Irish Catholic.' Today, 100 of the 400 wealthiest people in the United States have Irish roots. Yet the Irish in America have elevated misery to a form of artistic expression. No Irish event is complete without a reminder of the sign that greeted many nineteenth- and early twentieth-century immigrants: 'No Irish need apply.' Of course, you don't have to go back that far to find the everlasting truth of the Irish experience, as expressed by the late Speaker of the House of Representatives, Tip O'Neill: 'To be Irish is to know you will suffer.'

Misery does not square well with the cheerful sophistication of the last few years. Not surprisingly, many Irish-Americans have a hard time dealing with the forces that have changed their homeland. As a result, it is particularly difficult for many Irish-Americans to like my generation of native Irish immigrants. Those who left Ireland for America in the 1980s and 1990s built up new businesses in old, established Irish neighbourhoods, and in the process created an element of tension. *Boston* magazine began a fascinating cover story in March 1998 with this introduction: 'The Boston Irish have long wallowed in their grand but miserable past. But now that their ancestral homeland is suddenly the hottest country in Europe a new pride of enterprising Celtic Tigers has three words for the locals: Get over it!' The article reported that some local Irish-Americans referred to the entrepreneurial blow-ins as FBIs: Foreign-Born Irish. 'You like to get the feeling that you are helping the little beggars at home,' said one Irish emigrant settled in Southie, 'but I think the whole image is shot when the little beggars come over and start buying up all your property.' Before I returned to live in Ireland, I read an amazing story in an Irish-American magazine about a new Hilton Hotel at Boston's Logan Airport. An Irish theme restaurant was to be installed and long-time Hilton employees were pushed out to make way for people with Irish accents. The unions cried foul, describing the move as discriminatory. In less than a century, Boston had moved from the era of 'No Irish need apply' to 'Only Irish need apply'.

When I arrived in the United States in 1995, I would have celebrated that kind of role reversal. I did not have a high opinion of Irish-Americans, believing that they had a false notion of Ireland and did more to hinder the native Irish than help. I still don't think Irish-Americans completely understand their ancestral homeland, but I no longer think that really matters. The point is that in the years between Kennedy and Clinton, Irish-America has been evolving in a way the Irish back home in Ireland have not fully understood. That evolution was helped along by the change in Ireland's image in recent years, but the change in the Irish consciousness in the United States has its own dynamic. Today there is a more discriminating generation of American's tinkering with the Irish identity in a way that could have a profound impact on our side of the Atlantic.

I think this revival is more than a fashion statement by a new generation. I believe it has deeper roots in American society than are at first apparent. I hope it is not hijacked by commercial interests, and turned into some new version of plastic paddywhackery. Most of all, I hope it forces Irish-Americans to look more closely at their history and account for their past failures, even as they celebrate their well-deserved success. Irish America is stronger and deeper than many in Ireland think it is. It is certainly worthy of far more respect than we have given it in the 35 years since John F. Kennedy showed us our future.

It is a respect that we need to express now more than ever. No one needs to be reminded that of the more than 300 firefighters killed in the World Trade Centre tragedy, a significant proportion were first-, second- and third-generation Irish. On second thoughts, maybe we do need to be reminded, because we seem to have allowed the black and white debate over American foreign policy to diminish how we felt in the days immediately after the horror. Here was an event that forced the Irish, in a state of unaccustomed peace and affluence, to look to their cousins across the Atlantic and find sincere words of sympathy that would dull the pain of an inexplicable act of barbarism, just as the mainstream of Irish America had worried about us in the time of the Troubles in Northern Ireland.

As I looked at the portraits of the dead in the Irish-American magazines in the weeks that followed, I was struck by how much they looked like us. They looked like us because, save for multiple accidents of history, they were us: brother, sister, neighbour, colleague. Brenda Power wrote a moving piece in the *World of Hibernia* shortly after September 11. She wrote to Americans about the pain the Irish were feeling, and how that mirrored the pain of our grandparents and great-grandparents mourning the loss of an emigrant loved one: 'We felt again the echo of their worries for you, their anxiety about your welfare, their dread that you might never come home again, fears that seemed, up to that Tuesday, to be safely consigned to distant days.'

September 11 is an entire chapter in the long saga of the Irish in America. It is also a reminder to those of us who forget the scale of that story, or let it be diminished by the knowing cynicism of recent decades. On September 11, the native Irish were forced to look again at the story of those who left us for America, and we were forced to look at that story without the filter of irony and material certainty. We should never forget what we saw in those days. It was both our future and our past and a reminder that you cannot have one without the other.

# Eighteen

## Another Last Hurrah

The longer I stayed in the United States, the more I was unsettled by those big Irish-American extravaganzas – the awards ceremonies and charity events – especially those which focussed on Northern Ireland. In lavish settings like the ballroom of the Plaza Hotel in New York or the National Building Museum in Washington, they did their bit for peace in Ireland, donned in black ties and fancy jewellery. Over the years, corporate America ploughed millions of dollars into fundraising dinners for worthy causes like Project Children. The dinners were never quite complete until a speaker had invoked the name of Senator George Mitchell, quoted an Irish writer, and thanked the invited guests for their pivotal role in the affairs of Northern Ireland. After years of nasty headlines about death and destruction, the North was now all about peace and poetry. It no longer revolved around dollar bills in collection boxes in seedy bars in Queens; it was now thousand dollar tables at the Waldorf Astoria. The days of illicit support for men in balaclavas was over; now it was time for evenings with Gerry Adams and W.B. Yeats. All changed, changed utterly: a terrible beauty is born.

The week before St Patrick's Day was always a whirlwind of self-indulgence for well-heeled American supporters of the peace process. The celebrations kicked off with the annual *Irish-America* magazine awards in New York and then moved to Washington for the American-Ireland Fund dinner, where a substantial cheque bought you proximity to an impressive range of political celebrities and reformed terrorists. Of course, the week was not complete without an invitation to the White House for a night of Paddy's Day entertainment with the president and the first lady. The annual St Patrick's Day party began as a relatively modest event in Clinton's first term in office, with only the most senior Irish and Irish-American public figures invited to dine in the East Room. But, by the beginning of the second term, the party had become an ethnic orgy where the Irish-American aristocracy and the North's political elite whooped it up like a conquering horde. One year, President Clinton left the party telling the crowd to drink the place dry and turn out the lights. The following year the invitation list had grown so long, they had to move the party to an enormous tent on the lawn of the White House.

March 2000 brought the last St Patrick's Day party of the Clinton era. The guest list had been pared down and the crowd was small enough to fit back into the White House residence. There was plenty of saccharine praise for the peacemakers and their American backers, but the prospect of losing the best friend Ireland had ever had in the White House added a bittersweet touch to the evening. Taoiseach Bertie Ahern advised the crowd in the East Room to make the most of the night: 'I have a feeling you might not see the like of it again.'

Of course there were the poets and writers. Nobel Prize winner Seamus Heaney was brought to the stage to read and pay tribute to Bill Clinton. Heaney's *The Cure at Troy* had made such an impression on the president that he had adapted a line from the play and used it for the title of his book, *Between Hope and History*.

Seamus Heaney spoke in lyrical terms about Bill Clinton that night in the White House, and when the president rose to speak, he seemed deeply affected by Heaney's praise. But he quickly dispensed with the greetings and gratitude and began to talk as if there were no more than a handful of people in the room. He wanted to tell us about Philoctetes, the tragic hero of *The Cure at Troy*, who is so eaten up with bitterness that he cannot find a way out of his torment on a lonely island. The president's monologue seemed lost on some members of the audience, those who had come for the drink, the photo opportunity and the bragging rights. Even the president's staff began to lose the plot as Clinton started to explain the role of Odysseus and Neoptolemus in this play. 'Where is he going with this?' whispered a former close aide.

Where he was going was towards an explanation of his involvement in the Irish peace process. It was a long-winded and intricate account, expressed through the words of a beautiful play. The tone and length of his address seemed out of place that night, and I could hear the half-pissed mutterings of a few philistines by the exit. But there was silence as the president drew it altogether. With his finger pointing into the crowd, he quoted from the final chorus of *The Cure at Troy*:

'It was a fortunate wind
That blew me here'

The crowd cheered and hollered as if the final whistle of a cup final had just blown. I looked over and saw one of the Unionist Party's few prominent supporters in Washington raise his hands above his head and applaud so hard it looked like he would bleed. I was left stunned by the construction of the president's closing words. He had crafted the end of that speech with such precision and skill that I was reminded once again what a brilliant politician he was. He had made everyone in that room feel personally touched by the same emotion, even though we had taken different meanings from his words.

Was the president suggesting that Northern Ireland's political leaders were Philoctetes, freed from their torment by an outsider? Was he that outsider, Neoptolemus? Or was Clinton the tormented anti-hero, freed from his need for revenge by the 'fortunate wind' of his one great foreign policy achievement, the Northern Ireland peace process? Maybe Clinton was saying all those things. What I know for certain was that by the time he spoke those words in the East Room of the White House, the search for peace in Ireland had eaten into his soul in a way that almost no other issue had. It summed up his political outlook and his personality, but then so did his efforts to turn this foreign adventure into a myth of epic proportions.

During those last months in office, Clinton worked hard to write the first draft of the history of his presidency. He wanted to have that draft placed firmly in the minds of the people before his critics had had a chance to define his legacy. He launched a farewell tour and played to capacity crowds at fundraisers and rallies, delighting his audience with his greatest hits: the longest economic expansion in American history, falling unemployment, rising wages, urban renewal, budget surpluses and stable inflation. Somewhere in all this, Clinton sometimes reserved a little patter for his achievements abroad, a little patter that almost always involved Ireland. In his speech to the Democratic Party convention in August 2000, the president put peace in Northern Ireland at the top of the list of his foreign policy successes. Over a six-week period that final summer, Bill

Clinton talked about Northern Ireland at least eight times in various public settings. After the collapse of the Middle-East peace talks at Camp David in July, he delivered a pep talk to Jewish groups and advised them to look at Northern Ireland as an example of what could be achieved. 'It's a little, bitty place,' he told his audience. 'Smaller even than Israel.'

The president delivered one of his most revealing speeches on a warm and sticky night in Washington in late June. Irish-American Democrats had gathered in a hotel ballroom near the White House for their annual awards ceremony. There was a lot of talk that night about the 'risks' Bill Clinton had taken for peace in Ireland, and some of it came from Bill Clinton himself. 'I took a lot of flak for getting involved in the peace process,' he told the crowd. 'None of the elitists really thought I ought to do it but all us blue collar rednecks thought it was a pretty good idea.' Until that night, Bill Clinton had never explicitly endorsed the conventional wisdom that he had risked it all in an effort to bring peace to Ireland. That night in Washington, with the applause of the Irish-American Democrats ringing in his ears, he suggested that the conventional wisdom was true. But on his farewell tour, he also unwittingly drew attention to the flaws in the myth.

When Clinton allowed Sinn Féin leader Gerry Adams to visit the United States in January 1994, he enraged the British government and alienated some of his most senior advisers. It was a bold move, but a bold move taken by a politician who realised he could make a difference in Northern Ireland without exposing himself to any great risk at home. The Anglo–American relationship was heavily weighted in Washington's favour, so the British could never apply any meaningful sanction against the Clinton administration, except the political equivalent of a dirty look. Clinton's disapproving senior advisers could at worst turn up their noses if the president's decision resulted in no IRA ceasefire. There was certainly no risk in electoral terms. Northern Ireland was not Somalia, Haiti or Kosovo. American troops would never have to keep the peace by force of arms, and there was never a chance of body-bags being shipped back to grieving relatives in the United States. What was the worst that could have happened? The process might have collapsed and there would be a few sniffy editorials in the foreign policy journals and the odd 'I told you so' from some anglophile Republicans. But how many voters would actually blame the president for trying?

In the epic version of the Clinton story, the president is persuaded of the justice of the cause of peace in Ireland by that 'fortunate wind'. In reality, it required a lot of persuasion by mere mortals to get Bill Clinton on board in the early days. It took pressure from Irish-Americans to extract an initial verbal commitment from Clinton when he was still a presidential candidate, and it took considerable prodding from a cast of characters before the newly elected president seriously considered playing a central role in the process. Those who helped the White House negotiate the complexities of Northern Ireland say there were times when the president came close to backing out. One well-placed insider told me that if the peace process had collapsed in the early days, 'Clinton would have dropped it so quick, it would have made your head spin.' But ultimately he stayed the course and he did so because of many of the personal characteristics that inspired, disgusted and amazed a legion of Clinton-watchers.

You do not have to be a psychologist to know this is a man who really needs to be loved. He depends on the adoration of a crowd like others depend on oxygen.

During his first trip to Ireland in 1995 his desires were satisfied in a manner that would make him look at the peace process in a completely different way. The moment he stepped on the stage in front of Belfast City Hall the process was transformed from an intellectual challenge into a personal crusade. During a confessional interview before an audience of religious ministers in July 2000, Clinton was asked about the most memorable moments of his presidency. One of them was 'to walk down the Shankill and the Falls, the Protestant and the Catholic neighbourhoods, and see them there together, all these young people cheering for peace ... because they thought America stood for peace.' Of course, the point was that they were also cheering for Bill Clinton.

The president also needed to find some successful example of the correct use of American influence in the world, and he found it in Northern Ireland. Whether you were a Serb militia leader in Bosnia, or a senior official of the Palestinian Authority, you heard about the details of the Good Friday Agreement from the world's most powerful politician. 'I think the significance around the world is huge,' Clinton told me in December 1999, just after he had met all the main protagonists in the conflict in Kosovo. 'Their wounds are much fresher, and of greater magnitude, and I could talk to them about the Irish peace process. I could look them in the eye and say, you know, you can do this too. Sooner or later, you're going to have to do it.'

At times Clinton seemed to get carried away by the poetry of his Irish odyssey. 'Yeats was right when he said glory begins and ends in our friends,' Clinton declared at the American-Ireland Fund dinner. 'I can say truly and simply I tried to be a friend ... but good friends tell each other the truth; the loving truth.' Clinton got away with the seductive psychobabble because you always had the feeling that he really believed it, on some level. 'Any Irish person with any sense knows that the only things that count in life are affairs of the heart,' he declared at that reception to honour Irish-American senator Chris Dodd. 'If you're blessed by God with a pretty good mind, it's only supposed to be used to have a better understanding of the human heart and what counts.'

Sometimes with Clinton the heart gets the better of the brain. He began his presidency with no understanding of his Irish roots and yet, as he opened his farewell tour, he could not stop talking about them. At that last St Patrick's Day party in the White House, he joked that he was 'one of the few Americans who knows all the words to the second verse of 'Danny Boy'.' Four months later, he referred to himself as an 'apostate Irish Protestant'. He had become more Irish than the Irish themselves.

As the president came to the end of his farewell tour, Irish-Americans who really cared about the peace process took a long, hard look at the prospect of life without this 'apostate Irishman'. It was not a pretty sight. I had grown to respect the small number of people who really shaped the president's involvement in the peace process. And it was a small number. Nothing happened of any substance unless Senators Ted Kennedy and Chris Dodd signed off on it. In the House of Representatives, there were just a handful of congressmen driving policy towards Northern Ireland: Pete King, Richie Neal, Joe Crowley, Jim Walsh, Ben Gilman and Chris Smith. Then there were the skilled tacticians outside Congress: *Irish Voice* publisher Niall O'Dowd, Ted Kennedy's adviser Trina Vargo, and former congressman and Clinton friend Bruce Morrison. There were a few others, but they were outnumbered by the legions of Irish-Americans who took far more credit than they deserved. I sometimes stood at those big Irish-American events and looked at the people who mattered and wondered what they were thinking as the socialites and corporate Paddies patted themselves on the back. If they were sickened by that spectacle, they did not admit it. They were already focussed on the next battle: winning over President George W. Bush.

On 17 March 2001, President Bush held a decidedly low-key St Patrick's Day celebration at the White House. He said, 'It is in our national interest that there be a lasting peace, a real lasting peace, in Northern Ireland.' That statement, and the engagement of a senior State Department official, Richard Haas, was enough to calm the rumbling of discontent from Irish America, but it did not change the fundamental reality: the White House was not going to follow Bill Clinton on that epic Irish journey. If there were any doubts about that, they were dispelled in the wake of the terrorist attacks of September 11.

A week after the horror of the World Trade Centre, I bumped into a senior congressional adviser at a reception at the Irish Ambassador's residence in Washington. For years, he had been a strident critic of British policy in Northern Ireland, and I would have regarded him as one of Sinn Féin's most influential friends in Washington. But something fundamental had changed in a very short period of time. We started to talk about the arrest of three suspected IRA members in Colombia the month before. I expected him to rubbish the media coverage, which focused on the alleged links between the Republican movement and the Colombian rebel group, FARC. Instead, he removed a set of photographs from a brown envelope and gave them to me. They showed the aftermath of FARC attacks on police stations in Colombia: the charred bodies, the funerals and the grieving families. 'This is what it's all about now,' he said. 'When the IRA got involved with the people who did this, they crossed the line. For the first time, they are a threat to America's national interests.' This man had gone from one end of the political spectrum to the other in a matter of weeks, and a lot of senior Republican politicians in Washington had made the same journey. For all Americans, after the horror of September 11, the world had split in two: the civilised world and the world of terrorism. One world was led by the United States and the other was led by Osama bin Laden. It looked like the IRA was living in the wrong world. It was simplistic, but there was no room for nuance after the World Trade Centre; there was only black and white. With us or against us, the American people said. It seemed the IRA was against them.

In a broader sense, the entire peace process had been tainted. The poetry had disappeared and Northern Ireland was just another bad news story. Where once there was understanding of nuances, like decommissioning and police reform, now there was simply impatience. American policy on Northern Ireland could be about only one thing after September 11: ending terrorism forever. As long as there was any doubt about a permanent peace, there would be no more St Patrick's Day parties at the White House and no more cheering crowds in fancy New York hotels.

There were still people in the United States who cared about Ireland, but in the aftermath of September 11, they seemed increasingly lonely. Part of the problem is that even after years of heightened US involvement in Northern Ireland, there is still no well-developed Irish lobby group in Washington. There are six million Jews in the United States represented by a powerful lobby group with an annual budget in excess of ten million dollars. There are 44 million Irish-Americans without a national, broad-based pressure group in the American capital. A relatively new organisation called the US–Ireland Alliance has been established by Trina Vargo, but it's still in its infancy. Even Vargo warns that the special relationship enjoyed by Ireland during the Clinton era is over, and Irish politicians and Irish-Americans will have to fight hard to establish some new common ground with the Bush Administration. 'There is a vacuum in Irish America,' she observed after Clinton's departure. 'Irish America and Ireland must develop a dynamic new relationship which is broader than the narrow ground of Northern Ireland.'

It seems to me that Irish-Americans understand the dangers inherent in this new environment better than the people of Ireland. Never in history did the Irish enjoy such influence in the capital of the world's most powerful state as they did in the Clinton era. The White House driveway became a tourist trail for Irish political leaders. Politicians who would not have had enough votes to win a seat on Washington's city council got more access to the leader of the free world than the heads of state of most NATO countries. Former Tanaiste and Minister for Foreign Affairs Dick Spring said his EU counterparts were 'dumbfounded' that he had met Clinton eight times: 'I remember meeting the Dutch Minister in Brussels … and he asked how we managed to meet Clinton so often because he had been told he would have to wait six months before the president would be available.' Dick Spring understood this was a moment that would never come again. I am not so sure if all the Irish politicians who trooped up the White House driveway realised that.

I felt the end of the Clinton era provoked a surprising degree of indifference back home. It is possible that the impact of the American role in the Northern Ireland peace process had been exaggerated to some extent, but I wondered how much of this indifference was a reflection of a broader complacency about the permanence of the peace process. When I was growing up, if you needed to underline just how horrible the conflict in Northern Ireland had become, you would say: 'A generation has known nothing but violence.' Now there's a rising generation that has known nothing but relative peace. Kids that were twelve years old when the IRA declared its first cease-fire are now adults. There is still low-level paramilitary violence and there are ugly sectarian flare-ups, but for an awful lot of young people in Northern Ireland this is background noise in a society gorging itself on the economic and social rewards of years of restraint.

Just after the millennium celebrations, I travelled to Lurgan where my daughter, Sorcha, was staying with her grandparents. We went for a long walk, passing a mainly Nationalist estate on the edge of town. I looked over at a gable wall and read a piece of graffiti. It no longer posed a threat, but raised a question: 'If we give up our arms, how will we tie our shoelaces?' We walked into town, past the RUC station and up towards the Ashburn Hotel. As I got to the door of the hotel, I looked across the street and recognised the building opposite. In the summer of 1994, it had been a printing press and I had stood outside the building, interviewing witnesses to the murder of two young Catholic workmen, shot dead by Loyalist paramilitaries. Now, years later, I stood looking at the same building with my ten-year-old daughter. The building had been turned into a trendy bar. I could have bought a designer beer near the spot where those young men were murdered.

I sensed the complacency the following year on President Clinton's last visit to Belfast. In 1995 Clinton was the peacemaker with the Midas touch, but in 2000 he was simply a celebrity guest. The president's keynote speech was delivered in the Odyssey Hall, a huge new £100 million sports arena along the Belfast riverfront. It was surrounded by other new building developments that had not been there on my last visit to Belfast. The arena was home to the Belfast Giants, a team of hockey players with a truly non-sectarian following. The day Clinton spoke, thousands of schoolchildren had packed the arena. Looking around the hall, I wondered how many of those kids, with their Mexican waves and piercing screams, really understood why Clinton was there. I reckoned the hockey players in the audience behind the president had more relevance to their lives. For his part, Clinton delivered a warning to a generation growing up in a Northern Ireland defined by relative peace. 'No one can afford to sit on the sidelines,' he said in his speech. 'Remember, the enemies of peace don't require your approval. All they need is your apathy.'

As soon as President Clinton finished his address to the young people in the Odyssey Hall, I climbed into a clapped-out Ulsterbus coach at the back of the presidential motorcade. It was the beginning of a special journey, a favour from a friend in the White House press office. I was on my way to Aldergrove Airport where I would climb on board one of the most potent symbols of imperial power of the American presidency, Air Force One. On the drive out of Belfast, I listened as an RUC escort passed on his prejudices to the Air Force One press pool. He assumed we were all American, so when he was asked about the Republic of Ireland, he did not hold back: 'They are all thick, and I mean thick. And if you go down south, you will find potholes everywhere.' The more things change, the more they stay the same.

Within minutes the motorcade passed through the gates of the airport. The small army that travels with the president moved with military precision, hustling the contents of the presidential motorcade into the silver belly of the aeroplane. The whole process took a matter of minutes. The 'pool' of reporters assigned to trail the president was directed to a plush but cramped cabin at the back of the plane. Right in front of us, the Secret Service detachment settled in for the hour's flight to Heathrow, briefly dispensing with their trench-coats and jackets, but not their ear-pieces or side arms. Farther up the plane, senior staff members settled into bigger seats in bigger cabins, and right at the top of the plane, in an expansive suite of offices and private rooms, was the president of the United States. Seasoned travellers on Air Force One ignored the seatbelt signs and stood around chatting as the jet climbed steeply into the sky over Belfast.

For them, it was just another city, a footnote in the long and gruelling saga that comprised the Clinton years. But for me, the lights of the city had far more significance. I started my tour of duty as Washington correspondent with a flight into Belfast on President Clinton's first trip to Ireland in 1995. Five years later, I was finishing my posting with a flight out of Belfast on Air Force One. Something else occurred to me as the plane banked over Belfast Lough: it was the third time Air Force One and all those other presidential symbols had swept through Ireland, leaving lasting memories and a soothing dose of American sympathy. Witnessing those visits was an education in the correct application of the might of the world's last remaining superpower.

Bill Clinton had spent the past eight years travelling the world, touching the lives of people from West Africa to West Belfast with the reflected glory of the American presidency. That glory can be used for overwhelming good, as it has been on three occasions in Ireland, or it can inspire fear and loathing. From Vietnam to Chile to El Salvador, the global reach of the United States has been associated with the forces of oppression. During the Cold War, those presidential symbols were impossible to separate from the delicate balance between world order and global destruction. Yet those symbols are nothing but empty vessels until they are filled with the personality and philosophy of the person who occupies the presidency. The night I flew on Air Force One was the night the Florida recount came to an end and George W. Bush was declared president elect. As Air Force One approached the runway at Heathrow, I wondered how he would apply these symbols of power? What message would he bring on that great big jumbo jet? Would things really be that different? And was this where Northern Ireland and the White House parted company, on the runway at Heathrow?

In 1963, when Kennedy died, Daniel Patrick Moynihan wrote of the passing of an era for the Irish in America: 'It was the last hurrah. He, the youngest and newest, served in a final moment of ascendancy.' Clinton had tried to construct a Camelot-type mythology around his involvement in the peace process. The myth did not quite live up to the reality, but what Clinton did prove during his years of peacemaking was the potential for good that was invested in the symbols of American democracy. That night, when George W. Bush officially became Clinton's successor, a unique chapter in Irish history came to an end.

It was the end of a chapter in my life as well, so I was determined to enjoy every last moment of this journey. I walked down the stairs at the rear of Air Force One and turned to look back along the length of the plane. I looked up towards the president's quarters and caught a brief glimpse of activity before the blinds were pulled down. Inside, Bill Clinton was on the phone to Washington, where Democrats were trying to come to terms with the news that their presidential candidate, Al Gore, was about to concede defeat. I stood on the runway wondering how Clinton was feeling. He had grown apart from his vice president during the election campaign, but Gore's election would have been a symbolic popular endorsement of the Clinton legacy. As Air Force One sat parked on a runway at Heathrow, the Clinton era came to an end.

I turned away from the giant plane just in time to see a White House press officer approaching the press pool. 'OK pool, Nighthawk Four,' she called out above the noise of engines. We ran in single file towards the last in a line of Chinook helicopters. It was Nighthawk Four. Inside the aircraft, we put on the headphones and waited to begin the short journey to the British prime minister's residence at Chequers. I craned my neck to look out of the small window beside me. As we climbed into the darkness, I looked down at Air Force One and marvelled at the glorious finality of this moment. We flew higher and Air Force One began to look like a toy plane, not the imposing presence it had been a few minutes before. The fortunate wind that had helped foster a peace process had stopped blowing, and my journey was at an end.

# Nineteen

## E Pluribus Unum

My friends Bill Owens and Helena Fernandez finally got married in Seville in August 2000. It was less than five years since their first meeting in a bar in Madrid at the end of President Clinton's visit to Ireland and Spain. I was honoured to be part of the wedding party that gathered in front of the altar at the Iglesia de San Jorge, the stunning seventeenth-century centrepiece of Seville's Hospital de la Caridad. The men sat, in heavy woollen evening suits and waistcoats, on a narrow wooden bench by the altar. We struggled with the evening heat, but were thrilled to be witnesses to something so joyous, and so foreign to our lives in the United States.

The chapel was built by Don Miguel de Marane, the man who inspired the legend of Don Juan. It was penance for his wild ways, which he allegedly abandoned after he stumbled out of an orgy into a funeral procession that he was told was his own. During the wedding, I found myself playing the role of an American abroad, consuming the lush spectacle of a culture previously experienced through the clichés of a guidebook. After five years in Washington, my outlook was that of my American friends. I looked at the world through their eyes now, and during that weekend in Seville I took a crash course in Europe for beginners.

The wedding reception was held at a horse ranch in the Andalucian countryside and the last guests were dragged off the open-air dancefloor at 6.30 in the morning. After a few hours sleep, we all met up at the Plaza de Toros in Seville, where I watched my first bullfight. We had not prepared ourselves properly for the prospect of seeing an animal killed for our entertainment. One matador brought a bull within a few feet of our seats to deliver the *coup de grace*. I watched his face grow taut as he pulled the long silver blade level with his eyes and then made a final dash towards the animal. The sword disappeared behind the bull's shoulder blades and, within seconds, his legs buckled and his big black form crumpled into a lifeless heap. This was killing elevated to black art, and I was equally repelled and captivated by its malevolence.

We were all a bit shell-shocked as we made our way through the narrow streets of Seville's Old City to La Carboneria, a club established during the Franco era to promote artists and musicians banned by the government. For the second time in a matter of hours, we sat transfixed by the noise and the intensity of something entirely foreign to us. The flamenco dancer, her male partner and their guitarist pumped out a rhythm on the wooden stage that made our table tremble and my spine shiver. It was as beautiful as the bullfight had been barbaric, but the emotions it unleashed were just as elemental.

That weekend in Seville left me deeply unsettled. I was not prepared for how American my view of something so European would be. I was also surprised by how much I missed the raw attractions of life outside the United States. I had learned to love the grand spectacle of American life: the poetry of baseball at Yankee Stadium, the sense of history at a presidential inauguration and the pure patriotic joy of the Fourth of July celebrations. All these things remained deeply attractive to me, but after that trip to Seville I knew the time had come to choose. I had become more American than I would dare admit, but I still struggled with the loss of something I could not define. During that trip to Seville I looked in a mirror and, behind the contentment, there was a shadow.

Young Americans will be the first ones to tell you there are aspects of European culture of which they are jealous. The pace of daily life in the United States leaves little room for spontaneous charm, flair and non-conformity; that kind of thing is for the weekend. A foreigner seeking to make a life in the United States will begin to confront this uncomfortable reality just as they begin to prosper. Russian immigrants in Brooklyn began a fascinating debate in their local paper, the *Russian Bazaar*, in the summer of 2000. In a series of articles entitled 'Why they are leaving?', a former school principal who had moved from St Petersburg to New York bemoaned the lack of *Dukhovnost*, a spiritual dimension to life. 'When we were struggling to survive, we didn't think about this,' he said. 'But when we finally staggered to our feet, we started to look for America's *Dukhovnost* and we just couldn't find it.'

In Seville, I found a European *Dukhovnost*. I was back in a place where life is lived beyond the literal meaning; you look for beauty in colour, but also in shade; the joke is in the punchline, but also in the telling; passion is better than lust; happy endings do not always make the best stories; the meaning is in the silences as well as in the words. In the United States, what you see is what you get. By comparison, Europe has nuance, irony, and subtlety. In all of this is *Dukhovnost*.

After the trip to Seville, I began to feel more detached from my life in America. On my regular trips home to

Ireland, I was seeing the emergence of a new spirit, expressed in material and spiritual ways. The physical transformation of Dublin was mind-boggling. There was a slick vulgarity to the new hotels and apartment buildings, but there was also a refreshing eclectic sensibility about the city. Street life no longer had a shabby mid-Atlantic feel to it. The range of possibilities had expanded south and east; new shades, tastes and sounds had been introduced and embraced, and they were predominantly European, with a dash of Asian and African. There was an embryonic *Dukhovnost* in the city, unlike anything I had known in my youth. When I was growing up, I remember Dublin as a distinctly provincial place, but the years had washed away the bleakness. The last decade of the twentieth century brought my smug and confident generation home to harness the boomtown euphoria and encourage the growing demand for a cultural experience that was broader and more diverse than the pre-boom Ireland could support. The results were confusing, and all the better for that confusion. Japanese noodles, gourmet coffee, Samba, feng shui, focaccia and lap-dancing; you could be disgusted and inspired by what the traditionally finicky Irish palate was now savouring, but you could not be unmoved.

There was an emerging multicultural feel to my hometown that was inspiring, at least at first glance. I read with great pleasure that the first baby born in Ireland on New Year's Day 2001 was delivered to a Nigerian woman just a week after she had arrived in Ireland. The mother named the baby Nicole Ejomafuvwe, the second name meaning 'let me have peace'. The *Irish Independent* reported: 'In honour of her new homeland, the midwife who delivered her gave her an Irish name, Seamusina.' Everywhere I shopped, ate or drank, there were new faces, accents and nationalities with a distinctly non-Irish attitude to the concept of service. A couple of days into the New Year, I was in a Dublin pub having a drink with Tara. An Asian lounge girl served me a dark and delicious pint of Guinness. She had a shaky command of English, but a broad, infectious smile. As we were leaving, the same young woman was standing in the doorway of the pub with her hands lifted up in the air. It had started to snow and she was catching what were perhaps the first snowflakes she had seen in her life. At that moment, I could think of nowhere else in the world I wanted to be, or any other time in Irish history in which I wanted to live.

In January 2001, I said goodbye to Washington and moved back to Dublin for good. I had wedded my future to Ireland and was intent on enjoying the honeymoon, despite the warning signs ahead. I had heard so much about the dark side of Ireland's boom that I was prepared for the worst. Eventually, the constant whining about house prices and traffic was more distressing than the realities described. In my eyes, the traffic problems in Dublin paled into insignificance against cities like London and New York, and the rise in house prices was stunning but ultimately logical. The vitality of my surroundings allowed me to see the glass half-full, and not half-empty, although as time wore on, the glass started to drain. After a long exposure to life in the United States, there were things I discovered about the Irish psyche that began to make me question my optimism.

In his poem 'The Death of Irish', Aidan Matthews says there are 31 words for seaweed in the Irish language. That may be so, but I bet there is nothing in the Irish language that conveys the concept of personal space. When I returned home, I was confronted by a fundamental lack of awareness of the need to adjust behaviour in response to the physical proximity of another person: what political scientists call 'Partisan Mutual Adjustment'. As we charge towards each other in the supermarket aisle, or jostle in the queue for coffee, we assume there are no rules to be observed, no inviolate space for each individual, and because this is true, no one ever has the right to be surprised or offended. I have thought of getting a T-shirt printed expressing this principle: 'Weren't you the effin eejit for getting in my way.' Whenever I mention this to friends, I get raised eyebrows and comments that involve the word 'neurotic'. I take the point. While this is not, by itself, worth getting terribly excited about, it does suggest to me there is a wider problem with how we relate to the rest of the world.

From birth, all Irish people are taught that they have a natural flair for sincere friendship. We are convinced that because we protect ourselves from insincerity with thick layers of irony, we are genetically predisposed to having more meaningful relationships. We look at the Americans and laugh when we hear them saying, 'Have a nice day.' In Ireland, you know you have a friend when you can insult them and they can insult you back without offence being caused to either party. Yet we have failed to understand that most Americans really mean it when they tell you to 'have a nice day', while Irish friends are often *not* being ironic when they tell you: 'You are only an old bollocks anyway.'

For months after my return I was very sensitive about my accent, which had undoubtedly picked up an American twang in the years I had spent there. I would listen politely as people told me how unsuited the raised inflections and American aphorisms were to Irish ears. I wondered if the same people were aware of just how much their accents, and the accents of people around them, had changed in recent years. I have stood in hotel bars in Dublin, closed my eyes, and been transported back to the Whiskey Bar on Lexington Avenue in Manhattan. The developing Hiberno-American accent has expanded far beyond its original Southside Dublin origins, and become so polluted with false animation and jaunty inflection that it is simply a variation of the well-heeled chatter of any number of US cities. Most Irish people do not recognise this accent when they hear it because when they think of an American accent they think of Southern White Trash: 'You sure got a purty mouth' or Brooklyn Mafia: 'You tawkin to me?' Yet the mainstream middle-class accent in the United States is far less distinct and increasingly mobile, and it is playing in a town near you.

Maybe we understate the impact of American infl-uences because we have such heightened sensitivity to perceived American excess. While it is true that we have handled the quickening pace of life in a very Irish way (the 70 per cent increase in spending on alcohol in Ireland during the 1990s is testament to that), we are now prone to what were once regarded as purely American vices. We mock the obesity of our American cousins, while at the same time we stuff increasing amounts of fast and processed food into our groaning bodies. More than half the adult population of Ireland is overweight, and in 2001 more than 20 per cent of men were obese (ten years ago, the figure was eight per cent). Being fat is no longer a frailty: it has become a lifestyle choice, just as it is in the United States.

Maybe we are due a little pampering. After spending so much time in the shadow of others, enduring disdain in foreign countries, we are masters of a universe in which a new class of dependants looks to us for example. I was struck by a comment I read from an Irish businessman in the *Boston Globe* in June 1999: 'Go into any Dublin bar and most likely you will be served by a German or French kid. The Irish are moving up the value chain.' Immigrants are welcome to do the jobs we feel we have risen above, but the welcome is conditional: the new arrivals must accept our values and culture without question, or face isolation and suspicion. We celebrate what the Irish gained from their immersion in America's multicultural mix, but we have no intention of following the US example: we will not let our culture be changed forever by immigration. It's as though our history of subjugation and struggle relieves us of the burden to change.

I do not believe the Irish are a nation of racists. I believe we are close to resolving the broader, intellectual challenge posed by immigration, even while we still grapple with the vexed legal issues regarding asylum seekers and refugees. It is on this broader level that the United States could teach us a lesson. While we might have scoffed at the outpouring of national pride that followed the terrorist attacks on Washington and New York, I think many in Ireland understand the purpose it served. Patriotism can be used to blind citizens to injustice or flawed policies, but it can also be used to promote a deeper understanding of what makes a society work. American patriotism is the appreciation of the fundamental shared certainties that keep the United States intact and healthy, and the most fundamental principle is that anyone can become an American. *E Pluribus Unum* is how they sum it up on the face of their coins: 'Out of many we are one.'

In contrast, Ireland has traditionally been defined by nationalism, not patriotism, and so we have united on the basis of what makes us unique, what separates us from the rest of the world. You cannot simply choose to be Irish; you either are or you are not. The pure clinical framework of nationalism left us unprepared for the evolution of our nation, and yet I detect a real change. Among my daughter's generation, there is no compulsion to live down any historical inferiority or live up to some narrow definition of Irishness. Instead, these pre-teens see their national identity as a broad and inclusive concept. They have to. How else could they explain the increasing number of classmates and friends with different skin tones and exotic names? How could they feel pride every time footballer Clinton Morrison pulls on the green jersey or Samantha Mumba scales the British charts? If I am right, what the next generation will pass on to their children is a patriotism capable of reconciling the changes in our culture that immigration brings, with the enduring traits that define our identity.

Just as we will have to redefine Irishness in a new domestic setting, we will also have to try and resolve some of the mixed messages we are sending to the rest of the world. In the era of globalisation, 'Ireland' has become a corporate brand that is exploited on a worldwide scale. A week before St Patrick's Day in 2001, I stood at a corner on Omatesando, one of Tokyo's smartest shopping streets, watching eight Japanese men dressed as ninjas carrying a huge inflatable pint of Guinness. A month later, I sat in the Irish Village pub in Dubai Airport, sipping an almost perfect pint and eating shepherd's pie under an authentic currach. The following week, I drank whiskey in front of a Guinness poster in the United Nations club in the Afghan capital, Kabul. On a recent trip to the United States, I found rival brewers pitching rival 'Irish' beers to the American people. Anheuscher Busch sells Killarney's Red while Coors sells Killian's Red. Both are promoted as Irish; both are brewed in the United States.

Ireland is among globalisation's winners but, all too often, foreigners are presented with contradictory images of this country. The Irish brand is pitched to the lowest common denominator of globalised tastes, while at the same time it is sold as the next new thing. We may still be getting pissed and writing poetry, but we are also learning Japanese and designing software. And the wider world is picking up on these mixed messages. In 2001, the *Irish Times* received a letter from Dutch tourist J.M. Bobak in which he described an Aer Lingus flight from Amsterdam to Dublin: 'During the hour we had to wait for take-off, we were treated to "Rudolph the Red-Nosed Reindeer" and other American Christmassy gems, all in Hollywood arrangements, played over and over again at a solid forte. Aer Lingus parades W.B. Yeats, but gives us Walt Disney. It hints at leprechauns in the glen, but gives us Rudolph. May I suggest this is not what people have in mind when they head for Ireland.'

As a nation we are increasingly aware of how brands are monopolising public life, although it is harder to appreciate the extent to which Ireland's image abroad has been simplified rather than modernised. We may eventually rid ourselves of the 'potato-sucking moron' label but we may end up putting an equally meaningless image in its place. In the words of a US consular information sheet: 'Ireland is a highly developed democracy with a modern economy. Automated teller machines (ATMs) are widely available.'

Ireland's identity crisis has been sparked by affluence. Ireland's economic good fortune has changed who we are, and transformed the way we live our lives. Of course, the nature of the change depends on where you live. If you live in the city, your life has become increasingly complicated; if you live in the suburbs, you face heightened conformity. In the cities, the influences are more diverse but the farther you move out on the motorways the more things become generic in a truly American fashion. Many of us no longer have to go from suburb to town, and in this we are most certainly like the

Americans. 'Our lives are increasingly traced in large suburban triangles,' writes Robert Putnam in his study of the decline of civic involvement in the United States: 'At the beginning of the twenty-first century more and more of us commute from one suburb to another, more and more of our shopping is done in a mega-mall in a third suburb.' Putnam tried to quantify the social cost of the constant travel that life in the suburban triangle requires: 'In round numbers, the evidence suggests that each additional ten minutes in daily commuting time cuts involvement in community affairs by ten per cent.'

As Irish suburbs take on American proportions, the blandness of urban sprawl is beginning to shape the political consciousness. When the mock-period housing estates look the same, the shopping experience is the same, the cars are the same, the incomes are broadly the same and the accent is becoming the same, the emergence of a similar outlook on politics seems inevitable. The generic political philosophy of the American suburbs has made the journey across the 'common ground'.

There may be some very Irish reasons why Irish politics is increasingly consensual and soulless. The future of Northern Ireland, attitudes to church and state, and the pace of social change have traditionally been the engine of conflict in Irish politics, but these grand issues no longer provide the political spark they once did. Today, on all the big issues, politics has become a race to the cosy middle, where politicians differ in emphasis but not in basic political philosophy. Just as American election candidates aspire to be the suburban president, our leaders battle for power in the food courts of suburban shopping centres. Dublin 4 no longer defines the ethos of our political elite; the politicians now search for inspiration along the lethargic curve of the M50.

Perhaps this is a merely a stage we are going through.

It may well be that the comfortable consensus will be broken by hard times ahead. The economic uncertainty that will plague post-boom Ireland could turn out to be an opportunity, if the American experience is anything to go by. Perhaps the most important American trait we could import in the coming years is that beautifully elastic approach to failure: it is simply proof that you have tried. As we coast to a halt after the surging tide of economic expansion we may be forced to take a long, hard look at that philosophy. There is no intrinsic value in celebrating the failure of others, or lamenting your own short-comings. *Schadenfreude* and self-indulgence are things we do well in Ireland, but they have no place in nation that is looking for a compass in a changed world.

That's what I thought when I watched the workers file out of the Gateway factory in Clonshaugh, the day they heard the news that their plant was about to close. This is where Bill Clinton had heralded Ireland's pioneering role in the world, providing the symbolic bookend after three decades of change. Yet, like Clinton's career, in the hubris of the moment were the seeds of Ireland's next crisis of confidence. During that visit to Gateway, Clinton and Taoiseach Bertie Ahern signed a US–Ireland agreement using software developed by Ireland's high-tech pioneers at Baltimore technologies. In August of 2001, Gateway announced the closure of its plant with the loss of 900 jobs and Baltimore announced a 'restructuring', which led to more than 400 job losses in its operations around the world.

The job cuts robbed families of incomes, but for the first time in decades, there seemed to be an expectation among the workers that another job would come along. The closures were viewed as a painful symptom of changing global conditions, not some breast-beating exercise in Irish tragedy. 'The nature of the tech industry is that it recreates itself all the time,' said Gateway Ireland's managing director, Mike Maloney. We should always raise a sceptical eyebrow when a corporate executive tells us we have no choice but to take the pain, but there is something in this particular expression of business-speak: the principle of creative destruction. If the same principle could be applied to Ireland as a nation, then we need not worry about the future.

For all its flaws, what makes the United States special is the need for constant reinvention. We tend to regard the American people's unblinking faith in the future as naïve, but then we have failed to understand the power of that belief. The great irony in all this is that it was an Irishman who originally captured the beauty of this philosophy: In *Worstward Ho*, Samuel Beckett wrote: 'Ever tried. Ever Failed. No matter. Try again. Fail again. Fail Better.' Reality can be shaped to suit a nation's needs, not the other way. If we do decide to adopt this most American of ideas, we will once again be in a position to define a separate and unique course. We will be in a position to shape a *Dukhovnost* that matches the changed world we live in. Otherwise, Ireland will be a prisoner to those changes: unable to resist forces spawned by a society that it really does not understand.

Where we are clearly different from Americans, we often assume that we are better and in many cases we are wrong. Where we think we are alike, we are often deluding ourselves. We scour the maps, hoping to chart a course that is truly Irish, taking the best from our European neighbours and our American soulmates. Yet in some ways, we are like a boat adrift in the mid-Atlantic: our intellect draws us towards Berlin and our instincts draw us towards Boston. Even as we paddle towards the self-awareness and charm of Europe, the current pulls us towards the shiny shallowness of the

United States. As we flounder around, looking for a true measure of ourselves, we become increasingly disorientated. The trick is to stop paddling. What matters is the journey and not the destination.